Language Arts Handbook

Level 5

A Division of The McGraw-Hill Companies

Columbus, Ohio

► Consultants:

Jean Wallace Gillet, Charles Temple, and James D. Williams

► Acknowledgments:

Grateful acknowledgment is given to the following publishers and copyright owners for permissions granted to reprint selections from their publications. All possible care has been taken to trace ownership and secure permission for each selection included.

Excerpt from VOYAGER TO THE PLANETS by Necia H. Apfel. Copyright ©1991 by Necia H. Apfel. Reprinted by permission of Clarion Books/Houghton Mifflin Company. All rights reserved.

From CLASS PRESIDENT COPYRIGHT ©1990 BY JOHANNA HURWITZ. Used by permission of HarperCollins Publishers.

Copyright ©1988 by Russell Freedman. All rights reserved. Reprinted from BUFFALO HUNT by permission of Holiday House, Inc.

"The Story of Jumping Mouse" from SEVEN ARROWS copyright ©1972 by Hymeyohsts Storm. Retold and illustrated for children copyright ©1984 by John Steptoe. USE LICENSED BY THE JOHN STEPTOE LITERARY TRUST AND HARPERCOLLINS PUBLISHERS.

"Good Sportsmanship" Copyright ©1958 by Richard Armour. Reprinted by permission of John Hawkins & Associates, Inc.

SONGS OF THE DREAM PEOPLE: Chants and Images from the Indians and Eskimos of North America. Edited and illustrated by James Houston. Atheneum, New York, copyright ©1972 by James Houston.

"Roads Go Ever Ever On," from THE HOBBIT. Copyright ©1966 by J.R.R. Tolkien. Reprinted by permission of Houghton Mifflin Co. All rights reserved.

Excerpt from A KID'S GUIDE TO WASHINGTON, D.C., Copyright © 1989 by Harcourt, Inc. Reprinted with permission of Harcourt, Inc.

Adapted from WHEN SHLEMIEL WENT TO WARSAW by Isaac Bashevis Singer. Copyright © 1968 by Isaac Bashevis Singer. Reprinted by permission of Farrar, Straus, & Giroux, LLC.

► Photo Credits:

9, ©Hulton Archive; 11, ©CORBIS; 14, SRA photo; 16, ©CORBIS-Stock Market; 18, ©SuperStock; 20, ©CORBIS-Stock Market; 40, ©Tony Freeman/PhotoEdit; 45, ©CORBIS-Stock Market; 51, ©Michael Newman/PhotoEdit; 53, ©First Image; 67, 69, PhotoDisc; 70, ©Mary Kate Denny/PhotoEdit; 74, 76, PhotoDisc; 80, ©KS Studios; 83, ©Myrleen Ferguson Cate/PhotoEdit; 86, ©Eyewire Collection/Getty Images; 87, 90, PhotoDisc; 92, ©Stephen McBrady/PhotoEdit; 95, Corel; 96, ©NASA/Science Photo Library/Photo Researchers, Inc.; 101, PhotoDisc; 106, ©NASA/Photo Researchers, Inc.; 113, Corel; 125, ©David Ducros/Science Photo Library/Photo Researchers, Inc.; 138, SRA photo; 145, ©Davis Barber/PhotoEdit; 148, ©CORBIS-Stock Market; 152, (t, tr, cr) PhotoDisc, (br) ©Corbis, (bl) ©Myrleen Ferguson/PhotoEdit; 155, ©KS Studios; 160, ©Bloomsbury Publications (UK); 164, PhotoDisc; 167, ©Aaron Haupt; 171, ©Tom McHugh/Photo Researchers, Inc.; 172, ©CORBIS; 176, ©CORBIS-Stock Market; 178, ©CORBIS; 179, ©David Young-Wolff/PhotoEdit; 182, PhotoDisc; 183, ©E. Hanumantha Rao/Photo Researchers, Inc.; 184, ©First Image; 189, ©Michael Newman/PhotoEdit; 191, PhotoDisc; 194, ©Mary Ann McDonald/CORBIS; 196, ©Davis Barber/PhotoEdit; 199, 200, PhotoDisc; 202, ©Tony Freeman/PhotoEdit; 204, PhotoDisc; 206, ©Michael Newman/PhotoEdit; 211, PhotoDisc; 212, ©David Young-Wolff/PhotoEdit; 214, PhotoDisc; 215, ©CORBIS; 217, ©Tim Fuller; 220, PhotoDisc; 223, ©CORBIS; 227, Corel; 229, ©CORBIS; 232, ©Morton & White; 234, PhotoDisc; 236, Corel; 239, ©CORBIS-Stock Market; 240, PhotoDisc; 241, ©Morton & White; 243, ©CORBIS; 244, ©Morton & White; 251, ©CORBIS-Stock Market; 252, ©RubberBall Productions/CORBIS-Stock Market; 262, Corel; 264, ©Aaron Haupt; 268, PhotoDisc; 269, 273, ©CORBIS; 274, Corel; 277, 278, ©CORBIS; 280, ©N. Carter/North Wind Picture Archives; 281, ©Jeff Greenberg/PhotoEdit; 282, (t) (b) PhotoDisc; 283, ©CORBIS; 284, 285, Corel; 286, ©CORBIS; 287, ©James Noble/CORBIS-Stock Market; 289, 290, ©CORBIS; 291, ©Mary Kate Denny/PhotoEdit; 294, 295, ©KS Studios; 296, ©CORBIS; 299, ©KS Studios; 303, SRA photo; 308, ©CORBIS; 310, 312, PhotoDisc; 314, SRA photo; 316, ©CORBIS; 318, ©SuperStock; 320, 330, PhotoDisc; 332, Corel; 337, PhotoDisc; 339, ©KS Studios; 340, 342, ©Morton & White; 349, ©David Parker/Photo Researchers, Inc.; 351, ©KS Studios; 359, 365, 366, ©Morton & White; 370, ©CORBIS; 371, ©David Young-Wolff/PhotoEdit; 378, Corel; 380, ©First Image; 384, ©Renee Lynn/Photo Researchers, Inc.; 390, Corel; 393, PhotoDisc.

www.sra4kids.com

SRA/McGraw-Hill

*A Division of The **McGraw·Hill** Companies*

▶ Table of Contents

You Are a Writer. 8
The Traits of Writing 10

▶ The Writing Process 16

The Writing Process. 18
How Do I Get Started? (Prewriting) 20
Getting It Down on Paper (Drafting). 32
How Can I Improve My Writing? (Revising) 38
How Do I Edit My Writing? (Editing/Proofreading) 46
How Can I Share My Writing? (Publishing) 50
How Does It All Work Together?. 56

▶ Forms of Writing 66

Personal Writing 68

Journals 70
Notes and Cards. 76
Friendly Letters 82
Business Letters 86
Memos 92

Expository Writing 94

Summary 96
Analyzing Fiction. 100
Responding to Nonfiction 106
Book Reviews 110
Explaining a Process and Giving Directions 116
News Stories. 122
Expository Essays 128
Research Reports. 134

Narrative Writing 144
Personal Narratives 146
Autobiographies 152
Biographies 158
Mysteries 164
Adventure Stories 170
Historical Fiction 176
Fantasies 182
Plays 188

Descriptive Writing 198
Writing Descriptions 200
Observation Reports 206

Persuasive Writing 210
Persuasive Writing 212
Persuasion in Advertising 214
Letters to the Editor 216
Persuasive Reports 220

Poetry 226
Rhyming Poetry 228
Nonrhyming Poetry 232
Pattern Poetry 236

▶ Structures of Writing 238
Writing Sentences 240
Sentence Problems 246
Paragraphs 248
Types of Paragraphs 252
Graphic Organizers 256

▶ Writer's Craft **262**

Audience and Purpose 264
Ordering Information 268
Transition Words 272
Effective Beginnings and Endings 276
Variety in Writing 280
Combining Sentences 282
Figurative Language 286
The Sound of Language 290
Ways to Develop Expository Text 294
Ways to Develop Persuasive Writing 300
Ingredients for Writing a Story 304
Using Dialogue 308

▶ Vocabulary **310**

Compound Words 312
Antonyms 313
Synonyms 314
Analogies 315
Connotation 316
Homophones 318
Homographs 320
Words with More Than One Meaning 322
Greek and Latin Roots 324
Prefixes 326
Suffixes 328
Context Clues 330
Across-the-Curriculum Words 332
Adjectives and Adverbs 334
Precise Verbs 336

► Rules for Writing: Grammar, Usage, and Mechanics ... **338**

Grammar ... 340

Nouns ... 342
Pronouns ... 344
Verbs ... 346
Adjectives and Adverbs ... 348
Prepositions ... 350
Conjunctions and Interjections ... 351
Subjects and Predicates ... 352
Direct Objects and Indirect Objects ... 354
Modifiers—Words and Phrases ... 355
Clauses ... 356
Sentences: Simple, Compound, and Complex ... 358
Problems with Sentence Structure ... 360
Kinds of Sentences ... 363

Usage ... 364

Verb Tenses ... 366
Subject-Verb Agreement ... 368
Using Pronouns ... 370
Comparative and Superlative Adjectives ... 372
Comparative and Superlative Adverbs ... 373
Contractions ... 374
Double Negatives ... 375
Misused Words ... 376

Mechanics 378
End Marks 380
Abbreviations 382
Commas. 384
Colons and Semicolons 388
Quotation Marks, Underlining, and Apostrophes 389
Parentheses, Hyphens, Dashes, and Ellipses 390
Capitalization 391

Glossary. 396

Index. 404

You Are a Writer

Who are some writers you can name? When people think of writers, they most often think of novelists, journalists, or others who make a career of writing. In fact, we are all writers, and we can all be good writers with the proper tools and practice.

You have already started to hone your writing skills. Look at the following examples and think about the kinds of writing you already do.

Writing Around the House

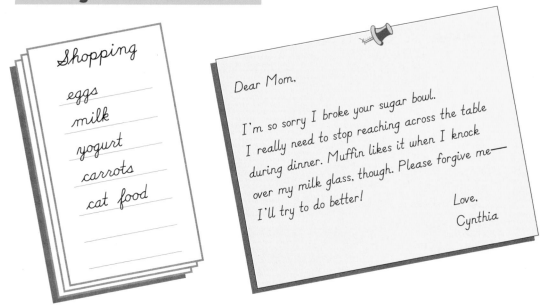

Shopping

eggs
milk
yogurt
carrots
cat food

Dear Mom,

I'm so sorry I broke your sugar bowl. I really need to stop reaching across the table during dinner. Muffin likes it when I knock over my milk glass, though. Please forgive me— I'll try to do better!

Love,
Cynthia

Cynthia's refrigerator note is meant to apologize for her mistake, while the shopping list will help the family remember what to buy at the grocery store. Writing notes can also help family members stay in touch and communicate deep feelings.

Try It

Think of some home situations where writing a note would be a better way to communicate than having a conversation.

Dear Ms. Kaplan,

I would like to try out for the part of Peter Pan in the spring show. I have seen the movie lots of times, and I already know all of the songs. I even know some of Peter's lines, and everyone tells me I'd be great as Peter. After all "I'll never grow up, never grow up, never grow up, not me!"

Yours truly,
April Carr

Fun Fact

Inventor Thomas Edison kept a mini-pencil (about 3 inches long) in his vest pocket for jotting down notes. Where do you keep your note-taking pencil?

This *persuasive* note is an example of trying to influence someone to see your point of view, and it is just one of the many types of writing you might use during the school day. Other types of writing are meant to *entertain*, *explain*, or *inform*.

As you can see, writing is an important part of our lives. Imagine what it would be like if you couldn't write letters or send e-mail messages to your friends. What if you couldn't take notes in class and you just had to remember everything your teacher said? It would make learning much harder.

This handbook will answer many of the questions you have about writing. You can use it to help you with your school assignments or when you want help with *any* kind of writing.

The Traits of Writing

We don't have to guess what features contribute to great writing. Through the years, language experts have discovered certain *traits*, or qualities, that are common in excellent writing. Let's take a look at these seven important characteristics of great writing.

Ideas

Ideas are the basis of all great writing. When writing is clear and focused, ideas are communicated. When writing is dull and confusing, ideas remain locked away, never reaching the intended audience.

Keys to Unlocking Ideas

Brainstorming

Get ideas for your writing by observing people and your surroundings and by thinking back on some of your own experiences.

Clarity

Your ideas must make sense to be understood by the reader. Try to figure out what might confuse a reader and fix it.

Focus

A topic should be narrow enough not to be overwhelming for either the writer or the reader. Don't try to cover too much in a single piece of writing.

Originality

Present ideas in fresh and different ways.

Data

Have all the information you need and more. Use resources from books, magazines, radio, TV, personal experience, personal interviews, and the Internet.

Details

Make your writing come alive with vivid and concrete details that help readers understand your ideas.

Organization

Have you ever seen the framework of a new building before the walls are put up? The organization of a piece of writing is like the framework of a building upon which everything else is hung or attached.

Keys to Unlocking Organization

Leads

Grab your reader's attention with a strong opening.

Direction

Provide your writing with a beginning, middle, and end section. Give it someplace to start—and someplace to go.

Building

The reader should have the feeling that your writing is building up to something, whether you are writing a mystery or an informational report.

Ending

Make sure your writing doesn't just stop, as if you ran out of time. Your ending needs to *sound* like an ending without saying "The End."

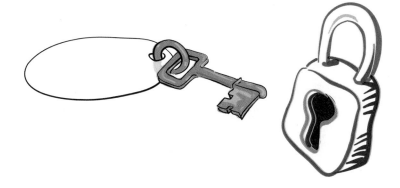

Voice

Voice is the trait that makes writing your very own. It's what separates your writing from someone else's writing. A writing voice full of enthusiasm and purpose will energize your reader from the very first sentence.

The voice you will use will change depending on what you are writing. If you are writing a story, you may want to use a writing voice that appeals to readers' emotions. Your goal may be to make them laugh or cry or have some other emotional response. If you're writing a report, you may want to use a voice that gives just the facts and that appeals to a reader's sense of reason. You may want to convince the reader that you are presenting a reasonable point of view.

Keys to Unlocking Voice

Uniqueness

Make your writing sound like your very own. Let it reflect your unique personality.

Influence

Write to influence your readers, whether it's to make them laugh or cry or feel admiration, concern, or astonishment.

Liveliness

Bring your ideas to life by painting vivid pictures for your reader to imagine.

Enthusiasm

Express energy and enthusiasm for your subject through the careful and deliberate choices you make in all aspects of your writing.

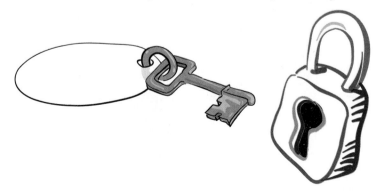

Word Choice

Language is the core of communication, so choosing the right word for the situation is important. There may be nine synonyms for the word *happy*, but only one will be the perfect choice in a particular sentence. Be a wordsmith, and choose your words carefully for maximum effect on your reader.

Keys to Unlocking Word Choice

Precision

Choose the most *precise*, or exact, word to express your intended meaning. Experiment using words you haven't used before in your writing.

Word Pictures

Choose words that paint strong, memorable images in the mind of the reader.

Avoid Repetition

Except for connecting words, try not to repeat the same words over and over in your writing.

Notice Word Choice

While reading, take note of unique word choices. Ask yourself, "Why is this word used perfectly here?"

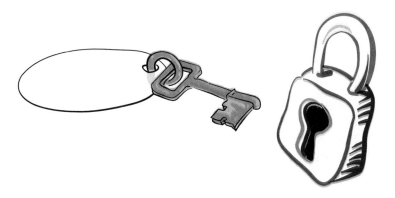

Sentence Fluency

This quality is achieved when sentences flow smoothly and with ease.

Keys to Unlocking Sentence Fluency

Read Aloud

Make sure your writing is easy to read aloud.

Variety

Vary the length of your sentences. Begin them in different ways and avoid repeating yourself.

Transition Words

Use transition, or signal, words to show how a sentence relates to the one before it.

Rhythm

Be aware of the rhythm, or flow of sounds, of your sentences.

Conventions

Conventions are the mechanics of writing. You will use conventions in the editing and proofreading phase of preparing a document for publication.

Keys to Unlocking Conventions

Correct Errors

Correct errors in spelling, punctuation, grammar, capitalization, and indentation.

Remove Distractions

Take out anything that may keep your reader from understanding what you've written. Make sure it's clear and easy to follow.

Presentation

Presentation refers to how your writing looks. It should appeal to the reader's eye.

Keys to Unlocking Presentation

Clean It Up

Make sure your paper is free from eraser marks and words that have been crossed out. Also look for any errors you may have made if you typed your paper.

Jazz It Up

Use graphics, charts, bullets, and subheadings where appropriate. Also try experimenting with bold and italic type for emphasis, but use these sparingly.

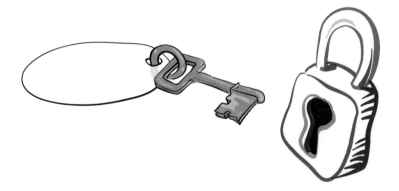

Try It

Can you add other keys that will help unlock the traits of great writing?

Reading Your Writing

The traits of great writing are keys to making your writing successful. Use them and you will keep your readers entertained and interested.

The Writing Process

Writing is a process that is done in stages. Each stage is different and has its own characteristics. These stages are prewriting, drafting, revising, editing/proofreading, and publishing. You can go back and forth between the stages as often as you like until you are satisfied with what you have written. Using the writing process in this way will help you improve your writing.

▶ **The Writing Process** **18**

▶ **How Do I Get Started?**
(Prewriting) **20**

▶ **Getting It Down on Paper**
(Drafting) **32**

▶ **How Can I Improve My Writing?**
(Revising) **38**

▶ **How Do I Edit My Writing?**
(Editing/Proofreading) **46**

▶ **How Can I Share My Writing?**
(Publishing) **50**

▶ **How Does It All Work Together?** . . . **56**

The Writing Process

Good writing cannot be rushed. It needs to be cared for, like a plant. Beautiful plants don't just pop up overnight—they require care and nurturing. The process that a gardener uses, from planting to weeding to fertilizing, helps the plant grow.

Good writing doesn't just happen automatically, either. Like a plant, it requires care and nurturing. The stages in the **writing process** will help you produce better work. It's important to be patient and not expect your writing to sound perfect from the very beginning. Keep in mind that each stage in the process will help you improve what you've first written, making it better and better, until you end up with a piece of writing that makes you proud!

▶ **Prewriting** What does the prefix *pre-* mean? Did you go to *pre*school? If so, you know that preschool is a school you go to **before** you begin kindergarten. Understanding this, can you figure out what *prewriting* means? If you came up with "**before** writing," you are correct!

Before you start writing about a topic, you'll need to perform three important tasks: *think*, *brainstorm*, and make a *list* or *web* to write down the thoughts you'll want to include.

think	brainstorm	list/web

- ▶ **Drafting** Also known as a *first draft*, or *rough draft*, this is where you'll begin to organize your ideas and start writing.

- ▶ **Revising** This is what makes good writing great. It's where you make your writing sound better by adding material, taking out material, and substituting more interesting words, phrases, and sentences.

- ▶ **Editing/Proofreading** This is your chance to correct all of your mistakes, including spelling, usage, and punctuation errors.

- ▶ **Publishing** Now that your work is ready to be shared with an audience, you'll need to neatly recopy it or type it on a computer. Finally you'll decide how you wish to share your writing with an audience. This is your chance to show the effort you've put into your work while you are sharing ideas that are important to you.

Not *every* piece of writing needs to be composed using the entire writing process, especially those that are intended for *your* eyes only. For example, journal entries and poems and stories that you write for your own pleasure often will not require that you fully use every phase of the writing process. On the other hand, for some writing you do, you may need to use every phase at least once. You may even need to move back and forth between some of the phases. For example, you could be writing a research report, and during the revising phase you discover that you need to add more information. That could require that you go back and do additional research and draft it into your original piece. Once you understand the purpose of each phase of the writing process, you'll be able to move from one to the next automatically.

Can you guess what percentage of pencils sold in the United States are painted yellow? The answer is 75 percent!

Reading Your Writing

Use the writing process to transform your ideas into a finished piece of writing. Your writing will be clearer and more readable if you do.

How Do I Get Started?

Getting started can be the most challenging part of any project. Fortunately, the **prewriting,** or planning, phase, of the writing process is also the most exciting portion in the life of a writing project—it's where *your* ideas come alive!

Decisions Before Writing

▶ **Prewriting** is the time when you create the ideas you'll be expressing in words, phrases, and sentences. It's also the time when you'll be making important decisions and setting goals. Following the steps below will help you during the decision-making process.

▶ **Choose a Topic** What's the assigned topic, or what topics interest you? What do you already know about the topic? What will you need to find out? What's the *focus*, or idea, you wish to concentrate on within the topic? What's the main idea you want to make sure that the audience remembers?

▶ **Identify Your Audience** Who is going to read, or hear you present, your writing? Is it classmates, your principal, your teacher, or your family? Knowing your audience will help you make decisions about the purpose, form, and length of your writing.

▶ **Define Your Purpose for Writing** What are you trying to accomplish? Do you wish to explain, inform, persuade, or entertain your audience? Which form might best suit the chosen topic and intended audience?

▶ **Select the Form of Writing** Should you create a realistic story, a classroom report, a persuasive letter, or some other form of writing? Check the following chart for some types of writing.

Take a Look

Reports	Essays	Directions
Notes	Recipes	Journal writing
Speeches	Summaries	Persuasive writing
Observations	Poetry	Realistic stories
Fantasies	Tall tales	Newspaper articles
Plays	Editorials	Weather reports

▶ **Length of Writing** Is there a *minimum* (smallest amount) or *maximum* (largest amount) number of pages required? If not, what length do you think would be appropriate given your topic, purpose, and audience? For example, something you wish to share with adults should be longer than something intended for kindergartners.

▶ **Deadline** A *deadline* is the final day or time that the completed project is due. What is your deadline? How much time do you have to complete your writing? How will you plan your time? What tasks will you perform, and on what schedule? Use a calendar to organize and keep records of your writing activities.

Targeting Your Topic

Now that you've made some decisions, it's finally time to decide on a topic. Where do you get topic ideas?

Topic Webs

Your teacher may assign a broad writing topic. Suppose your class is learning about cities, and you are asked to write about a city you have visited or would like to visit. Or you might choose to write about the history of a particular city. A *topic web* can help you decide what angle to use when beginning your writing.

Take a Look

When you are creating a web, start by drawing a small circle in the center of the page. Write the key word (in this example, *cities*) inside the circle. Think of words or phrases associated with the key word and write them around your center circle. Circle each word or phrase you come up with and connect them to the circles to which they relate. Look at the example below.

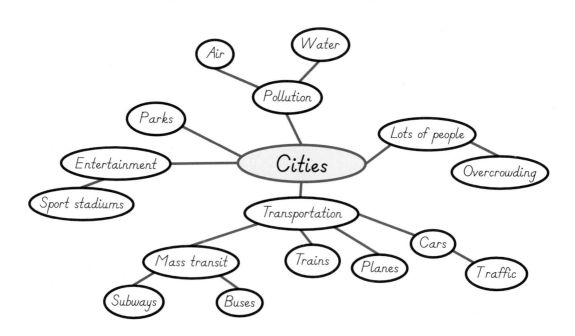

At other times, the responsibility of choosing a writing topic will be left up to you. Although finding your own topic is sometimes a difficult task, try making a chart like this to spark your thoughts.

About Me

My proudest moment
How I overcame a doubt about myself
My earliest memory
One thing I can do now that I couldn't do before
One thing I can't do that I could before

About the World

My best friend
My pet
Someone who has influenced me
The reason dogs have four legs
The reason shirts button up and down instead of side to side

No matter what topic you choose, always keep your audience in mind when you write.

Try It

Try adding some questions to the above list that may help you brainstorm possible writing topics.

Focusing Your Topic

Once you choose a topic, you need to narrow its *focus* so your writing is clear, concise (to the point), and specific. Sometimes, a writer chooses a topic that is too broad for the intended purpose and audience. When this happens, writing often lacks focus and direction, and this causes the audience to stop reading.

Here are some examples of topics that may be too broad to cover effectively. There's so much you could write about each one that it's hard to know where to start.

space

Washington, D.C.

music

my family

pets

the Civil War

electricity

computers

movies

Let's try to narrow some of these topics to focus on a specific portion of the topic.

Broad Topic	Focused Topic
Space	Black Holes
Washington, D.C.	The Day I (Almost) Met the President
Music	The Viola: The Glue of the Orchestra
My Family	My Twin Sister

Try It

See if you can think of a focused topic for each of the broad topics remaining on the list: pets, the Civil War, electricity, computers, and movies.

Collecting Information

Your assignment is to write about *cities*, but you know you need to narrow your focus. You've decided to concentrate on *mass transit*, because you've always been fascinated by subway systems. Check your assignment requirements to make sure you know what features must be included in your writing. Because the topic of mass transit is continually growing, your research will have to explore sources other than the general summaries usually found in social studies texts or encyclopedias.

Your school media center or neighborhood public library would be a logical place to begin your search for information. If you have access to the Internet, numerous search engines will speed and narrow your search through *billions* of pages of current data. Make sure to take notes on your Web journey, noting the addresses of the Web sites you found helpful. This will speed up your return trips to the same addresses. Print the most useful information for later use.

Check with the mass transit authority in your city. Write a letter to its main office, explain your project, and request brochures, data, pictures, or printouts that can be sent to you.

Documentary videos are another good source of information. Don't forget to check the video collections in the media sections of your school media center or public library.

Once you've assembled and examined your research materials, it's time to organize your information according to your purpose and audience.

Important note: When using information from sources for your writing, be sure to keep track of where you get your information. You will use it to document your sources in a bibliography. For more on writing a bibliography, see pages 141–142.

Organizing Your Writing

All creators need plans. Builders need blueprints. Film animators need storyboards. Fashion designers need sketches. Teachers need lesson plans. Without a clear plan of action, any project can become a jumble of confusion, wasting valuable time and effort.

The same is true for writing. Without a plan, writing will be disorganized and lack clarity, interest, and vitality. What might have been a thorough and thought-provoking project becomes unclear information without structure or purpose.

Because planning (prewriting) is one of the more important parts of the writing process, you should record your plans. One way to do this is to take notes and make an outline. Another way is to use a chart called a **graphic organizer.** These charts are designed to help organize your writing project into smaller parts. Writing short sections that are part of a larger piece makes the project more manageable.

Graphic organizers also help you visualize the structure of the piece. Once you've filled in some parts of your organizer, it will be easy to make changes based on the purpose and audience you've selected.

Once your organizer is complete, you'll have a map of your writing journey. All you'll have to do is follow the map to your final draft destination.

Organizing Story Writing

Specific types of writing call for specific graphic organizers. Writing a short story would require a different type of organizer than the one you would use for a report. For a story, you could plan its narrative elements using the *story map* shown on the next page. You'd have to consider your characters (*who* is involved?); the setting (*where* and *when* does the story take place?); the *conflict*, or problem, to be overcome; the *key events* in your plot; and the story's *resolution* (how do things turn out?). Use a *working title* at the top of the story map. A *working title* is used to identify a piece of writing while the writer is working on the story. Don't write your final title until the story is completed. To grab the reader's attention, titles must be thoughtfully chosen and should not give away too much of the plot.

Try It

Look at the story map shown on the next page and think about the words you would write in the boxes and ovals if you were planning a story based on cities or mass transit.

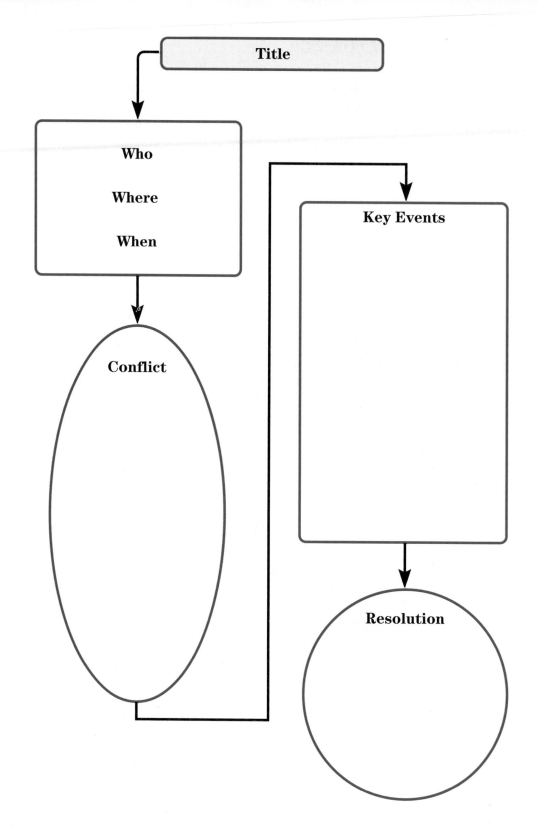

Organizing Informational Writing

The graphic organizer on the next page can be used to plan a piece of informational writing. Remember the example of a teacher-assigned writing project about *cities?* Under this broad topic, you chose the focused topic of *mass transit.* Once you began researching your topic, you found too much information and decided to narrow your topic even further. Now you have decided to concentrate on the New York City subway system, which is listed in the topic box at the head of the organizer.

Beneath the topic box are three *subtopic* boxes, each with room below for three supporting details. Having read through your research, you've chosen several areas that you believe would interest your intended audience—your class.

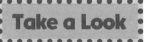
Take a Look

Topic

New York Subway System

Subtopic

Ridership

1. _____
2. _____
3. _____

Subtopic

History of the System

1. _____
2. _____
3. _____

Subtopic

Air Pollution Relief

1. _____
2. _____
3. _____

Try It

Your first subtopic is *ridership*. Here are some facts and ideas about ridership from your research and brainstorming. Which facts do you think would be the most interesting, fascinating, or eye-opening? Where would you place your selected details on the graphic organizer?

"Subtopic: Ridership"

▶ The New York City subway system officially opened on Thursday, October 27, 1904. One million people used the subway that first day.

▶ By 1946, daily ridership grew to eight million people.

▶ The number of people using public transit declined due to the car and highway boom of the 1950s and 1960s.

▶ How can the numbers be boosted to earlier levels?

▶ Who rides the subways?

▶ What is New York Transit currently doing about trying to increase ridership levels?

▶ Today, the subway serves 4.3 million customers on an average weekday and about 1.3 billion passengers a year.

▶ Ridership on the New York City subways is the fifth-largest in the world, behind Moscow, Tokyo, Seoul, and Mexico City. Moscow's subway system serves almost three times the number of passengers served by the New York City subway system.

Reading Your Writing

Prewriting is the process of choosing a writing topic and planning the content of your writing. It will help you make your thoughts clear so your audience will not be confused when reading your writing.

Getting It Down on Paper

Drafting is the second phase of the writing process. It's also called the *first draft* or *rough draft*. This is where you'll write your story or report in rough form, using the notes, research, and graphic organizers you've already completed in *prewriting*.

Take a Look

Here's the first draft of a paragraph from a student's essay about the New York City subway system.

NY City Subways

People often say that NYC has the biggest and best of everything. This is probably an exaggeration, but the "Big Apple" does shine in one respect: NYC's subway system is the fifth largest in the world!

Secrets of Successful Drafting

A **draft** is your first attempt at writing. The most important thing about a draft is to get your ideas down on paper.

Here are some tips on how to get your first draft written.

Tips for Drafting

▶ Write on only the front of each page, and leave a blank line beneath each line of writing. Later, you'll have room to make revisions and corrections in the extra space.

▶ Write quickly. What matters most in this step is content, or information you include in the writing. Write in complete sentences with a capital letter at the beginning and a period or other punctuation mark at the end.

▶ If you want to change something you've already written, do *not* start over. Just draw a line through it and keep going.

▶ Abbreviations may help you write faster if you can remember what your abbreviations mean.

▶ If you are having a hard time figuring out the spelling of a tricky word, sound out the word and circle it so you'll remember to look it up during the *proofreading* step of writing.

▶ Keep your purpose and intended audience in mind as you write. Adjust your drafting as you visualize your audience reading what you've written.

▶ If you can't think of an exact word or phrase you wish to use, leave a blank space and come back to it later.

Remember, the purpose of a draft is to get your ideas down on paper quickly, not to write a perfect piece. Try not to think about any single concern for too long. Leave that for later.

Turning Notes into Paragraphs

Now it's time to shape the ideas and information you've gathered into paragraphs. A paragraph is a group of two or more sentences that tells about the same thing. Many paragraphs have a topic sentence, which states the main idea, and supporting sentences, which provide details. Here are some tips for writing expository paragraphs. Keep in mind that narrative paragraphs (like those in stories) don't always follow all of these guidelines.

Tips for Writing Paragraphs

▶ Each paragraph should feature only *one* main idea.

▶ The topic sentence should state the main idea of each paragraph.

▶ This sentence is usually, *but not always*, placed at the beginning of the paragraph.

▶ Supporting sentences should add to the topic sentence, providing details to develop and back up the main idea.

▶ Don't include unnecessary sentences that seem out of place with the other supporting details.

▶ Be sure to *indent* the first line of each paragraph.

Creating a Paragraph

Let's return to the informational writing piece on the New York City subway system. On the graphic organizer shown on page 30, we chose *ridership* as one of the first *subtopics*. Check out the list of facts and ideas related to *ridership* on page 31. Remember to rephrase the information in your own words.

We're now going to turn some of the information chosen under the subtopic *ridership* into a paragraph about *ridership*. First, we'll need a topic sentence.

> *The New York City subway system is the fifth-largest in the world.*

Here are some details to support the topic sentence.

▶ The New York City subway system officially opened on Thursday, October 27, 1904. One million people used the subway that first day.

▶ By 1946, daily ridership grew to eight million.

▶ Today, the subway serves 4.3 million customers on an average weekday and about 1.3 billion passengers a year.

▶ Only Moscow, Tokyo, Seoul, and Mexico City have ridership greater than New York City's. Moscow's subway system serves almost three times the number of passengers served by the New York City subway system.

How do we form these separate details about *ridership* into a paragraph? Understanding how to use *transition words* can help.

Transition Words

Transition, or signal, words link sentences and paragraphs to each other. They help ideas flow smoothly. Transition words can be placed at the beginning of a sentence or paragraph and are used for different purposes, such as to show change, cause and effect, and the addition of more information and to signal order, time, or location.

Transition Words Showing Time and Order

yesterday	before	then
tonight	after	when
last night	first	finally
today	last	by
tomorrow	while	
the next day	the day after tomorrow	

Transition Words Showing Location

across	next to	in front of
under	as far as	into
over	behind	nearby
beside	above	

Transition Words Showing That There Is More Information to Come

furthermore	first of all	the principal item
moreover	remember	
also	a major event	it is important to note
keep in mind	in addition	

Transition Words Showing Change

although	on the other hand	different from
yet		rather
however	but	otherwise
	while	

Transition Words Showing Cause and Effect

because	therefore	so

Using what we have learned about transition words, we can form a paragraph using the details we chose about ridership.

Only Moscow, Tokyo, Seoul, and Mexico City have more riders than New York City. When it opened on October 27, 1904, one million people rode New York City's subway. By 1946, this figure had grown to eight million daily riders. Today, only half that number rides the trains each day.

Try It

Pick out the transition words in the paragraph about *ridership*. Which ones show time?

Next look at the *ridership* paragraph's *content* and ask yourself, *"What question or questions will my audience have after reading these sentences?"* You've introduced a bit of a mystery, telling readers that there were eight million riders in 1946 versus four million riders today. Why are fewer people riding the subway today than in 1946?

Your next paragraph should explore the reasons behind this dramatic drop in ridership. Present details that bring up thought-provoking questions. This will keep your audience reading because they will want to find the answers to their questions.

Reading Your Writing

Drafting is the time to get your thoughts on paper. Remember to use transition words so your reader can easily follow your thinking.

How Can I Improve My Writing?

Revising means changing. During this third phase of writing, your goal is to make your piece as clear, interesting, and as well organized as possible. In *revising*, you are not *rewriting* your story, report, or letter; you are searching for ways to make your writing better by making changes directly on your rough draft.

You can also use the revising step to make certain your writing is appropriate for your audience. If you are writing a story for first graders, you should use easy words and simple sentences so they can understand and stay interested. If you are writing an essay about the New York City subway system for your teacher, you will need to use more complex words and sentences.

You may want to consider setting aside your writing for a while before you begin your revisions. This will clear your mind so when you come back to your writing you will be refreshed and ready to make changes.

Revising is concerned with presentation of *content*, not mistakes. Revising comes down to five major operations:

ADDING

DELETING

CONSOLIDATING

CLARIFYING

REARRANGING

Adding

There are many ways to add to your writing. You can add ideas, characters, details, words, sentences, paragraphs, and sections. Adding material is probably the easiest of all the revising tasks. More details can make a sentence or paragraph more interesting.

Take a Look

Imagine you have written a personal narrative about your afternoon at the beach. The original sentence in your rough draft might look like this:

My grandma and I stood at the edge of the water.

After you revise your paper, your sentence might say,

*My grandma and I stood **close together** at the edge of the water **while the waves gently lapped at our feet.***

Try It

Revise this sentence. Make it more interesting by adding details.
▶ My mom left work early so I wouldn't be late for the appointment.

Deleting

Sometimes, reading over your first draft will reveal material that needs to be **deleted,** or removed. This material might be a word, phrase, or sentence you've accidentally repeated. Perhaps you've decided that certain items might be inappropriate or uninteresting to your audience. If you find something you want to delete, draw a line through it. Don't erase; you might want to use some of it later.

Take a Look

This paragraph contains some material that does not fit with the rest of the paragraph. Notice the deletions.

> *The African elephant is taller than the Asian elephant. A male African elephant is ~~is~~ about 13 feet tall, whereas a male Asian elephant is about 10 feet tall. ~~Both are shorter than a giraffe, which is 18-20 feet tall.~~*

Try It

See if you can find some words, phrases, or sentences that should be deleted from the following paragraph.

Parakeets have always been my favorite kind of pet. Ever since I can remember, ever since I can remember, my mom has always had a happy, chirping little green or blue birdie in the dining room. I like dogs, too. Seymour was the first parakeet I can remember. With his green chest and little yellow head, his chatter brought more life into our house. My cousin Richie had a finch named Fluffy.

Consolidating

When you are revising your writing, you may notice some information that could be **consolidated,** or joined together. Consolidating usually involves taking two or more sentences that have similar purposes or structures and combining them into one sentence.

Consolidating information can make your writing more to the point. This helps readers more easily understand what you are trying to tell them.

Take a Look

Here are a few sentences from a rough draft.

Our class took a field trip. We went to the aquarium yesterday. We saw sharks while we were there. We also saw dolphins.

Here is the same information after being revised.

Our class took a field trip to the aquarium yesterday. We saw sharks and dolphins while we were there.

Compare the original and consolidated examples. Do you see where words were added and deleted?

Try It

Try improving these sentences by consolidating them.

The aquarium was filled with salt water. Salt water is the natural habitat of seals and dolphins. I thought we would see walruses. No walruses were there.

Clarifying

Another way to make your writing better is to **clarify** it, or make it clearer to the reader. Perhaps your opening sentence is confusing or misleading. Maybe you've introduced a difficult idea or topic to the reader and you need to explain it more thoroughly. Clarifying requires that you look at your writing from the reader's point of view. Read your rough draft carefully and ask yourself, "Is the reader going to understand exactly what I am saying?"

Take a Look

Read this example sentence and ask yourself if there is a way to make the information clearer or more understandable.

> *We saw a killer whale and a calf in a separate tank.*

Now read the revised information.

> *We saw a killer whale and a calf, or baby whale. The whales were not in the same tank as the sharks and dolphins.*

The revised information makes two pieces of information clearer. The first sentence provides the meaning of the word *calf*. The second sentence makes it clear that the two whales were in the same tank with each other but that they were not with the other animals.

Try It

Try improving this sentence by clarifying any confusing information.

We ate lunch with the creatures in the aquarium.

Rearranging

Another way to revise your writing is through *rearranging*. When you rearrange your writing, you use the information that is already there, but you put it into a different order. The result is that your writing is easier to read and it makes more sense.

Rearranging may involve as little as switching two words in a sentence. Sometimes rearranging involves moving phrases, sentences, or even whole paragraphs of information.

Take a Look

Compare these sample sentences.

> *We excitedly watched as the shark ate and caught a piece of food.*
> *We watched excitedly as the shark caught and ate a piece of food.*

Rearranging the words *watched* and *excitedly* helps the sentence flow more smoothly. Rearranging *caught* and *ate* puts the events in better order.

Try It

Improve these sentences by rearranging the information.

The dolphins swam around the tank in circles. Some of them jumped through the air and out of the water.

A Revising Checklist

Below is a checklist you can use to make your writing better. It will help you think about what you have written and how to improve it.

Ideas

▶ Can I add information to make my writing clearer?

▶ Have I left out important information I need to add?

▶ Can I delete material that is off the topic or inappropriate for my audience and purpose?

Organization

▶ Does my opening sentence attract the reader's attention?

▶ Do I need to change the order of my sentences or paragraphs?

▶ Do I have a thoughtful conclusion?

Voice

▶ Does it sound like I wrote it?

▶ Have I involved the readers and made them care about the topic?

Word Choice

▶ Can I substitute words and phrases that are more exact?

▶ Have I painted "word pictures" for my readers?

Sentence Fluency

▶ Can I delete repeated or unnecessary words, phrases, or sentences?

▶ Can I use more variety in my sentences?

Conferencing with Classmates

After you've revised your writing on your own, you may wish to share your writing with fellow classmates. Called **peer conferencing,** these discussions can often provide you with additional ideas to improve your writing. This type of sharing can occur between two writers or within a small group.

Tips for Successful Peer Conferencing

Here are some things to keep in mind when you have been asked to read and comment on someone's writing.

▶ Avoid general comments such as "That wasn't very interesting" or "That was good."

▶ Make specific comments such as "I really liked the part where the wind blew the door open," or "I think it would be great to hear a description of the campsite."

▶ Always begin your comments with something positive before offering a suggestion for improvement.

Peer conferencing can be an effective tool for predicting your audience's response to your writing, but it will help to improve your writing only if you follow up on the comments made. Take notes on your classmates' responses. After the conference, carefully consider the reactions before making any changes. Do not change your writing just because a suggestion was made. Think about the suggestion and decide for yourself whether or not it would improve your writing.

How Do I Edit/Proofread My Writing?

At the **editing/proofreading** stage, all of your writing mistakes should be corrected. On your draft, where you also marked your revising changes, you'll carefully make sure that spelling, punctuation, and usage mistakes are corrected. A dictionary is helpful during this step for checking spelling and definitions of vocabulary words you used.

Read your work out loud to yourself in a soft voice. Listen to how it *sounds* as you read it. You'll be able to catch many more problems this way.

Another editing aid is a pencil eraser. While reading your draft, be sure to use your eraser to point to each word as you say it. Doing this will ensure that you read *only* the words that have actually been written down instead of unintentionally filling in sentences with the words that your mind knows should be there.

Take a Look

You might easily overlook a missing word unless you point to and say each word softly.

> *I enjoy going the lake on hot, humid days.*

You also could easily overlook an extra word unless you point to and say each word softly.

> *It's impossible to predict if if lightning will strike a certain location.*

Proofreading Marks

To make editing clear, quick, and neat, proofreading marks are used to indicate corrections.

Here's a list of proofreading marks and their meanings.

Mark	Meaning
Add ∧	caret Use this ∧when you want to add something.
Delete ℯ	This symbol means you want to ~~take out~~ℯ delete words.
Add a period ⊙	Use this symbol to add a period⊙
Capitalize ≡	These three small lines beneath a lowercase letter indicate the letters "d.c." should be made into capital letters.
Transpose ∼	Use the symbol⎤transpose to change the order of the words indicated.
Slash /	This slash mark through an uppercase letter shows that it should be changed to a small /etter.
Indent ¶	¶ Place this symbol before the first word of a sentence that begins a paragraph. The symbol indicates that you should indent.
Close up space ⌒	Use this symbol to close up space between words that should be joined, such as *play̑ground* and *hal̑ way.*
Add space ∧#	This symbol indicates that a space⌃#is needed between letters.
Check spelling ᵖ̶	Use this⁽sp⁾symbol to mark a word that you want to spell-check.

An Editing Checklist

Below is a checklist that you can use to check the conventions in your writing.

▶ Have I read over my writing carefully, speaking each word softly while pointing to it with my eraser?

▶ Have I used appropriate proofreader's marks for my corrections?

▶ Are there any missing or repeated words in my sentences?

▶ Are all of my sentences complete, or are there some fragments?

▶ Are there any run-on sentences?

▶ Are any punctuation marks missing?

▶ Do my subjects and verbs agree?

▶ Have I confirmed the definitions of words about which I am unsure?

▶ Have I misspelled any words?

▶ Have I written in paragraphs of appropriate length?

▶ Have I indented my paragraphs?

▶ Did I use a variety of words?

▶ Have I varied my sentence lengths?

▶ Am I positive that I have fulfilled the detailed requirements of the assignment?

Writing on a Computer

Although computers can help with certain writing functions, their usage, punctuation, and spelling checks are not very accurate. These computer aids should be used only as possible suggestions for corrections.

Tips for Writing on a Computer

▶ First, label your document with the title of your writing. Save this file in a location that you will remember.

▶ Type your rough draft (including revisions) carefully. Say the words as you type them.

▶ Increase the font size to make it easier to read. Try increasing it to 150 percent.

▶ Open your document to fill as much of your computer screen as possible.

▶ Save your work often. Remember that if your computer crashes, anything you've written since the last time you saved your work will be lost.

▶ Make corrections as you see them.

▶ After you've completed your corrections, read aloud what you've written directly from the computer screen.

▶ Finally, print your work and read it again. Looking at the printed version can alert you to mistakes missed when you were reading from a computer screen.

Reading Your Writing

Editing/proofreading is the process of correcting any mistakes in your writing. An error-free paper will make reading it a breeze.

How Can I Share My Writing?

Publishing is the last phase in the writing process. This is the step where you will prepare your writing to be shared with its intended audience. You will make certain that the *presentation* of your paper is pleasing to the eye of the reader. This means making certain the paper is neat and free from erasures. You can also consider adding graphics to make your paper look more appealing.

Publishing is also the step during which you'll decide *how* your writing will be shared. Will you *mail* the letter you've written? Will you *perform* your writing in front of an audience? Will you transform your writing into a *booklet, pamphlet,* or *folder,* complete with pictures, illustrations, or charts? Will you use a desktop-publishing computer program to design and lay out your work like a *magazine article?*

Here are some of the ways you might choose to publish your work.

Mail Your Work

Much of your writing can be published through the mail. You can write letters to family members, friends, celebrities, politicians, and even to newspapers, television, and radio stations. If you write these letters by hand, you should follow appropriate friendly or business letter formats, and the letters should be neat and free from errors. If you are using a computer for the final copy, see if the program has an automatic letter format. Learn the correct way to fold your letter before placing it in an envelope, and be sure to address the envelope correctly and neatly.

Present Your Work Orally

Oral presentation is an exciting way to share your writing. You'll need to practice your oral delivery, making sure you can be easily heard. Try practicing in front of a mirror, or have a friend or family member videotape your practice.

Ask yourself which audiences would most appreciate your performance and subject matter. Think about different types of audiences, such as your class, a younger or older class, adults at a faculty or PTA meeting, your after-school club, or relatives at a family reunion.

Try It

What audience would most likely appreciate an oral presentation of the following topics?

▶ an original fairy tale you wrote

▶ educational Web sites

▶ your family's history

If you decide not to perform your work, there are still lots of other opportunities for sharing it. Think of all the different types of printed material you come across in just one week: newspapers, magazines, brochures, booklets, fliers, comics—the list goes on and on.

Page Layout

Page Design Elements		
text	pictures	illustrations
diagrams	charts	graphs
borders	captions	titles

Many publications rely heavily on a combination of the written word and graphic design elements. An important part of an article's graphic design is its *layout*, or the way these different graphics and words are arranged on a page. Scan through this book. Are there some pages that catch your attention more than others? What is it about these pages that makes them interesting to view? Try using some graphic design elements in your work. For example, use colorful boxes to set off special parts, or put important phrases in italics or other type styles. They will add to the *presentation*, or eye appeal, of your paper. You may be surprised by the impact that graphics can have on your project.

Paste-Up

If you don't have a computer to design and print your completed pages, do it the way newspapers and magazines have for hundreds of years—use paste-up. Start by gathering the elements that you want to appear on a page. Cut out columns of text, pictures, charts, and even separate titles and captions. Then, using a blank page of the same size as your project, experiment with arranging the cut-out pieces into a clear and attractive whole page. Think of it as a jigsaw puzzle. When you've decided on a layout for that particular page, lightly mark (with pencil) the position of each cut-out piece on the blank page. Then, apply rubber cement to the back of the first piece you intend to paste up, and carefully rub it down onto the marked position. Continue pasting up each piece until you're finished.

Computer Page Layout

Today, many student-friendly page layout programs are available for your computer. To find one, try your media center or computer lab. If you have a computer at home, ask your parents what page layout programs they might have. If you can't locate one, use your computer to print all the page design elements, then use the paste-up technique outlined above.

Tips for Computer Page Design

Here are some ideas you can use with or without paste-up.

▶ Choose the page size of your final product.

▶ Decide on a color design for the elements of your page. Avoid putting too many colors on one page.

▶ Choose a font, font size, and color for your body text.

▶ Choose a number of columns for your body text.

▶ Choose a font, font size, and color for your titles.

▶ Choose a font, font size, and color for your pictures, illustration, or chart *captions*, which are short identifications or descriptions of graphics.

▶ Choose a style, size, and color for frames or borders that you want to place around text, graphics, titles, or pictures.

▶ Experiment with a variety of layouts, fonts, font sizes, colors, and borders until you find design combinations that are visually clear, strong, and appealing.

Bind Your Work

Stories, reports, poetry, and other types of finished pieces can be published in a number of ways. Directions for the binding of homemade books can be found in your school media center, where your work might be exhibited. Perhaps you could loan your piece to a class studying an issue related to your topic or enter it in a school, district, or state contest.

If you think your work is appropriate for publishing in a newspaper, magazine, or other periodical, you'll have to *submit*, or send, your work to the publication's editor. Although few submissions are selected for publication in magazines, your project may prove to be special and appropriate enough to be published. You'll never know if you don't try!

The first thing to do when submitting your work is to find out the publication's requirements. You can visit a library and check the *Writer's Handbook* for specific guidelines. You can also write to the magazine, journal, or Web site to which you want to send your work. In your letter, ask what the requirements are for submitting your work. Some publications will ask you to type and double space your writing. Some may require that you use a certain number of words in your piece. Be sure to follow the instructions that are given so you can increase your chances of having your writing published.

Reading Your Writing

Publishing is the part of the writing process when you show your work to the world. Choose the publishing option that is best for what you have written, and your audience will be sure to respond.

How Does It All Work Together?

Now that we've explored each of the stages of the writing process, it's time to put all this information to good use on another project. This time, let's imagine that Alec Levy's class has been involved with a unit on *consumerism*. The students have been focusing on customer service and protecting the consumer. For example, they learned that television commercials for toys sound really good, but sometimes when you get the toy home, it is not all that the advertisement promised. In other words, the class learned how *not* to be cheated, and their assignment was to publish a piece of writing on some aspect of consumerism.

Prewriting

Consumerism is a broad topic. The wide range of options makes it quite difficult to choose a specific topic and type of writing. Alec started by asking some questions: What do I already know about consumerism? Do I know anyone who has had to take consumer action? Do I have any reason to take some sort of consumer action?

Focusing Your Topic

With all these thoughts in his mind, Alec decided to make a topic web to brainstorm for a focused topic.

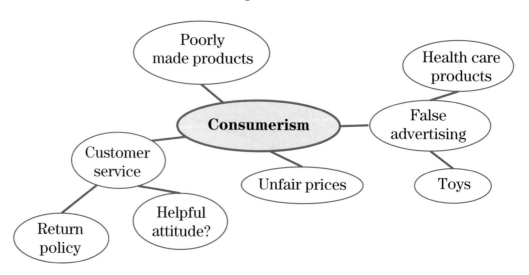

Decisions Before Writing

Suddenly, while making his web, Alec realized that he could fulfill the requirements of the writing assignment *and* stand up for his own consumer rights at the same time. Alec remembered that the personal tape player he had gotten for his birthday had been eating his tapes, so he and his dad took it back to the electronics store to exchange it for a new one. The salesperson said that the store did not exchange defective products and that Alec would have to mail the tape player to the manufacturer for repair. Because he had it for only a week, and it would take weeks or months for the repair to be completed, Alec decided to look into another way of resolving the problem. He wrote a **persuasive letter** to ask for a new personal tape player.

Alec's purpose was to persuade someone at the electronics store to exchange his defective tape player for a new one. He next had to decide on his audience. He asked himself who at the store would be the best person to whom to address his letter. Because a salesperson couldn't make the exchange, Alec decided to address his letter to the store's manager. He got the manager's name and the store's address by asking his dad to call the store.

Alec then made a plan for his letter. He decided to use a *business letter* format because he wanted to politely present his problem and ask for a replacement for his tape player.

Alec knew that the first step in writing a *letter of complaint* was to set up the *heading, inside address,* and *salutation.* You can find out how to do this by turning to pages 86–91.

The second step in Alec's process was to plan out what he wanted to say. First he would introduce himself and say why he was writing. Next he would explain his problem and the solutions that he tried to fix the problem. Then he would ask for what he wanted and thank the reader for her time.

Take a Look

Alec used the plan he made in the prewriting step to help him draft this letter to the store manager.

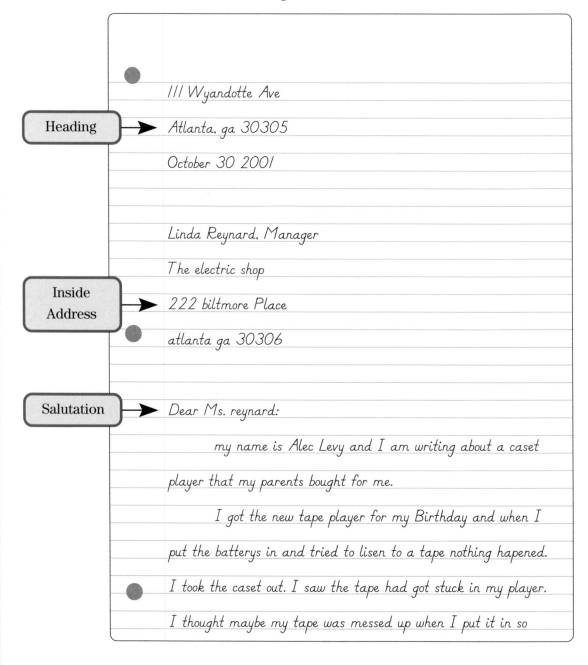

Heading

/// Wyandotte Ave

Atlanta, ga 30305

October 30 2001

Inside Address

Linda Reynard, Manager

The electric shop

222 biltmore Place

atlanta ga 30306

Salutation

Dear Ms. reynard:

my name is Alec Levy and I am writing about a caset

player that my parents bought for me.

I got the new tape player for my Birthday and when I

put the batterys in and tried to lisen to a tape nothing hapened.

I took the caset out. I saw the tape had got stuck in my player.

I thought maybe my tape was messed up when I put it in so

I tried another one and the same thing again happened.

My dad and me went back to your store. We talked to the salesperson who sold it to my parents. She said the store would not xchange my tape player and that I would have to send it in for repare and that it might take two to four weeks.

I should not have to wait two to four weeks to get my caset player repared since it was broke when I got it. I hope you will be able to exchange it for me.

Thank you for reading my letter. Please call me at (404) 555-5555 if you have questions.

Sinceerly,

Alec Levy

Try It

Before moving on, read the letter again and look for words, phrases, or sentences that can be *revised* to make the letter better.

This is a revised copy of Alec's letter.

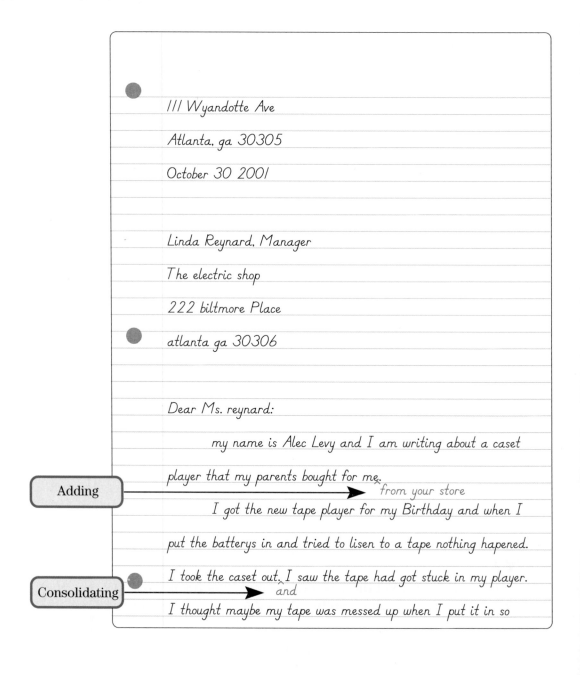

111 Wyandotte Ave

Atlanta, ga 30305

October 30 2001

Linda Reynard, Manager

The electric shop

222 biltmore Place

atlanta ga 30306

Dear Ms. reynard:

   my name is Alec Levy and I am writing about a caset

player that my parents bought for me.

Adding   → *from your store*

   I got the new tape player for my Birthday and when I

put the batterys in and tried to lisen to a tape nothing hapened.

   I took the caset out. I saw the tape had got stuck in my player.

Consolidating   → *and*

I thought maybe my tape was messed up when I put it in so

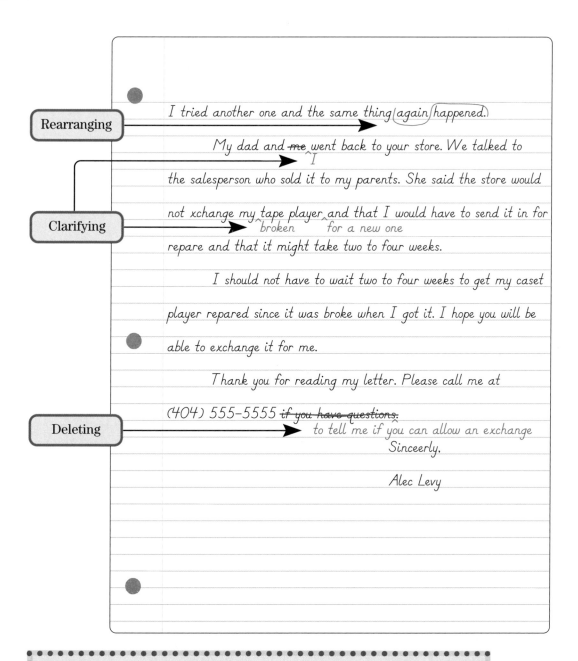

Rearranging

I tried another one and the same thing (again) happened.

My dad and ~~me~~ went back to your store. We talked to
                    ^I

the salesperson who sold it to my parents. She said the store would

Clarifying

not xchange my tape player and that I would have to send it in for
              ^broken   ^for a new one

repare and that it might take two to four weeks.

I should not have to wait two to four weeks to get my caset

player repared since it was broke when I got it. I hope you will be

able to exchange it for me.

Thank you for reading my letter. Please call me at

(404) 555-5555 ~~if you have questions.~~

Deleting

to tell me if you can allow an exchange
                            Sinceerly,

                            Alec Levy

•••

Try It

Read the letter again now that the revisions have been made.
Can you see any changes that you would make for the
editing/proofreading stage?

•••

Take a Look

This is a copy of Alec's revised and edited letter. Look for the proofreading marks that Alec made.

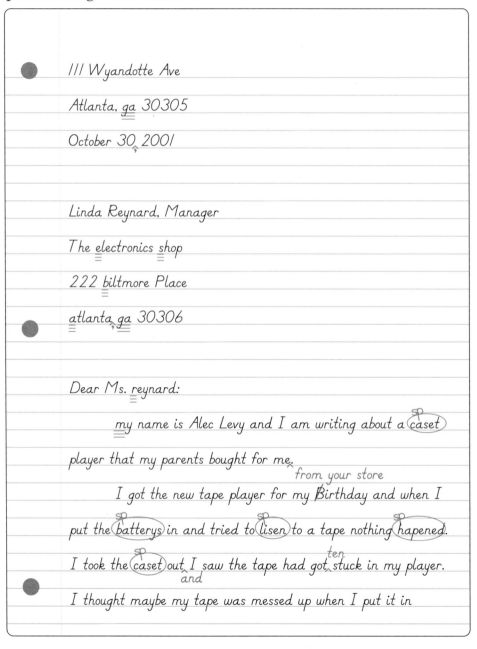

111 Wyandotte Ave

Atlanta, ga 30305

October 30, 2001

Linda Reynard, Manager

The electronics shop

222 biltmore Place

atlanta, ga 30306

Dear Ms. reynard:

my name is Alec Levy and I am writing about a caset player that my parents bought for me. from your store

I got the new tape player for my Birthday and when I put the batterys in and tried to lisen to a tape nothing hapened.

I took the caset out I saw the tape had got stuck in my player. and ten

I thought maybe my tape was messed up when I put it in

so I tried another one and the same thing (again) happened.

My dad and ~~me~~ I went back to your store. We talked to
the salesperson who sold it to my parents. She said the store
would not (xchange) my tape player, and that I would have to
broken   for a new one
send it in for (repare) and that it might take two to four weeks.

I should not have to wait two to four weeks to get my
(caset) player (repared) since it was broke when I got it. I hope you
will be able to exchange it for me.

Thank you for reading my letter. Please call me at
(404) 555-5555.
to tell me if you can allow an exchange
(Sinceerly).

Alec Levy

This is Alec's letter after all the changes have been made.

111 Wyandotte Avenue
Atlanta, GA 30305
October 30, 2001

Linda Reynard, Manager
The Electronics Shop
222 Biltmore Place
Atlanta, GA 30306

Dear Ms. Reynard:

My name is Alec Levy and I am writing about a cassette player that my parents bought for me from your store.

I got a new tape player for my birthday and when I put the batteries in and tried to listen to a tape nothing happened. I took the cassette out and saw that the tape had gotten stuck in my player. I thought maybe my tape was messed up when I put it in so I tried another one and the same thing happened again.

My dad and I went back to your store and talked to the salesperson who sold it to my parents. She said the store would not exchange my broken tape player for a new one and that I would have to send it for repair and that it might take two to four weeks.

I should not have to wait two to four weeks to get my cassette player repaired since it was broken when I got it. I hope that you will be able to exchange it for me.

Thank you for reading my letter. Please call me at (404) 555-5555 to tell me if you can allow an exchange.

Sincerely,

Alec Levy

Reading Your Writing

The writing process has transformed this letter from an idea to a persuasive letter that is sure to keep the attention of the reader.

Forms of Writing

The purpose of writing is to communicate a message. When you write, it's important to choose a form of writing that fits the message you want to convey.

Sometimes the message is very simple. For example, you want to thank a friend for a gift. You write a thank-you note. At other times, the message is more complex. You want to communicate to your classmates your concern about the need for more recycling. You have some choices about how to communicate that message. You might write a poem. You might write a story in which the events of the plot and the actions of the characters reflect your message. You might prepare an informational report. These are just a few of your choices. There are many others.

In this unit you will learn about the different forms of writing: personal, expository, narrative, descriptive, persuasive, and poetry. Think about how and when to use them when you write.

▶ Personal Writing **68**

▶ Expository Writing **94**

▶ Narrative Writing **144**

▶ Descriptive Writing **198**

▶ Persuasive Writing **210**

▶ Poetry **226**

Personal Writing

Do you write notes to your friends? Do you make lists to remind yourself to do things? Do you write in a journal? These are all examples of personal writing. In these kinds of writing, you can express yourself in a more personal, or individual, way.

Some kinds of personal writing, such as lists and notes, are very practical. Others, such as journals, are more reflective. Think about how you can use each of them.

▶ Journals **70**

▶ Notes and Cards **76**

▶ Friendly Letters **82**

▶ Business Letters **86**

▶ Memos **92**

Journals

You can use a **journal** to write about your thoughts, feelings, ideas, and observations. Many people find it helpful to write in their journals every day. Writing in a journal helps you organize and understand your thoughts and ideas. When you add to your journal, you write a **journal entry.**

A journal keeps good ideas from getting away and can be a wonderful resource for a writer. You can use a journal to store the interesting and meaningful things that catch your attention throughout the day.

Your journal writing can be useful for other writing you do. You may have written a few lines that can be expanded into an essay, or you may have written a description of an unusual person that could become the basis of a short story. You won't use everything in your journal, but a journal can serve as a valuable writer's tool.

Journals come in many shapes and sizes. A spiral-bound notebook keeps everything in one place and can be taken anywhere. A loose-leaf binder allows you to add and subtract pages. Folders with pockets allow you to insert things you've collected, such as magazine clippings, songs, poems, and pictures. You can also keep your journal on a computer.

September 5, 2003

It is so strange how the weather changes right after Labor Day. It's almost like the weather knows that swimming and the other fun stuff of summer are over and that we have to get back to the business of going to school. Mom thinks that we will get some hot weather again, but I feel a change in the air. The trees don't look as green, and I've seen some apples on the trees.

The weather isn't the only thing that's different. My clothes feel different. I finally got to wear the new shoes we bought last week for starting school. I like them, but they make my feet sweat. My new jeans feel funny, too.

Try It

For which type of writing might a student use the above journal entry?

▶ historical fiction
▶ business letter
▶ personal narrative

Although your journal entry should be readable, it does not have to have all of the elements of a finished piece of writing. Journals give you the chance to be freer and more creative. Some of your best ideas can begin in your journal.

Other Kinds of Journals

Some journals have more specific uses. They may overlap in use with your personal journal, but each type has a different focus.

Dialogue Journal

In this kind of journal, two people write back and forth to each other as if they are having a conversation or dialogue. Topics may include books, movies, people they've met, ideas they've thought about, and other experiences. You can share a dialogue journal with a teacher, a parent, or a friend.

In this dialogue journal, a student and teacher discuss a story that was read in class.

> Dear Ms. Griggs,   October 12
> I really liked the story that we read in class this week, "Class President." I thought it was neat how Julio's friends stood up for him and how he had the courage to go talk to the principal. I think it would be great to have Julio as a friend.
>   Karla Waters
>
> Dear Karla,   October 13
> I'm glad you liked the story. I also liked the part in which Julio's friends stood up for him when he was running for president. What other things did you like about the story? I really liked the way the class had a good competition for class president. I thought the speeches were very good.
>   Ms. Griggs

You can use a **learning log** to take notes as you learn about something. You may find it helpful to write about subjects that you wish to understand better. Suppose something doesn't make sense in science. You may want to write down your questions so you can research them later or ask your teacher. In reading, you may want to list vocabulary that you don't understand.

Take a Look

Karla wrote this entry in her learning log when she had a question about something she learned in class.

> Science
>
> We are studying butterflies in science. Mr. Nanapush told us that monarch butterflies that live east of the Rockies migrate 2,000 miles south to one village in Mexico. I think I can understand how a bird can migrate this far, but how can something as light and slow-moving as a butterfly do it?

Here's Karla's entry in her learning log after she experimented with some new ideas with her camera.

> Photography
>
> I took picture A-1 and A-2 of our dog Leo with my camera. I was standing in the sun, and Leo was sitting in the shade. The photos turned out too dark. Leo is just a fuzzy shadow. I took A-3 and A-4 when we both stood in the sun. The camera shutter must have let in just the right amount of light, because Leo came out clear and colorful.

Other Ways to Use Learning Logs

Summarize

Make a list of key words or see if you can come up with a sentence that summarizes what you've learned.

Question Box

Write down any questions that you may have for your teacher or another expert. Some tough questions might require research when you have time.

Visual Cues

Drawing a diagram, a word web, or a simple picture may help you understand and remember your subject.

Take a Look

A word web may help stimulate your thinking on a topic.

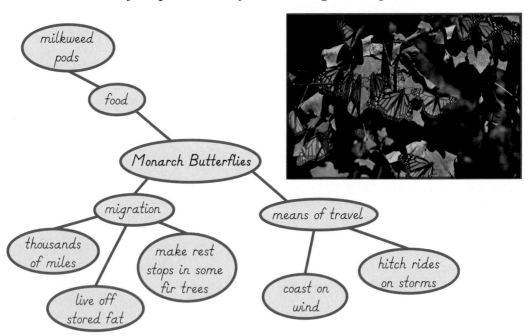

Hints for Keeping a Learning Log

Use separate, small notebooks for each subject or one large notebook that can be separated into sections. Write the date before each entry. Focus on ideas and questions you have about the subject.

Literature Response Journal

This type of journal is similar to a learning log, but it deals with the special problems and questions related to reading a book. Here are some things to think about as you write.

Characters: Write down each character's name and what you learn about that character.

As You Read: Are there things you don't understand about the events? Have the characters changed? Are things turning out differently than you expected? What do you think might happen? Do certain characters or events remind you of anything you've experienced?

Wrapping Up: Did the book end in the way you expected or hoped? How did the main characters change? Did the book cause you to grow or change your views? Would you recommend the book to a friend?

Take a Look

David had trouble remembering who was who in the short story "The Abacus Contest," so he described the characters in his response journal.

Gao Mai – main character, worried about winning, works carefully	
Li Zhi – Gao Mai's best friend, likes practical jokes, carefree	
Gao Mai's father – encouraging, provides helpful hints	
Gao Mai's mother – encouraging, believes in Chinese traditions	
Kun Pei – Gao Mai's classmate, likes to win, turned answers in first, brags	

Reading Your Writing

Most journals are meant for your eyes only and are used to write personal ideas, thoughts, and concerns.

Notes and Cards

You can write a **personal note** or **card** when you want to invite, thank, congratulate, or encourage someone. Notes and cards are shorter than friendly letters and contain key features related to their purpose.

Personal notes begin with a greeting or salutation, contain a short body with just a few lines that state the purpose, and end with a closing followed with your signature. The closing may be even less formal than that used for the friendly letter. "Love," "Your student," and "Your friend," all work.

Personal notes are a great way to show your creativity. You may choose to create a personal note from art materials such as construction paper, markers, colored glue, and glitter.

Premade cards require little of your own writing. To add a personal touch to these cards, write a short note under the preprinted message. Then add the closing and sign your name.

Try It

What kinds of personal notes would you send for the following?

▶ You are having a party to celebrate the end of the school year.

▶ Your scout troop leader has a serious illness.

▶ Your grandmother sent you a new watch.

Thank-You Notes

A **thank-you note** is written to someone who gave you something or did something for you. If you are thanking someone for a gift, be sure to describe the gift in the letter. This will let your reader know that you remember exactly what gift they gave you. If the gift is not your favorite, find something positive to write about it.

Thank You

Dear Aunt Gale,

Thanks for driving all the way from San Francisco to come to my party. It was great seeing you. The hair braiding kit you gave me was perfect. My friends and I have been braiding hair after school lately. The kit gave us new ideas and lots of extra beads and ribbons for braiding. Maybe I'll try it on your hair when you visit for Thanksgiving. Thanks again.

Your niece,

Tamara

Dear Ty,

Thanks for helping out at the car wash. I know you were looking forward to staying at my house. Washing cars probably wasn't what you had in mind, but I promised the band director I would be there. I really appreciate how you pitched in and helped make it a success. Everyone else did, too.

Your Friend,

Eric

Get-Well Cards

A **get-well card** is sent when someone you know is sick or injured. The purpose for writing is to encourage people and let them know you are thinking about them. Get-well cards can be purchased in stores with preprinted poems or messages. Whether you send a purchased card or one you have designed, take the time to write a few words of your own. It will add meaning to the card and make it personal.

Take a Look

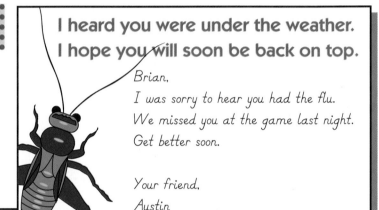

I heard you were under the weather.
I hope you will soon be back on top.

Brian,
I was sorry to hear you had the flu.
We missed you at the game last night.
Get better soon.

Your friend,
Austin

Dear Grandma,
    I was really sorry you had to go back into the hospital. You must be tired of seeing the same old walls every day. Owen and I think about you all the time. Mom has been watering your plants and getting your mail. We will visit you again this weekend.

Love,
Emma

Birthday Cards

Birthday cards honor a person on the day he or she was born. Write a birthday card to give with a gift or to be given or sent on its own. Birthday cards may be purchased, or they can be created at home with stickers, photos, special paper, and other art materials. A homemade card or one designed on a computer might include a clever message or poem.

Take a Look

Hope your birthday's extra special, just like you.

Jamie, Are you really turning twelve? It seems like just yesterday we were fighting over building blocks. I hope you have a great birthday.
Your cousin,
Kyle

Kelly,

When I heard about your birthday, I knew it was true.
Roses and violets would never do.
So I worked on this card
And had a good time of it too!
Have a great birthday.
Love,
Yolanda

Telephone Messages

Telephone messages are another type of personal note. They may seem less important than some other kinds of notes, but if you have ever missed one, you know how important they can be. Avoid trying to remember a telephone message. Instead, write it down and deliver it as soon as possible or place it where it will be seen. Be sure to write down the name of the caller and the return number. The person getting the message may find it helpful if you include all of the following:

▶ **The date**
▶ **Who** called (first and last name)
▶ **When** the person called
▶ **Why** the person called or what the caller wanted (if the caller gives you this information)
▶ **The caller's return telephone number**
▶ **Your name**

Take a Look

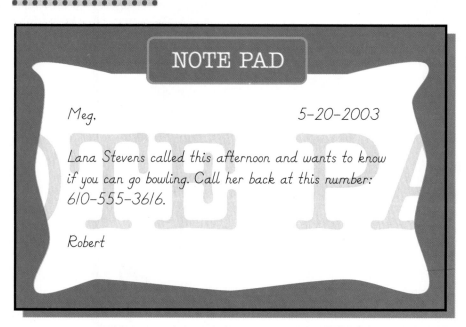

> ## NOTE PAD
>
> Meg,   5-20-2003
>
> Lana Stevens called this afternoon and wants to know if you can go bowling. Call her back at this number: 610-555-3616.
>
> Robert

Invitations

Invitations invite people to a party or a special event. The people who receive invitations need to know certain things in order to decide whether or not they can come.

▶ **What/Why:** What is the purpose of the event or party? What does it celebrate?

▶ **Who:** For whom is the party?

▶ **When:** When will the party take place? Give the date and time.

▶ **Where:** Where will the party be held? Provide an address and directions, if needed.

▶ **Given By:** Who is giving the party?

If you want the persons who are invited to let you know whether or not they can come, print the capital letters RSVP with your telephone number at the bottom of the invitation.

Some invitations say "regrets only." This means that those who receive the invitation should respond only if they *cannot* come.

Fun Fact

R.S.V.P. stands for *repondez, s'il vous plait*, a French phrase meaning "answer, if you please."

Take a Look

You're Invited!

What: _A birthday party_

Who: _Sam Cavenaugh_

When: _5:30–8:30, Friday, October 21st_

Where: _360 Hudson Street_

Given by: _The Cavenaugh family_

Reading Your Writing

Notes and cards are a great way to keep in touch with friends and relatives. Remember to double-check your spelling and grammar so your writing will be clearer.

Friendly Letters

You can send a **friendly letter** to a friend, a relative, a pen pal, or someone you just met and want to get to know better. Include any or all of these things in a friendly letter.

▶ Updates on the interesting things you've been doing
▶ Questions for the person receiving your letter
▶ Tips on good books, movies, and videos
▶ Stories, poems, and jokes that you want to share

Parts of a Friendly Letter

These are the parts of a friendly letter:

Heading

This is your address and the date. It goes in the upper right corner.

Salutation

Use the word *Dear*, followed by the name and a comma. The Salutation goes by the left margin, two lines below the heading.

Body

This is the message part of the letter. Start it two lines below the salutation. Indent each paragraph in the body of your letter.

Closing

Yours truly and *Sincerely* are commonly used as a closing. The Closing goes two lines below the body by the left margin. Capitalize just the first word, and use a comma at the end of the closing.

Signature

Sign your name under the closing.

Jason replies to a letter from Tyrone, a friend he made on vacation.

Heading ▶ 4992 Illini Avenue
Rockford, IL 61109
April 2, 2003

Salutation ▶ Dear Tyrone,

Body ▶ It was great to hear from you. I really miss camping at Huntington Beach too. Can you believe all the baby crabs we caught in the ocean stream? I have never had so much fun. I'm glad we threw them all back because my teacher at school told me that some crabs are getting scarce. The fiddler crabs up on the beach were pretty funny. I still think about how they ran across the sand and disappeared at the slightest noise.

My dad and I have been doing a lot of fishing where we live. We catch mostly sunfish and bluegills, but last weekend I caught a smallmouth bass. Do you ever go fishing? Wouldn't it be great if we could get our dads to takes us on a fishing trip together?

What do you like to do for fun in Kentucky? Is it warm down there now? It's still pretty cold where we live. We've been riding our bikes a lot and playing with scooters, but we will probably have to wait until the middle of June before we can go swimming.

My mom finally said I could take Tang Soo Do lessons. It's kind of like karate only it's Korean. Do you do any martial arts?

Write soon and tell me what you're doing.

Closing ▶ Your fishing buddy,
Signature ▶ Jason

E-mail

E-mail stands for "electronic mail." Many people use e-mail messages in place of friendly letters. Writers use e-mail addresses to communicate by computer. An e-mail message is sent through the Internet.

To send an e-mail message, follow these steps:

▶ Open your e-mail program. Go to "start a new e-mail message."

▶ Where it says "to," type the e-mail address of the person to whom you are writing. After "subject," type a word or short phrase describing your topic, such as "vacation" or "birthday."

▶ Begin typing your message. For an e-mail message to a friend or relative, you may wish to follow the friendly letter format. Include a salutation (Dear _____,). Indent the paragraphs of the body. Type your closing, followed by a comma with your name underneath. Your tone may be casual.

▶ For a business e-mail message, follow the business letter format.

Take a Look

Here's an e-mail message sent by Jack Bodo to his favorite author, Jerry Spinelli.

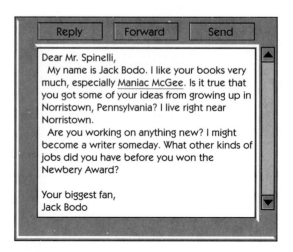

Tips for Writing a Friendly Letter

Prewriting Plan What You Want to Say

▶ Choose a friend or relative to whom you wish to write.

▶ List questions you want to ask and jokes, stories, and ideas you want to share.

Drafting Get Your Ideas on Paper

▶ Work on the body of your letter. Include everything you want to say. Refer to your prewriting ideas.

▶ After drafting the body of your letter, add the heading, the salutation, the closing, and your signature.

Revising Make Sure It Makes Sense

▶ **Organization** Make sure your letter has five parts.

▶ **Sentence Fluency** Make sure your reader can understand your ideas and that they flow well.

▶ **Voice** Check your tone. It should be friendly and not too stiff or formal.

Editing/Proofreading Check the Details

▶ **Conventions** See pages 82–83 to make sure you used the proper format. Use a comma after the salutation, and indent paragraphs.

▶ **Conventions** Make sure you capitalized names and any other proper nouns used in your letter.

Publishing Prepare to Mail Your Friendly Letter

▶ **Presentation** Neatly type or write your final copy.

▶ **Presentation** See page 90 for how to fold your letter and address your envelope.

Business Letters

A **business letter** is a formal letter written to a company, organization, or professional person for a specific reason. Your tone should be less personal and even more polite and direct than that normally used for a friendly letter. Below are the parts of a business letter:

Heading

The heading consists of the sender's address and the date. It goes in the upper left corner.

Inside Address

The inside address includes the name and address of the person receiving the letter. It goes two lines below the heading.
   Ms. Greta Frederick, Ph.D.

Salutation

The salutation is the greeting. Put a colon after it.
       Dear Ms. Samartino:
You may use salutations like these when you don't know the person's name:
       To Whom It May Concern: Dear Sir or Madam:
       Dear National Geographic Society:

Body

The body includes what you want to say. Be brief and polite but not overly formal or stiff. Begin the body two lines below the salutation. Leave a single line of space between each paragraph. Do not indent.

Closing

The closing goes two lines below the body, at the left margin.

   Yours truly,   Sincerely,

Signature

Sign your name under the closing.

The Three Types of Business Letters

You will have different reasons for writing business letters. Your purpose will determine which of the three types of business letters you write.

A Letter of Request asks for information.

You write to an amusement park to find out about the safety of its rides and whether it has any record of accidents.

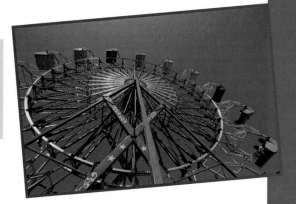

A Letter of Concern states your concern about an issue that affects a group of people such as your school, your neighborhood, or the general public.

You write a letter to the editor of your local paper to raise awareness about the lack of community parks in your area.

A Letter of Complaint complains about a policy, a product, or a service.

You write a letter to a nearby rock-climbing gym to complain about its inconvenient hours.

Try It

Which of the three types is each of these?

▶ A letter to the governor about the lack of bicycle trails in your state.

▶ A letter to a bicycle catalogue company telling them about a problem with the bicycle accessories they sent you.

▶ A letter to the state parks department asking them to send you bicycle trail maps.

This is a letter of complaint that Kevin Chang wrote to the makers of the Super Whiz-Bang Zoomer.

Heading

147 Mayfield Street
Campbell, FL 67043
November 3, 2003

Inside Address

Karen Nelson, Customer Relations Coordinator
The Sky's the Limit, Inc.
3300 Atmosphere Ave.
Star City, KS 17970

Salutation

Dear Ms. Nelson:

Body

I am writing about the Super Whiz-Bang Zoomer made by your company. Last week I gave one to my brother. Just a few hours later, the Whiz-Bang broke. The store where I bought the toy didn't have any left. They offered me a refund, but my brother really wants another Whiz-Bang Zoomer.

I am sending you the original store receipt along with the broken pieces in this package. Please send us another Whiz-Bang Zoomer.

Thank you for your attention to this matter. You can write to me at the above address.

Closing

Sincerely,

Kevin Chang

Signature

Kevin Chang

The Business Letter Body

Use these checklists for writing the body of a letter of complaint, a letter of request, or a letter of concern.

Letter of Complaint

- ▶ Explain the problem.
- ▶ Describe the product, service, or policy.
- ▶ Tell what you think is the cause of the problem.
- ▶ Explain what you expect of the reader—whether a replacement, a refund, a change of policy, or other outcome.
- ▶ Thank the reader for looking into the problem.

Letter of Request

- ▶ Introduce yourself and explain why you are writing.
- ▶ Include any specific questions you want answered.
- ▶ Inform the reader of any dates or deadlines you must meet.
- ▶ Thank the reader for his or her help.

Letter of Concern

- ▶ Describe the issue or situation and give your opinion.
- ▶ Explain how you would correct the problem or change the situation.
- ▶ Tell the reader how your suggestions or solution will work.
- ▶ Ask that action be taken to change the situation.

Mail Your Business Letter

After you have checked and corrected your letter, you are ready to send it. First you will need to fold your letter.

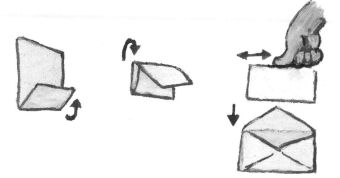

Now you are ready to address the envelope.

▶ In the center, just slightly to the left, write the name and address of the person receiving the letter.

▶ In the upper left corner, write your name and address. When addressing your envelope, you should write in only capital letters and leave out all punctuation. This makes it easier for the Postal Service to process mail.

▶ Put the stamp in the upper right corner.

Fun Fact

Will your letters be worth something someday? The highest price paid for a signed letter is $748,000. The letter was written by Abraham Lincoln.

Reading Your Writing

Write a business letter when you want to make formal contact with a company or professional person. Be sure to use the correct format so your reader can easily read your letter.

Tips for Writing a Business Letter

Prewriting Plan What You Want to Say

▶ Refer to the checklist on page 89 to plan the body of your business letter.

Drafting Get Your Ideas on Paper

▶ After drafting the body, add the heading, inside address, salutation, closing, and signature.

Revising Make Sure It Makes Sense

▶ **Organization** Make sure your letter has six parts.
▶ **Organization** Delete sentences that stray from the central idea of each paragraph.
▶ **Voice** Check your tone. It should be polite and straightforward.

Editing/Proofreading Check the Details

▶ **Conventions** See page 86 to make sure you correctly formatted your letter. Use a colon after the salutation, and do not indent paragraphs. If you are writing your letter on a computer, use the automatic business letter tool to set up your letter for you.

Publishing Prepare to Mail Your Business Letter

▶ **Presentation** Neatly type or rewrite your final copy.
▶ **Presentation** See page 90 for how to fold your letter and address your envelope.

Memos

A **memo** is a short message that communicates something to a person or a group of people with whom you are working. The word memo is short for **memorandum,** which means "written reminder."

Memos do not have closings or signatures. Instead, writers may initial their names by the headings. The format of a memo is much different from the format of a business letter.

Take a Look

Heading ▶

Memo
Date: April 14, 2003
To: Dogwood Festival Float-Building Committee
From: Ava Gregorio, Chair A∨
Subject: Donations
CC: Fred Cushing and all
              Community Center
              Maintenance Staff

Body ▶

Please collect large- and medium-sized cardboard boxes. We will need them for building our float. Also, we need the following donations: white sheets; brown felt; cans of blue, green, and yellow latex paint. Items may be left Tuesday through Friday, April 15–18, at the Community Center garage between 3 p.m. and 8 p.m.

Memos sometimes use the label *CC*. *CC* stands for carbon copy (even though most memos today are photocopied). Write *CC:* at the end of the heading before a list of other people who will receive copies.

The label *Re:* is sometimes used in place of *Subject:* to describe the topic.

Tips for Writing a Memo

Prewriting Plan What You Want to Say

▶ Decide who should receive your memo. Should it go to just one person or a group of people?

▶ Limit the memo to one main point or two or three related points.

Drafting Get Your Points on Paper

▶ Use your prewriting ideas for your writing. Keep the memo brief and to the point.

Revising Make Sure It Makes Sense

▶ **Organization** Your heading should contain four heading labels, five if you are listing those getting copies *(CC:)*. For formatting, check the sample memo on page 92.

▶ **Word Choice** Make sure your readers can understand the information and will know what to do with it.

Editing/Proofreading Check the Details

▶ **Conventions** The first letters of the date, name, and subject should line up underneath each other. Do not indent paragraphs. Instead, separate each with a single line of space.

▶ **Conventions** Make sure that heading labels, all names, and other proper nouns have been capitalized.

Publishing Get Ready to Deliver the Memo

▶ **Presentation** Neatly type or write your final copy.

▶ Make copies of your memo and distribute.

Expository Writing

Expository writing does two things. It explains how to do something, or it presents information about something. The steps in the explanation are arranged in a logical way so that the reader can follow the procedure or repeat the activity. When information is presented, it is clear, correct, complete, and well organized.

Much of the writing you do for school is expository. Some of the lessons in this unit can help you improve your reports and book reviews. You can use the others to try types of expository writing that may be new to you.

▶ Summaries 96

▶ Analyzing Fiction 100

▶ Responding to Nonfiction 106

▶ Book Reviews 110

▶ Explaining a Process and Giving
Directions 116

▶ News Stories 122

▶ Expository Essays 128

▶ Research Reports 134

Summary

When someone asks you about a movie you saw, do you tell them every single thing that happened in it? Of course not! You'd give a **summary,** or a condensed version of the movie, highlighting the main events, ideas, and characters.

A summary is used as a way to communicate in a brief and to-the-point manner. Summaries on the back covers of paperback books are written to grab your interest and make you want to read the book. At other times, summaries help us decide whether we wish to explore more detailed information. Internet search engines, for instance, often feature summaries of recommended Web sites.

Often, we summarize the main points of a reading selection to help us remember what we feel is most important.

Take a Look

On the next two pages is the first part of Necia H. Apfel's book *Voyager to the Planets*. The headings to the left of the excerpt represent some notes that a student, Ling, made while she was reading the Voyager 2 story.

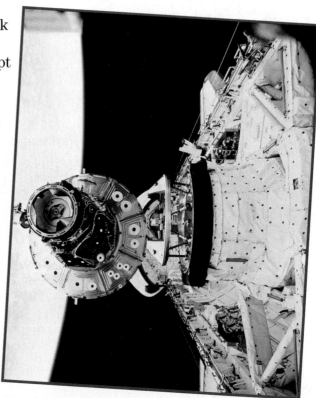

What Voyager 2 was ▶ Voyagers 1 and 2 are space probes, spacecraft sent to explore other planets. Space probes carry instruments that collect information and send photographs and other data back to Earth. Before the Voyagers, space probes had been sent to gather information from Mars, Venus, Jupiter, Saturn, and Mercury. Voyager 1 flew by Jupiter and Saturn. Voyager 2, however, was the first space probe to go on a "grand tour" of several planets.

When it lifted off ▶ On August 20, 1977, Voyager 2 was placed atop a Titan 3-E/Centaur rocket at the United States launching site on Cape Canaveral in Florida. The rocket blasted off and rose majestically into the clear blue sky.

All was well. But now the real countdown began. Voyager would take two years to reach its first destination—the giant planet Jupiter.

Where it went ▶ Voyager is a strange-looking machine with tubes and boxlike structures sticking out all over it. These contain its many instruments, including cameras, radio receivers, and ultraviolet and infrared sensors. The instruments were

What the mission was ▶ designed to collect data from places Voyager would visit and to send this information back to Earth, where scientists and engineers were eagerly awaiting the reports.

Sometimes instructions had to be sent from stations on Earth to Voyager, telling it when to change its position, what data to record, or which instruments to use. Voyager was equipped with a big umbrella-shaped antenna to receive

How messages were sent and received ▶ these directions.

Problem ▶   In designing Voyager, the engineers tried very hard to anticipate any problems or emergencies that might arise on its long journey. But the first difficulty occurred much sooner than they expected. Only eight months after Voyager was launched, its primary radio system stopped working and the backup radio receiver developed a short circuit. These defects drastically reduced Voyager's ability to receive instructions from the scientists. New computer programs

Possible Solution ▶ had to be sent to Voyager so that it could respond to future commands. The scientists could only hope that the defective radio system would last for the entire journey. Otherwise, there would be no way for them to communicate with Voyager.

Here's Ling's summary of the selection. Notice how she organized the summary based on the notes she made. First, she carefully read the selection and chose *what, where, when* and *how*. She then looked at the material and chose a sentence that contained the main idea of the selection. She put that sentence first, using it as her topic sentence. Finally, she organized the supporting details and combined some sentences for her summary.

> Voyager 2, launched on August 20, 1977, was the first space probe to visit several planets. Its first destination would be the giant planet Jupiter—two years away. Voyager 2 had many instruments for collecting and transmitting data from space to Earth. It also had a giant antenna for receiving instructions from home. Engineers tried hard to plan ahead for possible Voyager 2 problems, but its main radio system shut off after eight months. If Voyager couldn't be fixed with new computer programs from Earth, scientists wouldn't be able to direct it.

Tips for Writing a Summary

Prewriting ▸ Plan What You Want to Say

▶ Read the material you are summarizing and figure out the main idea.

▶ Locate the supporting details.

Drafting ▸ Get Your Ideas Down on Paper

▶ Start with a sentence that states the main idea of the selection you are summarizing.

▶ Use your own words. Don't copy from the book.

Revising ▸ Make Sure It Makes Sense

▶ **Organization** Arrange your sentences logically so the reader can follow along with your summary.

▶ **Voice** Make the summary sound like *you* wrote it.

▶ **Organization** Have you left out any important details or added things that aren't necessary?

Editing/Proofreading ▸ Check the Details

▶ **Conventions** Proofread for spelling errors.

▶ **Conventions** Check for mistakes in punctuation and capitalization.

▶ **Sentence Fluency** Read your paper out loud to make sure the sentences flow together well.

Publishing ▸ Get It Ready to Go

▶ **Presentation** Neatly type or write your paper if you are turning it in for an assignment.

Analyzing Fiction

In fiction writing, characters and plot combine to tell an interesting story. The way to tell if a character or plot is developed well or poorly is to analyze it. When you analyze something, you look critically at the separate parts that make up the whole. This process can help you better understand the story.

Character Analysis

One way to analyze a character is to use a character web. A web is a good way to visually lay out the things a writer has shown about a character.

Here is a web that a student, Lisa, made about Julio, the main character in Johanna Hurwitz's story "Class President."

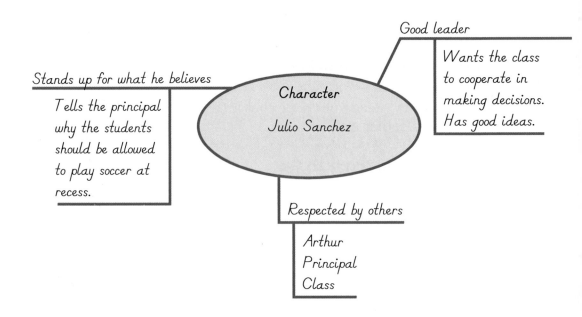

Character Web

Stands up for what he believes

Tells the principal why the students should be allowed to play soccer at recess.

Character
Julio Sanchez

Good leader

Wants the class to cooperate in making decisions. Has good ideas.

Respected by others

Arthur
Principal
Class

This is the character analysis that Lisa wrote using her web. Notice how she included a paragraph for each trait.

The Right Person for the Job

Julio Sanchez is the main character in "Class President." Julio is a strong and interesting character for a lot of reasons.

We find out from the story that Julio is someone who is not afraid to stand up for what he believes. When he finds out that the students at his school won't be allowed to play soccer at recess anymore, Julio goes to the principal of the school. Julio is able to talk to the principal about all the reasons the children should be allowed to play soccer, and the principal agrees that Julio is right.

Another thing we learn from the story is that Julio is respected by others. His principal tells Julio that he has "a good head on his shoulders." Julio's friend Arthur tells the entire class that Julio is fair and does nice things. The class elects Julio as its president.

Julio is also a good leader. When he makes his speech to become president, Julio tells the class that he thinks they should all cooperate and make decisions together. When he wins the election, he suddenly gets lots of good ideas for his class.

Julio has many traits that make a good class president. I would like to have someone such as Julio for president of our class.

Exploring Plot

The *plot,* or story line, of fiction introduces characters, presents a problem, and follows the characters as they attempt to solve the problem. Effective plots contain the following elements:

▶ a beginning section, a middle section, and an end section

▶ a problem to be solved, or a goal to be achieved, which is introduced in the beginning section

▶ conflict in the middle section as characters try to solve the problem or achieve the goal

▶ a **climax,** or high point of action, which usually occurs in the first part of the end section

▶ a **conclusion,** or resolution, occurring after the climax, which sometimes explains how the problem is solved and ties up loose ends in the story

Take a Look

Lisa asked herself the following questions about "Class President" and wrote the answers on a graphic organizer so she could analyze the plot.

▶ What problem is introduced in "Class President"?

▶ What's the story's conflict?

▶ What might be the story's climax?

▶ What might be the story's resolution?

Graphic Organizer for "Class President"

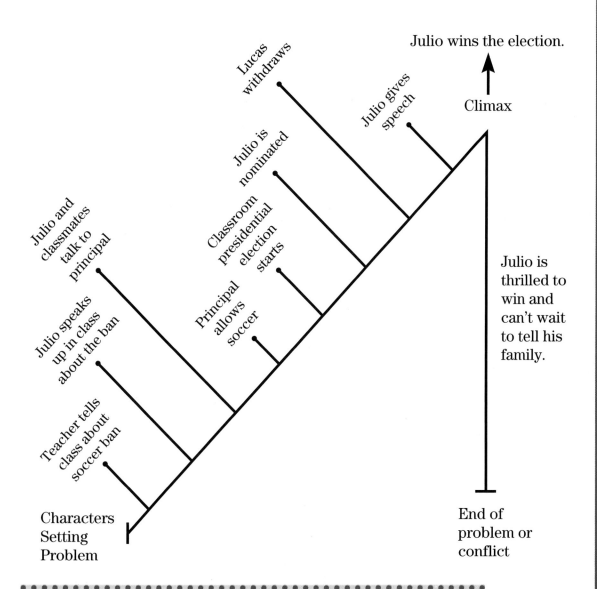

Plot Line

Julio wins the election.

Lucas withdraws

Julio gives speech

Climax

Julio is nominated

Julio and classmates talk to principal

Classroom presidential election starts

Julio is thrilled to win and can't wait to tell his family.

Julio speaks up in class about the ban

Principal allows soccer

Teacher tells class about soccer ban

Characters
Setting
Problem

End of problem or conflict

Try It

Think of the plot of your favorite book. Can you pinpoint the problem, conflict, climax, and conclusion?

This is the paper that Lisa wrote after she completed her graphic organizer of the plot.

Julio's Big Day

Julio Sanchez is excited about beginning the school year. He has volunteered to help his friend Lucas win the election for class president. During recess of the first day of school, Arthur Lewis, one of the boys in class, breaks his glasses while the boys are playing soccer. This is where the main problem in the story begins.

The next thing that happens continues to build the excitement in the story. During class the next day, the teacher announces that there will be no more soccer during recess. This is when the conflict begins in the plot. Julio and some classmates get permission to tell the principal that the soccer ban is unfair.

When Julio and his classmates meet with the principal, Julio presents his points very clearly. The principal agrees that the students should be allowed to play soccer. The tension has decreased in the story, but it doesn't stay that way for long.

When Julio and his classmates get back to the classroom, Arthur Lewis nominates him for class president because Julio is such a good leader. This could be the beginning of another problem because it means that Julio will be running against his best friend, Lucas! At that moment, Lucas withdraws from the election and tells the class that everyone should vote for Julio.

When the campaign speeches start, the excitement begins to build again. The climax of the story is when Julio wins the election. After that, the action slows down. The story ends with Julio running home to tell his family about the election, and all the problems are resolved.

Reading Your Writing

Knowing how to analyze character and plot will help you better understand the stories you read. It will also help you write better stories for your readers.

Tips for Character and Plot Analysis

Prewriting Plan What You Want to Say

▶ Provide examples from the text to support the points you are making.

▶ **Character Analysis** Use a graphic organizer to plan what you want the reader to know about the character.

▶ **Plot Analysis** Identify the problem, conflict, climax, and conclusion of the plot on a graphic organizer.

Drafting Get Your Ideas Down on Paper

▶ Use your web and graphic organizer to draft paragraphs for your paper.

▶ Be sure to put your own thoughts and words on paper rather than copying from the book.

Revising Make Sure It Makes Sense

▶ **Organization** Did you use a topic sentence in each paragraph?

▶ **Organization** Make sure that your paper is arranged logically and that your paragraphs connect.

▶ **Voice** Does it sound like *you* wrote the paper?

Editing/Proofreading Check the Details

▶ **Conventions** Proofread for mistakes in spelling and punctuation.

Publishing Get It Ready to Go

▶ **Presentation** Neatly rewrite or type your paper.

Responding to Nonfiction

Nonfiction is about people, events, and situations. It is true and factual. Good nonfiction can make you think of things you've never even considered. For instance, a biography can tell you about how a person responded to a particular situation and cause you to think of how you might have responded if you had been in the same situation.

Nonfiction can spark your creative energy. That's exactly what happened to Sam when he read Necia H. Apfel's book *Voyager to the Planets*. When his teacher asked the class to respond to *Voyager to the Planets*, Sam knew exactly what he wanted to do. Some students wrote about the scientific impact that Voyager 2 had because it was the first to tour all the outer planets. Others wrote about whether or not it was a good idea to spend the money to send Voyager into space. Sam decided to imagine that he was the chief scientist responsible for Voyager 2. The graphic organizer he used to write down some of the main ideas and details from the book is below.

Look at the graphic organizer Sam created. First, he broke down the book about Voyager 2 into subtopics, then he included details about each of the subtopics.

Topic

Voyager 2's Journey to the Planets

Subtopic

The Launch

1. August 20, 1977—blue sky
2. From Cape Canaveral on a Titan 3E/Centaur rocket
3. First space probe to visit several planets

Subtopic

Description

1. Looks like alien robot
2. Instruments collect and transmit data to Earth
3. Giant antenna receives data from Earth

Subtopic

Problems and Solution

1. We planned to avoid problems
2. Radios break within 8 months of launch
3. If we can't fix it, we're sunk!
4. Sent new computer programs

Conclusion

New commands received. Voyager takes pictures and measurements of Jupiter's clouds.

Can you identify how Sam organized his response using his graphic organizer?

It's My Voyage, Too

I was so excited as Voyager 2 blasted off into the deep blue sky from Florida's Cape Canaveral on top of a Titan 3E/Centaur rocket. It was August 20, 1977. As chief scientist for the project, I felt responsible for this historic space probe. Its first stop was the planet Jupiter. Its estimated time of arrival was two years.

Voyager looked like some sort of alien robot. It had strange-looking rods and shapes sticking out of it. These were instruments to collect and send data from space back to my lab on Earth. Voyager 2 also had a giant antenna for receiving instructions we would send out.

Even though my engineering team spent years trying to plan for possible problems, Voyager 2 had its first major problem within eight months of its launch. Voyager 2's main radio system shut off, and a short circuit killed its backup radio. If it couldn't be fixed quickly, we wouldn't be able to direct the space probe's movements and activities.

Without wasting any time, we sent Voyager 2's radio some new computer programs. On July 9, 1979, two years after launch, Voyager 2 arrived at Jupiter, a planet so large that 1,300 Earths could fit inside it. Our commands were received, and Voyager 2 responded by taking pictures of Jupiter's clouds. All our hard work was worth the effort.

How is Sam's response different from a summary? Sam did not simply restate what the original book said. Instead, he made something new of it. He did this by changing the narration of the story to the first-person point of view. He shifted the story from one being told from an outside observer's point of view to one being told by himself.

Reading Your Writing

Taking the time to write an original, thought-provoking response will help you keep your reader's attention.

Tips for Responding to Nonfiction

Prewriting Plan What You Want to Say

▶ Decide how you will respond to the piece.

▶ Identify the main idea and supporting details from the piece to which you are responding.

▶ Create a graphic organizer to get your thoughts in order.

Drafting Get Your Ideas on Paper

▶ Use your graphic organizer to draft paragraphs for your paper.

▶ Be sure you have a topic sentence and supporting details for each paragraph.

Revising Make Sure It Makes Sense

▶ **Organization** Is there anything you would like to add or clarify?

▶ **Voice** Will your audience be able to tell that *you* wrote the paper?

Editing/Proofreading Check the Details

▶ **Sentence Fluency** Read your paper aloud to make sure it flows smoothly.

▶ **Conventions** Proofread for correct punctuation, capitalization, and spelling.

Publishing Get it Ready to Go

▶ **Presentation** Add any drawings, diagrams, or charts that will make your writing clearer.

Book Reviews

Book reviewers, also known as book critics, write essays about the books they have read. **Book reviews** are part summary and part opinion, and they help people decide which books they may want to read. A book review may steer you toward or away from reading a certain book.

Reviewing Fiction

In reviewing any book, you'll first want to read it thoroughly from beginning to end. Then, complete a graphic organizer to clearly identify both the plot summary and your opinions, in addition to the reasons behind these opinions.

Take a Look

Look at the following graphic organizer and review of Sheila Burnford's book *The Incredible Journey* written by Damon for an assignment.

The Incredible Journey by Sheila Burnford

1. Introduction

- Title—*The Incredible Journey*
- Author—Sheila Burnford
- Main Characters—Luath, Bodger, and Tao
- Setting—Ontario, Canada

2. Character Descriptions

- Luath—Independent and encouraging
- Bodger—Old and loves to fight
- Tao—Intelligent and brave

3. Summary

- Begins in Longridge's house
- Animals decide to make their way home
- Face obstacles along the way
- Reunite with their owners

4. Opinion and Recommendation

- Book is about the value of friendship
- Reader cares about the animals
- Recommend to anyone who likes animals

The Incredible Journey by Sheila Burnford: A Review

The Incredible Journey by Sheila Burnford is a story about a Labrador retriever named Luath, a bull terrier named Bodger, and a Siamese cat named Tao. These three animals cross hundreds of miles and face many obstacles to be reunited with their owners.

The story begins in the house of John Longridge in northwestern Ontario, Canada. The animals' owners, the Hunters, give them to Longridge to take care of while the family is away from home.

One day, Longridge lets the animals out of the house. They usually don't stray too far, but this day they decide to go home. Their natural instincts tell them to head west, and so they set out on their journey.

Luath, the young Labrador, is the leader. He is an independent dog that distances himself from the other two but encourages them when they are weak or afraid.

Bodger is an old bull terrier that loves to fight. He helps Luath fight another dog and beat him. Bodger has a hard time keeping up the pace because of his age, but the others help and feed him when he can't do things for himself.

Tao is a strong, intelligent cat that has no fear. He shows his bravery when he rescues Bodger from a bear cub. His intelligence helps him outsmart a lynx that wants to eat him.

My favorite part of this book is the animals' reunion with their owners. While the Hunter family is at their cabin, Elizabeth Hunter believes she hears Luath's bark. Soon, Tao and Luath are reunited with the family. Bodger appears later, and until then, the reader is unsure if he will make it home.

I like this book because it shows the value of friendship. No single one of the animals could have made the journey home alone. Their dedication to helping each other makes the reader care about them. I recommend this book to anyone who likes animals.

Reviewing Nonfiction

Because plot is not a feature of a nonfiction book, reviews generally discuss what the book has to offer the reader. The reviewer will look at the organization of the book and judge whether it is presented in a logical order. The reviewer will also examine tone and language. Is the book humorous, serious, or somewhere between the two? A reviewer may also check the information in the book. Is it accurate, up to date, and appropriate for the book's audience?

When reviewing a nonfiction book, you can choose to complete a graphic organizer to gather your points. You can list points that summarize the book. Also list important features of the book. Finally, evaluate the intended purpose of the book, and offer an opinion as to whether the author achieved this purpose. Look at the following graphic organizer and review of *A Kid's Guide to Washington, D.C.*

Take a Look

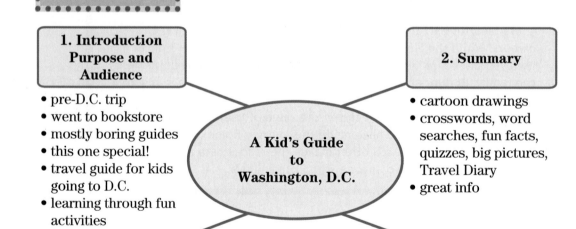

1. Introduction Purpose and Audience

- pre-D.C. trip
- went to bookstore
- mostly boring guides
- this one special!
- travel guide for kids going to D.C.
- learning through fun activities

A Kid's Guide to Washington, D.C.

2. Summary

- cartoon drawings
- crosswords, word searches, fun facts, quizzes, big pictures, Travel Diary
- great info

3. Highlight and Feature

- Travel Diary
- show an example of one

4. Opinions and Recommendation

- interesting and exciting!
- I recommend it!

A Kid's Guide to Washington, D.C.

A few weeks before our spring vacation trip to Washington, D.C., my mom and dad took me to our neighborhood bookstore. We spent a lot of time looking at all of the Washington, D.C., travel guides. Most of them were written in tiny print and seemed sort of boring. It was hard to tell one from the other. Then, I spotted one that looked different from all the others. It's called A Kid's Guide to Washington, D.C., and it's written just for kids.

I knew right away that it was the perfect guide for me. It's bigger than most guides, with lots of cartoon drawings. There are history crossword puzzles, museum word searches, big pictures, fun facts, mini-quizzes, art projects, and a really good feature called Travel Diary.

Every few pages a half page is devoted to the Travel Diary. The traveler can complete a paragraph that's already partly written. Here's an example:

Travel Diary: The Museum of American History

My favorite part of the Museum of American History is the
_____, because
_____.
I saw the _____ that belonged to
_____. The most amazing invention I saw was the
_____.

This book is so interesting that it made my trip to Washington, D.C., really exciting! I recommend it, even if you're not really going to Washington!

Reading Your Writing

A book review is an essay that is part summary and part opinion about a book. A thoughtful and well-written review can help other kids who are searching for books to read.

Tips for Writing Nonfiction Book Reviews

Prewriting Plan What You Want to Say

▶ Plan your review. Include the purpose, intended audience, important features, and your opinion of the book.

▶ Pull in your audience with a unique, attention-getting opening sentence.

Drafting Get Your Ideas on Paper

▶ Use the graphic organizer you created to help you draft paragraphs for your review.

Revising Make Sure It Makes Sense

▶ **Organization** Be certain that your paragraphs flow well and that your paper is arranged logically so your readers can follow along with your review.

▶ **Voice** Can your reader hear *you* in your review?

Editing/Proofreading Check the Details

▶ **Conventions** Correct mistakes in grammar, spelling, capitalization, and punctuation.

Publishing Get It Ready to Go

▶ **Presentation** If possible, include something visual such as a photo, chart, or a graph to add interest to your review.

Tips for Writing Fiction Book Reviews

Prewriting Plan What You Want to Say

▶ Plan your introduction, summary, and opinion of the book.

Drafting Get Your Ideas on Paper

▶ Use the graphic organizer you created to help you draft paragraphs for your review.

▶ Pull in your audience with a unique, attention-getting opening sentence.

Revising Be Sure It Makes Sense

▶ **Organization** If you have revealed too much of the plot of the piece, try changing your review so you will not ruin the enjoyment of the piece for your readers.

▶ **Voice** Can the reader hear *you* in your writing?

Editing/Proofreading Check the Details

▶ **Sentence Fluency** Read your paper aloud to make sure it flows well.

▶ **Conventions** Correct mistakes in grammar, spelling, capitalization, and punctuation.

Publishing Get It Ready to Go

▶ **Presentation** If possible, include a piece of artwork to add interest to your review.

Explaining a Process and Giving Directions

How does this work? What do I do? How do I get there? Has anyone ever asked you these questions? If so, you've probably answered by explaining how a process works or by giving directions.

Explaining a process requires giving step-by-step instructions about what is involved. Your math teacher explains a process every day when he or she tells you how to solve a problem. When you explain a process, you teach a person what steps to take to do something. Giving directions is different than explaining a process. When you give directions, you tell a person how to physically get from one place to another.

Explaining a Process

We're often asked to explain how to do something. Sometimes, we'll be asked to write it down for later reference. For example, your friend may want to know how a VCR records TV shows for later viewing. He won't be able to remember everything you tell him so he asks you to write down the process.

Start by identifying your purpose and audience. For example, an explanation of the VCR recording process for a fifth-grader would be too hard for a first- or second-grader. Then, gather all the information necessary to explain the process, such as the VCR manual. Remember that transition words will help clue your audience to the order, location, and importance of certain information. The transition words in the model have been bolded for easy identification.

Be sure to include all the steps necessary to complete the process. A graphic organizer can help you remember everything.

PROCESS: Programming a VCR

> **FIRST:**
> Plug in the VCR.

> **NEXT:**
> Set the date and clock.

> **THEN:**
> Choose the type of recording from the menu.

> **NEXT:**
> Set recording time and speed.

> **FINALLY:**
> Turn off the VCR.

VCR Programming Process

Programming a VCR for timed recording has always been a mystery, especially for adults. Luckily, I have always been good with electronic devices and will explain how this process works.

First it's important to make sure your VCR is plugged in and getting power. **Next** the VCR's date and clock must be set. **Then** locate the programming menu and choose the type of recording you wish. You'll **next** be asked to set the start time, stop time, channel, and recording speed. **Finally** remember to turn off the VCR. This places it in the timed recording mode.

Reading Your Writing

When you explain a process, you tell how to do something. Remember to include all the steps in your explanation, or the process may not work.

Giving Directions

If you have ever been lost, you probably understand the importance of good directions. It is very frustrating to be late getting somewhere because someone left out an important detail when he or she gave you directions. It is even worse when you get completely lost and never arrive at all. Learning how to give good directions is a practical skill that you will use again and again.

Begin planning how to give directions by thinking about your audience. What might the person who will be following your directions already know about the area? If you are trying to tell your cousin who lives out of state how to find your house, your cousin will need more specific information than someone who lives a mile away from you.

Let your audience know how easy or difficult it will be to find the way. Also include how long it will take to get there.

Remember that transition, or signal, words will help your audience understand the order, location, and importance of certain information. The transition words in the following example are bold for easy identification.

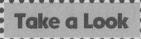

How to Get to Charla's House from School

These are the directions for getting to my house for my birthday party. Tell your parents it should take only about 15 minutes by car.

From the parking lot beside the cafeteria, turn **turn left** (east) onto Main Street. Continue on Main for four blocks until you see Elm Street. Turn **left** on Elm and **stay** on that street for about three miles. At the stop sign at Elm and Pine Avenue, turn **right** onto Pine. You will see a fire station on the corner. Pine curves around Chambers Park. Then there will be a stop light. Go **straight** through the light for two blocks until you get to Van Buren Drive. Turn **left** on Van Buren and go one block to Madison Court. Turn **left** on Madison and look for the white house with the chain-link fence. Take Madison to the end of the street. My house is 1903 Madison Court. Look for the balloons!

Reading Your Writing

Directions tell someone how to get from one place to another. Good directions will include all the important information to keep your reader from getting lost.

Tips for Explaining a Process

Prewriting Plan What You Want to Say

▶ Think about the audience for whom you are writing.

▶ Use a graphic organizer to plan the steps in the process.

Drafting Get Your Ideas on Paper

▶ Use your graphic organizer to help you write your draft.

▶ Use signal words such as *first, next, then,* and *finally* to alert your audience to what is coming next.

▶ Explain the process in logical order.

Revising Make Sure It Makes Sense

▶ **Organization** Use enough signal words to help your reader follow your explanation.

▶ **Organization** Include all the necessary details.

▶ **Organization** Ask someone to read your explanation to make sure it makes sense.

Editing/Proofreading Check the Details

▶ **Conventions** Be sure all the words are spelled correctly and that you've used complete sentences.

Publishing Get It Ready to Go

▶ **Presentation** Prepare a handwritten or typed copy of your work.

Tips for Giving Directions

Prewriting Plan What You Want to Say

▶ Determine your audience.

▶ Use a graphic organizer to help you get your thoughts in order.

Drafting Get Your Ideas on Paper

▶ Use your graphic organizer to help you write your directions.

▶ Use transition words such as *left, right, straight,* and *turn* to alert your readers about what to expect next.

Revising Make Sure It Makes Sense

▶ **Organization** Be sure you haven't left out any details that will be helpful to your audience.

▶ **Organization** Include the necessary transition words.

▶ **Organization** Ask someone to read your directions to make sure they make sense.

Editing/Proofreading Check the Details

▶ **Conventions** Make certain all street names and landmarks are spelled correctly.

Publishing Get It Ready to Go

▶ **Presentation** Make a final copy of your directions. Either type them or neatly write them.

▶ **Presentation** Consider drawing a map to include with your directions.

News Stories

News stories focus on reporting of events. People around the world depend on newspapers to tell them about what is happening.

News stories provide the reader with information about a specific topic. The information provided needs to be accurate. To be effective, news stories should include facts to answer the following six questions:

▶ *What* happened?   ▶ *When* did it happen?

▶ *Where* did it happen?   ▶ *Why* did it happen?

▶ *Who* was involved?   ▶ *How* did it happen?

Collecting Information

Collecting information is an extremely important activity when writing a news story. One way to get information is by doing research. You can look up information at the library and on the Internet. Depending on your topic, you may also be able to get information by visiting government buildings and historical sites.

Another way to collect information for a news story is by observing what is happening around you. For example, if your school is holding a track meet, you could go to the meet and report what you see.

Interviews are also a good way to get information. You may want to interview people who are a part of the story, such as a participant in the track meet mentioned earlier. You could also interview experts to get information. For example, if you are writing a news story about the stray animal population in your town, you may want to interview someone who works at your local animal shelter or a veterinarian. You can use the tips on the following page when interviewing people for news stories.

Interviewing Tips

▶ Have your questions ready before you meet with your interviewee.

▶ Contact the interviewee and set up a time for the interview.

▶ Ask the interviewee the questions you wrote down. Listen to the responses and ask additional questions when necessary.

▶ Ask permission from your interviewee to take notes or use a tape recorder to help you write your news story later.

▶ Ask the interviewee to spell any names of which you are unsure. This will help you be accurate in your news story.

▶ Thank your interviewee for his or her time. Tell the person where and when your news story will be published.

Taking Notes

Take complete research notes and keep them organized in a notebook. Include the date, subject, and source of the information that you gathered.

Parts of a News Story

Organization

Make it short, clear and to the point. Capitalize proper nouns. Write the headline after you finish the news story so you can accurately tell the reader what to expect from your story.

Byline

The reporter's name goes here.

Lead

The lead is the beginning of a piece of writing. In a news story, the lead answers many of the *who, what, when, where, why,* and *how* questions. It should be a brief and simple summary of the most important information.

Body

This is the informational text of the article. Each paragraph starts with a topic sentence, followed by sentences that contain supporting details of interest to the reader.

Quotation or Callout

This feature helps draw the reader into the article. It is a quotation or interesting portion of a sentence printed in large, bold type in the middle of a column.

Photo Caption

Use short, simple captions in small, bold typeface.

Close

In a news story, the writer's opinions are not used for a conclusion. Instead, the closing wraps up the story, often with an answer to *why* or *how* or *what else would the reader want to know?* Sometimes, the closing looks ahead to the future or quotes one of the people involved.

Here's a news story that was written in the summer of 2000.

Headline ▶ # Astronauts Visit Space Station

Byline ▶ **by Mark Morrison**

Lead ▶ The International Space Station had visitors late Monday night, as the crew of the space shuttle *Atlantis* floated into *Unity*, the U.S.-built section of the station. Their mission: to prepare the space station for its first residents.

International Space Station

Callout ▶ *"It's great to be here," said Commander Terrence Wilcutt*

Body ▶ Just before 11 P.M. ET, the crew opened the first of 12 hatches connecting the shuttle and space station and entered the 140-foot-long station. "Welcome aboard," blared the radio greeting from Mission Control. "It's great to be here," said Commander Terrence Wilcutt.

For the next week, the *Atlantis* crew will move nearly three tons of supplies into *Zvezda*, the Russian-made service module and other parts of the station, including laptop computers, vacuum cleaners, clothing, medical equipment, and exercise machines. Beginning this fall, two Russians and an American will live in *Zvezda* for four months.

Close ▲

Writing Effective Leads

The first few sentences of your writing are always the most important because they are what gets the attention of your reader. In many types of writing, leads are intended to put questions in the minds of the readers so that they want to continue reading.

In news writing, however, a lead paragraph should be short and clear, offering the reader the article's primary information in a nutshell.

Of all professions, journalists have the largest vocabulary—approximately 20,000 words.

Take a Look

Here's a different lead for the space station story. Does it give you the same information?

> *Yesterday, laptop computers and clothing were moved into the International Space Station. The crew opened the first of 12 hatches connecting the shuttle and space station.*

Without giving too many supporting details, this lead tells you what the article is about by summarizing the main information.

Try It

Pick out the lead's answers to these five questions:

▶ *Who* was involved?   ▶ *When* did it happen?
▶ *Where* did it happen?   ▶ *Why* did it happen?
▶ *What* happened?

Reading Your Writing

News stories focus on reporting of events, without the writer's opinions. Answering *who, what, when, where, why,* and *how* in your news story will provide your readers with the information they need to know.

Tips for Writing News Stories

Prewriting Make a Plan

▶ Know your purpose and intended audience.

▶ Do research and take detailed notes for later use.

▶ Brainstorm and list answers to *who, what, when, where, why,* and *how.*

Drafting Get Your Thoughts on Paper

▶ Begin with a clear, concise lead of the basic facts.

▶ Each paragraph should have a topic sentence followed by sentences that contain supporting details.

Revising Be Sure It Makes Sense

▶ **Word Choice** Be sure to present all information clearly.

▶ **Organization** Present information in a logical order.

▶ **Sentence Fluency** Use sentences of different lengths.

Editing/Proofreading Look Closely at the Details

▶ **Conventions** Make sure you've spelled the names of people and places correctly.

▶ **Conventions** Double-check all facts used.

Publishing Get Your News Story Ready to Print

▶ **Presentation** Add pictures with captions, if possible.

Expository Essay

In an **expository essay,** the writer explains or presents the reader with information about a specific topic. While it is similar to a research report, an expository essay may also include the writer's thoughts and personal opinions.

Getting Started

Prewriting, or planning, is an essential step in the writing process. Research grounds your presentation in facts, making you a confident and knowledgeable author.

There are several ways you can get information about your topic. You can read articles and books, which may be the most common form of research. You can interview people who are experts on your topic. Or you can use your powers of observation. The approach you use will be determined by your topic, your audience, and what you want your essay to do.

Look at the following example of an expository essay about the Cyclorama, a panoramic representation of the Civil War's Battle of Atlanta. The student who wrote the essay performed the following research:

▶ observed the Cyclorama presentation

▶ read about its history in the attraction's brochures, in local guide books, and on the Internet

▶ arranged for and received a private tour of the facility

▶ interviewed the manager of the Cyclorama

Take a Look

With all necessary materials and notes in hand, the writer completed the following graphic organizer.

Topic

Cyclorama

Introduction

125 Years Ago

1. There were no amusement or water parks. There were no Braves–Dodgers baseball games.
2. The Yankees and the Rebels fought the Civil War.
3. The Cyclorama takes you back to the 1860's.

Subtopic

History and Size of Painting

1. On July 22, 1864, Generals Hood and Sherman fought in the Battle of Atlanta.
2. The painting Battle of Atlanta weighs 9,334 pounds (the weight of three small cars). It is 42 feet high and 348 feet around. It's the size of 360,000 wallet-sized photos taped together.

Subtopic

Description of Painting and Diorama

1. The painting was originally a touring exhibit.
2. The diorama has over 120 figures, cannons, trees, and railroad tracks.
3. In 1979, the painting was cleaned and repaired. It took four years and cost $11 million.

Subtopic

Computer Operated

1. A computer controls the lighting, sound effects, revolving platform, and narration.

Conclusion

The Cyclorama takes you back to the days of the Civil War.

Here is the essay based on the graphic organizer.

That's One Big Picture!

One hundred twenty-five years ago, Atlanta's kids weren't concerned with amusement or water parks. In 1864, the Battle of Atlanta was not staged at Fulton County Stadium between the Braves and the Dodgers but was a real life or death struggle between the Yankees of the North and the Rebels of the South. Modern technology helps bring that July day back to life at Atlanta's Cyclorama.

A trip to the Cyclorama is like stepping into a time machine. The present is forgotten and the 1860s become very real with the help of the museum's exhibits, including the famous steam locomotive "Texas." The feature attraction here is the massive Civil War painting and three-dimensional diorama.

The painting, called The Battle of Atlanta, shows the events of a hot July 22, 1864, when Confederate troops under the command of General John B. Hood made a desperate attempt to save Atlanta from Major General William T. Sherman's Union forces. The painting weighs 9,334 pounds (about the weight of three small cars) and is an incredible 42 feet high and 348 feet around. Try to picture over 360,000 wallet-sized photos taped together and hung in a circle. That's one big picture!

The painting was originally shown as part of a touring exhibit where it was rolled up on 50-foot poles and transported from city to city. It came to Atlanta to stay in 1898, and the diorama was added in 1936.

This impressive diorama makes the scene come to life with more than 120 figures, cannons, trees, and railroad tracks coming toward you as if right out of the picture.

By 1979, the painting had gotten very dirty and so ragged that it was beginning to crumble in places! It took four years and $11 million to fix up the Cyclorama. A revolving seating platform was added along with sound effects and a narration.

Stashed away in a hidden corner of a building is the computer that controls the lighting, sound effects, revolving platform, and narration with the touch of one button. Spend an hour of your time and let the Cyclorama take you back to a time when brother fought against brother in our country's only war between the states.

Analysis of the Essay

Now, let's look at some features of the Cyclorama essay. Read about a feature here, then turn back to the essay and check the text for an example.

Voice

Voice is the writing trait that makes a piece of writing your very own, separating your writing from your classmate's. A writing voice full of enthusiasm and purpose engages your reader from the very first sentence. An example of the writer's voice is the first paragraph of the essay. The writer's personality comes through when comparing the concerns of Atlanta's kids today to the concerns of kids 125 years ago.

Sentence Fluency

This quality is achieved when sentences flow smoothly and with ease. Vary the length of your sentences and begin them in different ways. Look at the first two sentences in the second paragraph. The writer used a simple sentence followed by a compound sentence. The writer could have chosen to write three simple sentences in place of the compound sentence. *The present is forgotten. The 1860s became very real. The museum's exhibits includes the famous steam locomotive "Texas."* Do you see how combining the three simple sentences into a compound sentence makes the paragraph easier to read?

Word Choice

Choosing just the *right* word for the right situation can make language sing. Be a "wordsmith," and choose your words carefully for maximum effect on your reader. The words *staged* and *struggle* in the first paragraph and *ragged, crumble,* and *revolving* in paragraph six create vivid pictures for the reader.

Ideas

Present ideas in fresh and different ways, and make your writing come alive with vivid, descriptive images that put your reader in the middle of the action. Notice the description in paragraph three about the weight of the painting. Telling the reader that the painting is about the weight of three small cars is a fresh way to describe the painting.

Organization

Notice how the essay begins 125 years ago and ends in the present. Chronological order tracks events from oldest to most recent and is one of the most logical and effective methods of organization.

Reading Your Writing

An expository essay explains information about a specific topic. Providing your readers with interesting information will keep them involved in your essay.

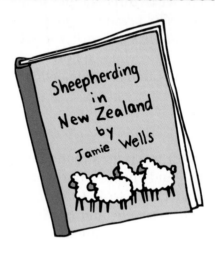

Tips for Writing Expository Essays

Prewriting Make a Plan

▶ Know your purpose and intended audience.

▶ Conduct research and take detailed notes for later use.

Drafting Get Your Thoughts on Paper

▶ Lead with an attention-getting sentence.

▶ Order events chronologically.

▶ Allow your personality to come through in your writing.

Revising Be Sure It Makes Sense

▶ **Word Choice** Use interesting words to make your writing come alive.

▶ **Ideas** Use descriptive images and easy-to-understand comparisons.

▶ **Sentence Fluency** Use smooth, easy-to-read sentences of varied lengths.

Editing/Proofreading Look Closely at the Details

▶ **Conventions** Make sure you've spelled the names of people and places correctly.

▶ **Conventions** Double-check all facts used.

Publishing Get It Ready to Go

▶ **Presentation** Try including illustrations or photos.

Research Reports

A **research report** is written to give in-depth information about a specific topic. Information should be obtained from many different sources.

Let's make our way through a research report, from beginning to end.

Targeting Your Subject

The first thing to do is to choose a topic. In many cases, your teacher may give you the overall subject and it will be up to you to choose the topic within that subject. Be sure to choose a topic that interests you, or you might find yourself becoming bored with your topic.

Imagine that your teacher has assigned the broad subject of *health* for your paper. Your task is to decide on a topic that relates to health. Start by brainstorming all the ideas you can think of related to health. You might want to make a web like this one to list your ideas.

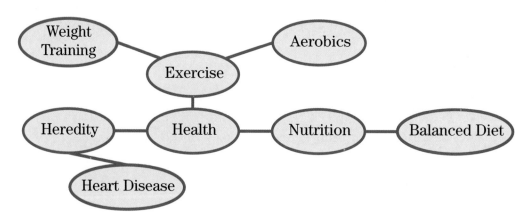

Study your web for ideas for your paper. As you look through the possible topics, *balanced diet* catches your eye. Your next task is to come up with some questions you think your report should answer.

Write the Questions

▶ What do our bodies need to keep going?

▶ What's in the different foods we eat?

▶ What different nutrients do our bodies need?

▶ What happens when our bodies don't get the right stuff?

▶ How can we balance the bad stuff with the good?

Find the Answers

Detailed answers to these questions may come from a variety of sources, including the following.

▶ books, magazines, encyclopedias, dictionaries, almanacs, atlases, videos, and newspapers

▶ personal interviews, museum visits, and brochures from businesses or organizations

▶ research findings from experiments you conduct at school or at home

▶ information from the Internet

Ask yourself these questions when choosing a research source:

▶ Can I trust this source to provide me with accurate and thorough information?

▶ Does this source provide enough information?

▶ Is this information up to date? Check the copyright to see when it was published. Get the most recent data available.

Finding Information Fast

Here are some tips for finding important information fast, without reading an encyclopedia entry or magazine article word for word.

Skimming Tips

▶ Search for words or phrases printed in CAPITALS, *italics*, or **bold** lettering.

▶ Search for clues in section headings.

▶ Read the article's introduction to decide whether it has information you need.

▶ Read the topic sentence of each paragraph to discover if the information contained applies to your targeted topic.

▶ Read the captions of photos, charts, graphs, and illustrations.

Key Words

As you take your notes, make a separate list of any key words that sound like they'll be important for the reader to know. If they are not included in your text's titles or section headings, these words are often *italicized*, **bolded,** or frequently repeated in the text. If your research doesn't already provide it, use a dictionary to find the definition of each key word.

Note Cards

Take notes on index cards of information you think will be important to your report. Be sure to use your own words rather than copying straight from your source. Don't write full sentences—only words and phrases. Use one card for each time you get an answer or part of an answer to one of your questions. Experiment with organizing them into an order that suits your plan and provides your report with a beginning, middle, and end section.

> ### Minerals
> for bones — blood — to make body parts strong
> calcium — milk — cheese — yogurt — broccoli
> iron — red meat — whole grain breads —
>   cereals — eggs — seafood — nuts

The Final Plan

Finally, plan your report. You can use your note cards or a graphic organizer like the one shown here.

Topic

Eating the Right Things

Subtopic

Food Processing and Nutrients

1. Protein—fish, chicken, turkey, nuts, eggs, meat cheese, milk for hair, muscles, bones, brain, teeth
2. Carbohydrates—pasta noodles, potatoes for energy
3. Fats—slow, steady energy but can cause heart problems because of cholesterol

Subtopic

Vitamins and Minerals

1. Vitamins—fuits, vegetables, carbohydrates, protein, fats
2. Minerals—calcium from milk and cheese, iron from red meat, eggs, cereal

Subtopic

Balanced Diet

1. Eat balanced foods from each group to avoid getting sick
2. Stay away from too much sugar
3. Burgers and pizza: too much fat!

Conclusion

Eating right can be a balancing act, but worth it for your health.

Here is the report that was written using the graphic organizer.

Eating the Right Thing—A Balancing Act

Introduction ▶
Clearly state the topic of your report.

The food you eat affects your health. Eating nutritiously is a matter of balance and choices; the more you know about it, the better prepared you'll be to eat healthfully.

The body is a food-processing factory that needs different kinds of food to get all that you need. To start off, you can't live without protein from foods such as fish, chicken, turkey, nuts, eggs, meat, cheese, and milk. Your hair, muscles, bones, brain, and teeth are mostly made of protein.

Carbohydrates provide nearly all of your energy. They come from noodles, potatoes, bread, peas, beans, cereal, and fruit. These foods also provide fiber for a healthy heart and good digestion. Carbohydrates can also come from sugar, but sugar is not the best choice because it doesn't have any fiber or other nutrients. Your body will store leftover carbohydrates as fat.

Body ▶
Topic sentences and details in this section.

Some fats are good for you, providing a slow, steady source of energy. There's fat in all foods labeled as protein. There is also fat added to food, such as butter on toast and oil used to cook meat and vegetables.

Scientists have discovered that too much of the wrong kinds of fat can lead to heart problems. This happens when the wrong kinds of fats and a substance called cholesterol work to clog your arteries (one of the types of "roadways" in your body that circulate blood). For a healthy heart, choose fish or chicken (without skin) instead of hamburgers or steak. Limit butter, and if you drink whole milk, try switching to 1 percent fat or nonfat milk. You may not even taste the difference!

To stay healthy, you need vitamins. Vitamins from fruits and vegetables help with basic body functions such as changing food into energy. Carbohydrates, protein, and fats also contribute to your daily dose of vitamins.

You need minerals, too. Minerals make your bones, blood, and other body parts strong. Most people need extra calcium and iron. Sources of calcium include milk, broccoli, cheese, and yogurt. Iron is found in red meat, seafood, nuts, eggs, and whole-grain breads and cereals.

Burgers and pizza provide vitamins, minerals, protein, and fat. Add vegetables or a salad to create a nutritious meal. Have a burger once in a while, but try to have skinless chicken or turkey, fish, or pasta more often.

Conclusion ▶
Leave the reader with something to ponder.

A balanced diet means eating foods from each of these different groups to give your body all the different foods it needs to work well. Eating too many carbohydrates and fats or skipping your fruits and vegetables could overload your body's system. Then you might not feel well or have enough energy to get through the day. Eating right is a balancing act that will keep your body factory running smoothly.

Bibliography

A **bibliography** is a list of the research materials used and referred to in the preparation of an article or report. Placed at the end of your report, each entry identifies the name, author, title, publisher, date published, and sometimes the page numbers of the source. Each type of entry has a specific format that must be followed. Readers often want to know the source of the author's information or where they can read more about the subject.

Take a Look

Here are some bibliography entries.

BOOKS: Author (last name first). <u>Title of Book</u> (underlined). City of Publication: Publisher, Copyright date.

Kaplan, Francine. <u>The Kid's Guide to Nutrition</u>. Chicago: Snoopy Press, 1999.

MAGAZINES: Author (last name first). "Title of Article" (in quotations). <u>Title of Magazine</u> (underlined) date of publication (month day year): Page numbers of the article.

Martin, Patricia A. "Eat to Live." <u>The Nutrition Guide</u> February 26 2001: 3–7.

ENCYCLOPEDIAS: Author (last name first). "Title of Entry" (in Quotations). <u>Title of Encyclopedia</u> (underlined). Edition or version. If no author given, begin with "Title of Entry."

"Nutrition." <u>The Children's Encyclopedia of Health</u>. 2000 ed.

INTERNET: "Post Title" (in quotations). <u>Site title</u> (underlined). Post date or last update. Site sponsor. Date accessed. <Electronic address>.

"The ABC's of Nutrition." <u>The Ultimate Nutrition Website</u>. July 19, 2003. Nutritionists of America. October 17, 2003. <http://www.unw.net/nutrition/abc's.htm>.

INTERVIEW: Person interviewed (last name first). Type of interview. Date (month day year)

Clark, Patricia. Personal Interview. October 20, 2003.

Pay close attention to the exact format and punctuation used in your bibliography. Ask your teacher about the required format for other types of sources, such as magazine and newspaper articles, encyclopedias, videos, and Web sites.

As you do your research, list your source entries on a proposed bibliography sheet. Later, you can choose which ones need to be included on your final list. Avoid having to go back and find the information needed for the bibliography after you've already returned materials to the library.

Reading Your Writing

A research report is a paper that gives in-depth information about a topic. Use different sources such as books, magazines, encyclopedias, and the Internet to add variety to your research and provide your reader with the most up-to-date information.

Tips for Research Reports

Prewriting Make a Plan

▶ Know your focus and intended audience.

▶ Use notes on cards to plan your report. Use a graphic organizer.

Drafting Get Your Thoughts on Paper

▶ Each paragraph should have a topic sentence followed by sentences that contain important supporting details.

▶ Give your report an introduction (beginning), body (middle), and conclusion (end section).

Revising Be Sure It Makes Sense

▶ **Organization** Tie the end of one paragraph to the beginning of the next.

▶ **Organization** Give your readers an ending that will make them think!

Editing/Proofreading Look Closely at the Details

▶ **Conventions** Make sure you've spelled the names of people and places correctly.

▶ **Conventions** Double-check all facts used.

▶ **Conventions** Make sure your bibliography is accurate.

Publishing Get It Ready to Go

▶ **Presentation** Consider including illustrations in your report.

Narrative Writing

   Narrative writing tells a story. The story can be true, such as a biography or autobiography. These stories are about real people and real events. The story can be fictional, or make-believe. Some fiction stories can be realistic, with characters and events that could really happen. Others, such as fantasy and science fiction stories, contain characters and events that could never really happen.

   When you do narrative writing, you are telling your readers what happened. Narrative writing has a beginning, a middle, and an end. It also needs a setting, a problem and solution, and characters. It may also need dialogue. Look on the following pages for some different kinds of narrative writing.

▶ Personal Narratives 146

▶ Autobiographies 152

▶ Biographies 158

▶ Mysteries 164

▶ Adventure Stories 170

▶ Historical Fiction 176

▶ Fantasies 182

▶ Plays 188

Personal Narratives

A **personal narrative** is a true story you write about something that happened in your own life. When preparing to write a personal narrative, you should reflect on an experience that caused you to learn something or grow or change in some way. That doesn't mean that you have to write about a record-setting or life-changing event, though. Your narrative can be a simple story about something that caused you to think of something in a different way.

Getting Ideas for Personal Narratives

To get ideas for your writing, think about things that have happened to you that made you happy, excited, sad, or some other emotion. Reviewing old journal entries may also give you good ideas.

You might choose to write about any of these: losing a pet, a birthday party that was a flop, winning a poetry contest, or being replaced in the starting line-up of your basketball team. Just keep in mind that the goal for your personal narrative should be to share what you learned from your experience with your reader.

Making a Point

Have you ever noticed how some of your friends are great at telling stories, but other friends' stories will go on and on with no point? If you've ever had to sit through a story like that, then you know how boring it can be.

Before you start writing your narrative, put yourself in your readers' shoes. Think about how to make your story the most interesting for your reader. First determine the point you want to make. Once you've made that decision, then you should figure out how you want to guide your reader to your point. Finally think about the special moment in your story where you realized that you had learned something. Be sure to describe that moment to your readers.

Putting the Reader There

Using vivid descriptions in your personal narrative can help the reader feel as if they are there with you. Try to paint pictures for your readers by using words. For example, instead of writing, "We saw the deer by the pond," you might try, "The doe and fawn, alert to our every move, were grazing by the murky pond."

You may also want to include dialogue in your narrative in order to add interest to your writing. Instead of saying, "The hike leader told us there were deer by the pond," you could say, "The hike leader whispered to the group, 'Look at the deer near the pond.'"

Organizing Your Personal Narrative

When you are ready to start writing your personal narrative, you may want to use a graphic organizer. Keiko used the story map shown here to help her organize her ideas.

Story Map

Title
"The Wrong Present"

Who
Keiko Ozawa

Where
Fourth-Grade Classroom

When
The end-of-the-year party

Key Events
1. We were to bring something we made or something costing no more than five dollars.
2. I hoped to get the present purchased by my friend.
3. We passed the presents to music.
4. I passed faster when I thought her present was coming.
5. The teacher stopped the music and I thought I got the gift my friend bought.
6. I was disappointed when I didn't get what I wanted.

Conflict
I hoped to get the present purchased by my friend, but I ended up with something completely different.

Resolution
I learned about the gift I received and felt lucky to have gotten it instead of the present my friend bought.

The Wrong Present by Keiko Ozawa

At the end of every school year we have a party with a gift exchange. We play a few games, talk about summer vacation, and exchange gifts. When I was in fourth grade, things did not go according to plan, at least not according to my plan.

For the gift exchange, our teacher, Mrs. Babinchak, told us to bring either something we made ourselves or something that cost five dollars or less. My friend Haley and I went shopping together for the gifts. We dragged our moms to our favorite stores at the mall.

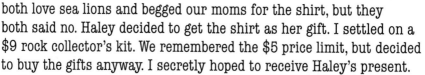

Haley found a $10 T-shirt silk-screened with sea lions. We both love sea lions and begged our moms for the shirt, but they both said no. Haley decided to get the shirt as her gift. I settled on a $9 rock collector's kit. We remembered the $5 price limit, but decided to buy the gifts anyway. I secretly hoped to receive Haley's present.

The next morning at school, kids were louder than usual, laughing and yelling in the halls. Everyone was excited because it was the end of the school year. It was hard to concentrate that morning. During the spelling test, all I could think about was Haley's gift. I kept wondering which one in the jumble of presents was the T-shirt. The morning went by so slowly that it seemed like an entire school week. Finally, at 1:30 the party began.

When it was time for the gift exchange, Mrs. Babinchak told us to get in a circle. She was going to play "Yankee Doodle" while we passed the presents. When the music stopped, we were to keep the present in our hands. A flat box that looked like a shirt box went around the circle. Mrs. Babinchak looked ready to stop the music, so I quickly passed the other gifts. I was hoping the box I thought was Haley's would make it to me. When the music stopped, I looked down and saw the long, flat box in my hands. Very slowly I unwrapped the gift, lifted the lid, and looked inside.

My heart sank. Poking out of the tissue paper was something I had never seen before, but it was definitely something homemade. The top of it was round with something that looked like a spider's web inside it. There was a hole in the middle of the web. Some long cords that were covered with beads dangled from the object. There was also a feather on it. I lifted the gift out of the box and looked at it, trying to hide my disappointment over not getting Haley's T-shirt.

Mrs. Babinchak must have seen the look on my face, because she said, "Wow! What a beautiful dreamcatcher! Who made it?"

A voice came from a boy named Michael who sat in the corner of the room, "I made it! Do you like it?"

Mrs. Babinchak looked over at Michael and asked him to tell the class about the dreamcatcher. Michael told us that he learned all about dreamcatchers from his grandmother. He said that I could hang it from my bed at night. All my good dreams would get caught in the web of life and would stay with me forever and all my bad dreams would go through the hole and disappear.

I felt so lucky to get something that had so much meaning. My dreamcatcher has been hanging from my bed ever since that party. I'm so glad I got the wrong present!

Analyzing the Model

Organizing Events

Take a look at "The Wrong Present." Do you see how the narrative takes the reader from beginning to end? Does it follow the story map? Keiko sets the scene and opens her story by describing the end-of-year party. She tells when the events happened to her and ends her first paragraph with a phrase that catches her readers' attention. She ends the story with a reflection of what she learned.

The Beginning

The student model begins well before Keiko receives the dreamcatcher. Because of this, we get a real feeling about the shopping trip and how much Keiko wanted to get the T-shirt that Haley had bought. We wouldn't know how much she wanted the shirt if the story had begun with "When it was time for the gift exchange . . ." Starting with the shopping trip helps the reader understand Keiko's disappointment when she doesn't receive Haley's gift.

The Special Moment

The special moment begins when Mrs. Babinchak asks Michael to tell the class about the dreamcatcher. The reader can sense that the point of the story is coming. The reader discovers along with Keiko that we don't always get what we wish for—sometimes we get something better.

Description and Dialogue

Keiko's personal narrative includes descriptions of the T-shirt and the dreamcatcher. She also provides sensory information and dialogue. Do you hear the kids laughing and yelling? Can you see the dreamcatcher? Can you hear the teacher ask Michael about the dreamcatcher? By including these details in her writing, Keiko makes the scene seem more real to her readers.

Reading Your Writing

A personal narrative is a story you write about something that happened in your own life. Try to use sensory details to make your writing come to life for your reader.

Tips for Writing a Personal Narrative

Prewriting Make a Plan

▶ Search your memory or journal for interesting things that happened to you.

▶ Choose your approach. You may wish to simply describe an experience with lots of detail or reflect on something that happened.

▶ Plan a beginning, a middle, and an end.

▶ Create a story map with what you want to include.

Drafting Get Your Thoughts on Paper

▶ Refer to your story map and write your narrative.

▶ Focus on including descriptive detail in your story.

Revising Be Sure It Makes Sense

▶ **Ideas** Is what happened described in detail? Do you use sensory description, and is your story interesting?

▶ **Organization** Do events occur in a logical order that will make sense to readers?

▶ **Voice** Does your narrative show that you care strongly about what is happening and does it encourage the reader to identify with you?

▶ **Word Choice** Did you use precise verbs, colorful adjectives, and specific nouns?

Editing/Proofreading Look Over the Details

▶ **Conventions** Proofread your piece to check for spelling mistakes.

▶ **Conventions** Check punctuation and capitalization.

Publishing Get Ready to Share Your Narrative

▶ **Presentation** Neatly type or rewrite a final copy.

Autobiographies

An **autobiography** is a story that you write to tell about your own life. It covers a string of events, sometimes from your birth to the present. An autobiography is like a personal history written by you. It is different from a biography, which is a story about a person's life written by someone else.

Like a personal narrative, an autobiography may include details about how the writer thinks and feels about things. An autobiography differs from a personal narrative by focusing on a longer period in a person's life instead of on just one event or experience. An autobiography may tell about one important period, or it may cover the whole lifetime of the writer.

For example, for your autobiography, you might choose to write about the major events from kindergarten through fifth grade, or you could write about just one year of your life. An autobiography usually covers a longer period.

Gathering Information

If you're writing an autobiography that begins at your birth, you will need to interview your family members. They can give you information and details about your early days. They may have a baby book or photo album that tells about where you were born, when you walked, and what your first words were. Ask them about any funny or unusual things that you did. As with other types of writing, the details will make your autobiography interesting to your readers.

Organizing the Information

An autobiography that covers an entire life is most often told in chronological order, the order in which the events occurred in time. Another way to organize would be to begin with a key event in the present, such as winning an athletic tournament, and then go backward in time telling about each event in the last few years that led to the recent accomplishment. Whichever way you organize, you will want to make sure your method makes sense. You may find it helpful to list key events on a chain-of-events graphic organizer such as the one shown here.

Take a Look

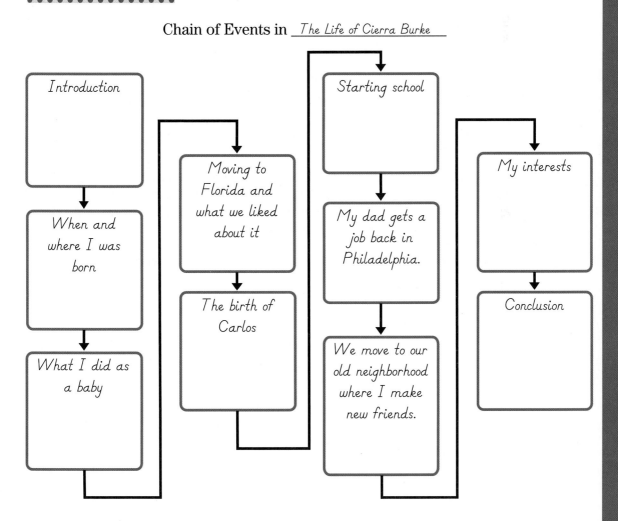

Chain of Events in _The Life of Cierra Burke_

Introduction

When and where I was born

What I did as a baby

Moving to Florida and what we liked about it

The birth of Carlos

Starting school

My dad gets a job back in Philadelphia.

We move to our old neighborhood where I make new friends.

My interests

Conclusion

My Life: Florida and Back by Cierra Burke

I was born during a huge ice storm on January 25, 1993, at Thomas Jefferson Hospital in Philadelphia. When my mother was ready to have me, my parents had to walk to the hospital because taxis couldn't get through all of the ice and snow in the streets. I weighed seven pounds exactly.

I learned to walk at thirteen months and said my first word, "fan," when I was fifteen months old. My dad said I liked to watch the ceiling fan whirling from the ceiling of our house. When I was still a baby, my parents used to take me to Fairmount Park to walk Harvey, our basset hound. I used to get excited and pant like a dog when other dogs came up to my stroller.

When I was three, we moved to Miami to be closer to my grandparents. The thing I liked about Florida was the weather. Our apartment complex had a pool, and we could swim in it just about every month of the year. I also liked being able to pick lemons and oranges from trees right in my grandparents' backyard. My mother loved the fresh mangoes we could buy. It reminded her of Venezuela, where she was born. Soon after my fifth birthday, my mother told me she was going to have a baby.

We named my baby brother Carlos, after my grandfather. In no time at all, he was crawling around and getting into my stuff. For the most part, I like having a brother. He can be pretty funny sometimes. After he was born, I was ready to begin school.

I started kindergarten at Mangrove Elementary School. My first teacher's name was Mrs. Cavendish. The main thing I remember about her was a shirt she always wore. It was aqua with pink seahorses and bubbles. I went to that school through third grade. Then we moved back to Philadelphia. My dad got a really good job with a big bakery here. It was hard to leave our grandparents, but the place where my dad worked in Florida was shutting down.

We moved back to Spring Garden, our old neighborhood. We bought a three-story house, so we were all very excited. I started going to Greentree Elementary School in fourth grade and made some new friends. My mom said my best friend, Alicia, is actually an old friend that I don't remember!

My interests include listening to music, drawing, and riding my bike. In fifth grade, I started taking Spanish. I'm hoping to be able to surprise my grandparents next time we visit them in Florida. They speak Spanish and so does my mother, but she never taught me much.

I'm glad I got to live in Florida, but I like my life here, too. I guess the saying is true— Philadelphia really is "the place that loves you back."

Try It

Think about the events that have shaped your life. What would you choose to focus on in your autobiography?

Analyzing the Model

Organizing the Events and Connecting the Ideas

Do you see how this autobiography is organized in chronological order? In the first paragraph, the author tells about her birth. Each paragraph after that moves us forward one to three years in time until the present.

Notice how the paragraphs are connected. The last sentence of most paragraphs provides the transition to the next. Transitional sentences make it easier for readers to follow the sequence of events.

The Introduction and Conclusion

Just as with any form of writing, this short autobiography has an introductory paragraph and a concluding paragraph. In the introductory paragraph, the student captures the readers' attention with an interesting first sentence. In the concluding paragraph, she reflects on the major events in her life: moving to Florida and then back to Philadelphia. Her concluding sentence, ". . . Philadelphia really is 'the place that loves you back,'" echoes her title, "My Life: Florida and Back." Her autobiography isn't simply a telling of events from birth to the present. It is also a comparison of the two places Cierra has lived and a reflection on moving away and back to the original place.

> **Fun Fact**
>
> The prefix *auto* means "self." Just as an *autograph* is a person's own signature, an *autobiography* is written about oneself.

> ### Reading Your Writing
>
> An autobiography is a true story that a person writes about himself or herself. To keep the reader's interest, be sure to use only the most interesting facts, not every little detail about your life.

Tips for Writing an Autobiography

Prewriting Make a Plan

▶ Interview your family to learn interesting and important facts about your background, birth, and early years.

▶ List the major events of your life. Include topics on which you might want to reflect and possibly a theme that may tie it together.

▶ Use a chain-of-events graphic organizer or just list events chronologically on a piece of paper.

Drafting Get Your Thoughts on Paper

▶ Use your chain-of-events organizer or your list to write your autobiography.

▶ Focus on interesting details in your autobiography.

Revising Be Sure It Makes Sense

▶ **Ideas** Are events accurately described? Will the things you chose to write about be interesting to your reader?

▶ **Organization** Do you write about events chronologically? Do the events and ideas connect, and do paragraphs end with transitional sentences?

▶ **Voice** Does your writing involve readers, providing them with a sense of who you are?

Editing/Proofreading Look Over the Details

▶ **Conventions** Proofread your autobiography for spelling, punctuation, and capitalization errors.

Publishing Get Ready to Share Your Autobiography

▶ **Presentation** Neatly type or rewrite a final copy.

Biographies

A **biography** is the story of a real person's life that is written by *another* person. Unlike a story written about a fictional character, all the events in a biography are supposed to be true. Unlike a research report, which is written on a specific topic, the subject of a biography is always a person.

A biography contains important information about a person's life. It includes the major events. It may also include information about how the person thinks and feels about things. Biographies often include what other people have to say about the subject. A biography may cover a person's life from birth to the present, or it may focus on an important period in a person's life.

Biographies usually organize events in chronological order, or the order in which the events occurred in time. A biography that focuses on just one period may order events from a key event and go backward.

Gathering Information

The sources you use will depend on your subject. If your subject is no longer living, encyclopedias and other reference books may provide you with the most information. For well-known living subjects, use reference books, magazines, Web sites, CD-ROMs, and video- and audiotapes. If your subject lives nearby, you may be able to interview both your subject and the people who know him or her. If you arrange an interview, be sure to come prepared with a list of questions. You may wish to record the interview. No matter which type of source you use, remember to write down where you got your information. For more information on documenting your references, see pages 141–142 on Bibliographies.

Organizing Your Information

A graphic organizer such as a time line may help you focus on key events as you gather information. The dates used in this model are years only. You may want to include exact dates such as the day, month, and year of the event. Dates help the writer put the events in order.

Subject of Time Line: _J.K. Rowling_

Date:	1965 – 1971	1971 – 1975	1975 – 1981	1981 – 1985	1985 – 1990	1992 – 1993	1993 – 1994	1996 – 1997

Event:

J.K. Rowling is born in Chipping Sodbury, England.

She moves to the country and goes to a new elementary school. She attends Wyedean Comprehensive School.

She works in offices and comes up with the idea for Harry Potter.

She moves to Scotland as a single mother and finishes her book.

She writes her first story. She moves twice and makes friends with a family named Potter.

She attends Exeter University and studies French.

She moves to Portugal, marries, has a daughter.

British and U.S. publishers agree to publish her book, and she becomes a full-time writer.

J.K. Rowling

Joanne Kathleen Rowling is the author of the Harry Potter books. She was born at Chipping Sodbury General Hospital in England on July 31, 1965. As a writer who loves funny names, she is amused at the unusual name of her birthplace.

When she was little, she often played by herself and loved to use her imagination. When she was five, her younger sister, Di, who was three at the time, became her first audience. Joanne loved to tell stories, especially about rabbits. The first one she wrote down was about a rabbit who got sick with the measles and had many visitors, one of whom was a giant bee named Miss Bee.

Her family moved first to Yate and then to Winterbourne, England. In Winterbourne she played with a group of kids and had two very good friends, a brother and sister named Ian and Vickie Potter. She says she always liked their last name: Potter.

When she was nine, her family moved again, this time to a small town in the English countryside. She had a hard time adjusting to the new school. On the first day, the new teacher gave her a test on fractions that she failed because she had never done them. Her teacher arranged students from left to right, with those on the left being those she thought were the smartest. After the test, she sat Joanne very far to the right. By the year's end, Joanne proved herself smart enough to earn the seat that was second from the left.

After elementary school, she went to Wyedean Comprehensive School, which is like high school in the U.S.A. She wrote all the time. Most of the time she wrote just for fun. Sometimes she wrote to entertain other people. Her teachers encouraged her to keep writing, but she never told anyone about her dream to become a writer. Her parents didn't even know about Joanne's dream. Even Joanne herself thought a writing career would not be possible. She decided to go along with her parents' suggestion to study French at Exeter University. After she graduated from Exeter, she worked different jobs as a secretary for six years. Sometimes she got into trouble for writing stories at work. One day, riding home from work, she was looking at cows from the train window. Suddenly the idea for Harry Potter popped into her head. She began working on the first book in her spare time, but she kept the project secret.

She turned 26 in 1992 and went to Portugal to teach English. She got married while she was there and had her daughter Jessica in 1993. Her marriage failed, and she went to live in Edinburgh, Scotland, near her sister Di.

She rented a tiny apartment with poor heating. Joanne could not afford to pay someone to stay with her daughter while she was at work. She decided to stay at home with her daughter and finish her book. It was a very hard time for her, and she often went to bed hungry. She finally finished her first Harry Potter book and found the courage to look for a publisher.

In 1997 Bloomsbury Press agreed to publish the first book, called Harry Potter and the Philosopher's Stone. They paid her only a small amount, and she had no hopes of making any kind of living from writing. She wanted only to see her work in bookstores. In 1997 Scholastic Press decided to publish the book in the U.S. They paid her a very large amount that allowed her to become a full-time writer. Her first book become a worldwide success as did the other books in the Harry Potter series. Her lifelong dream of becoming a published author had been fulfilled.

Try It

What is the main thing the author of this biography wants us to know?

▶ Interesting information about Rowling's family

▶ Information about how Rowling became a writer

Analyzing the Model

Choosing a Key Issue

When gathering your information about the person, you may want to focus on a key issue related to the person. Notice how the model includes early interests and influences and how they helped J.K. Rowling become an author.

Organizing the Information

Now go back to page 159 and see how each event listed on the time line matches a paragraph in the biography. While you are gathering your information, you may find it helpful to use a time line or chart to list dates and events. It will keep you on track as you take notes. It will also help you organize your writing chronologically.

Making It Readable

Notice how some of the paragraphs end with a concluding sentence that provides a transition for the next paragraph. As with other forms of writing, a biography should also have an introduction and a concluding paragraph. In the model, the introduction tells us who the subject is, what she is known for, and where and when she was born. The conclusion tells us how Rowling's lifelong dream to be a writer was fulfilled. The rest of the biography sticks to the topic of J.K. Rowling and her writing career.

Reading Your Writing

A biography is the true story about a person that is written by another person. When writing a biography, use a time line of events to help you keep events in order. This will make it easier for the reader to follow along.

Tips for Writing a Biography

Prewriting Make a Plan

▶ Pick your subject. Think of a person who interests you about whom you would like to know more.

▶ List ways to get information about your subject.

▶ Make a time line to help you focus on key events.

Drafting Get Your Thoughts on Paper

▶ Use your time line to write the biography.

▶ Focus on details that interest you and will interest your readers.

Revising Be Sure It Makes Sense

▶ **Ideas** Are events accurately described? Does what you included relate to the things for which the subject is known?

▶ **Organization** Do events and ideas connect, and do most paragraphs end with transitional sentences? Do you tell about events chronologically?

Editing/Proofreading Look Over the Details

▶ **Conventions** Proofread the biography for spelling mistakes.

▶ **Conventions** Check to make sure the names of the people in your subject's life and any other proper nouns are capitalized.

Publishing Get Ready to Share Your Biography

▶ **Presentation** Neatly type or rewrite your final copy.

Mysteries

A **mystery** is a type of story in which a crime, puzzle, or mysterious happening is solved or explained by a central character.

Like other types of fiction, mysteries contain the following:

Setting

The setting is a description of a time and place in which the events occur. In mysteries, the setting helps create the mood. For example, the setting of the mystery *The House of Dies Drear* by Virginia Hamilton is a large, old house on the edge of a dark woods. In addition to having many pillars, eaves, and gables, the house holds a secret.

Characters

Characters in a mystery talk and act in ways that make them seem real. In most mysteries, at least one of the characters, usually the main character, tries to solve a mystery. In *The House of Dies Drear*, Thomas, the oldest son, wants to learn the secret of the house.

Famous Crime Solvers as Characters

In many stories and novels, characters hired as detectives or younger people, acting as detectives, solve mysteries. You may be familiar with the Nancy Drew, Boxcar Children, Encyclopedia Brown, and Hardy Boys mysteries.

Plot

The plot is a chain of events in which there is a problem that is solved or an unexplained event that is finally explained.

The main feature of a mystery's plot is a crime or mysterious happening. In *The House of Dies Drear*, the mystery has to do with house's role as a stop on the Underground Railroad. Why does the family who rents the house more than 100 years later feel unwelcome? What is the family's connection? What is the house's secret?

Clues

Clues are a major feature of the plot included in and used to solve mysteries. Clues are the important details communicated through action, conversation, or a character's observation. The main character uses clues to solve a mystery. So does the reader. In the *Encyclopedia Brown* series, fifth-grader Leroy Brown, known as "Encyclopedia," solves one crime after another using clues and his own encyclopedic store of facts. In each story, the reader has access to the same clues or details observed by Encyclopedia.

For example, in *The Case of the Three Vans*, a neighbor saw three vans pull up to Harry Dunn's house the day he was kidnapped. The first clue was that each had its company name printed on the side—*Bill's Fish Market*, *ABC TV Repair*, and *Sun Drug Store*.

Suspense and Surprise

Suspense is what you feel when you are nervous and unsure about what is going to happen. **Surprise** is what you feel when an event catches you off guard. These elements are great mystery writing tools. You can create suspense by describing unusual sounds, using descriptive adjectives and verbs, and by suggesting danger. For example, Mary D. Hahn creates suspense in *Dead Man in Indian Creek* when she describes Matt and Parker hiding in a workshop just inches way from the criminals who are talking about them. You can create surprise by including unexpected events and by adding plot twists. Hahn creates surprise when she has Parker's normally troublesome dog make a surprise appearance that saves the day.

Mystery Model

How does this story include the elements of a mystery?

Derek and Aaron:
Worm and Clue Hunting Specialists

Setting ▶

Phineas Felch retreated into the garden shed. We saw his scrawny back disappear just as we approached. He was the caretaker of the vacant Pennypacker mansion. Aaron and I wanted to ask if we could dig for night crawlers in the mansion's old rose garden. Night crawlers are great fishing bait, and the old rose garden was the best place to find them.

First Clue ▶

When we knocked on the rotting door, he opened it, scowled, and asked us what we wanted. The shed smelled overwhelmingly of mildew, and inside we saw a faded fern-print sofa with broken springs. Phineas' own smell and appearance weren't much better. He was wearing an old torn shirt with fraying corduroy pants. His shoes looked clean and new, but his teeth and gums looked like they had never felt a toothbrush.

Second Clue ▶

We introduced ourselves—Aaron and Derek—and asked him politely if we could go digging for worms. He said he wasn't sure if he should let us. There had been some problems lately. Kids were stealing valuable statues from the gardens. After we showed him our bait cans, Phineas reluctantly gave us permission. He told us to stay away from the east garden. He said it was nothing but a muddy mess from all the rain. Then he told us not to bother him again because he wanted to take his long afternoon nap.

**Characters ▶
Who Solve
a Mystery**

Aaron and I planned to follow through on our plan to get night crawlers, but we couldn't resist a good mystery. We decided to dig for worms like we had told the caretaker and then look for clues to the missing statues. If anyone caught us snooping, we could show them our reason for being on the property. As soon as we started digging, we pulled up one plump night crawler after another. We quickly filled our bait containers. Mud oozed all around us, caking our shoes and pant legs.

Suspense ▶

Nothing in the rose garden seemed suspicious, so we walked to the back of the house. We found an abandoned bathtub, a refrigerator without its doors, and lots of ants. We had the creepy feeling that someone was watching us. We hunted around outside the house for

Surprise ▶

another half hour. Then we were startled by a noise coming from the opposite end of the property, near the east garden.

It sounded like people talking and grunting. Were they taking statues? We crept toward the noise. We heard someone saying something about being there four hours too early. Before we could get close enough to see who the people were, we saw a van pull away. It came around to near where we were hiding, so we were able to

Suspense ▶

memorize the license plate number. We nervously waited. When we thought the van was gone, we sneaked the long way back to the garden shed and knocked on the door.

The caretaker took his time answering the door. He grumbled about us interrupting his nap, but when we told him what we had seen, he quickly called the police. The officer who came first searched the property. She met us back at the shed. Like everybody, her boots were

Final Clues ▶

caked with mud. In fact, four sets of muddy footprints covered the stone walkway to the shed.

The officer thanked us for getting the plate number and said she would do a search. Phineas Felch said he hoped they would catch the statue thieves. I said I wasn't so sure tracing the plate number would put an end to the problem. We noticed an extra set of muddy footprints on the walkway. Whose were they?

Try It

Think of a mystery that you have read. Who were the main characters? What was the mystery? Can you think of some of the clues that were presented in the story?

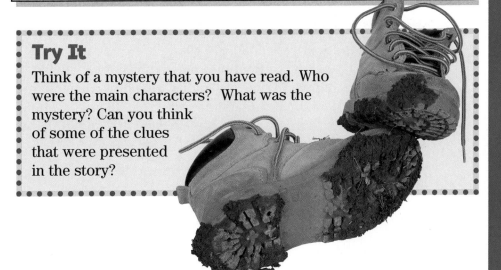

Analyzing the Model

Begin by looking at the basic features of the story. Notice how the setting creates the mood. Descriptive words like *vacant, old, rotting,* and *mildew* describe the mansion and its grounds. We learn at the end of the first paragraph that the events take place in the afternoon. The crime in this mystery story is the theft of valuable statues. The main characters who try to solve the crime are Aaron and Derek.

Now take a look at the parts of the story that make it a mystery. Did you pick up on the story's clues? Derek's observation of Felch's clean, new shoes was the first. The final clue, another observation by Derek, comes at the end. *Everybody* had muddy shoes, and there were four sets of muddy footprints. The model uses suspense when Derek and Aaron feel like they are being watched and when they sneak toward the voices and hide. Surprise is used when the boys are startled by a noise.

Solution to the Mystery

Remember the appearance of Phineas Felch at the beginning? He was mostly a mess except for his shoes, which were clean and new. The boys noticed an extra set of footprints, and they also noticed the state of Felch's new shoes after his so-called nap—muddy. Phineas Felch hadn't napped at all because he was busy moving statues into the van.

Fun Fact

The most famous crime detective of all time, Sherlock Holmes, was created by Sir Arthur Conan Doyle, who wrote mystery novels more than 100 years ago.

Reading Your Writing

A mystery is a type of fiction in which a crime or other mysterious happening occurs and is solved by a character in the story. To keep your readers interested, be sure to include good clues in your story that hint at the solution but do not spoil the mystery.

Tips for Writing a Mystery

Prewriting Make a Plan

▶ Brainstorm ideas from which to create a story about a crime or mysterious event.

▶ Plan the setting, develop the character(s) who solve the mystery, and list the clues that will be used. You can use a story map to help you plan.

Drafting Get Your Ideas on Paper

▶ Refer to your story map or notes to write your story.

▶ As you describe the setting and characters, focus on descriptive detail.

Revising Be Sure It Makes Sense

▶ **Ideas** Is your story original? Did you include elements of suspense and surprise? Did you add descriptive touches to add interest?

▶ **Organization** Are the events mysterious or just confusing? Be sure to explain what happens in a way that makes sense to the reader.

▶ **Organization** Do you catch the reader's attention in the opening paragraph? Do you provide enough clues? Is the mystery solved?

▶ **Voice** Do you write with a style that involves the reader and complements the mood of the story?

Editing/Proofreading Look Over the Details

▶ **Conventions** Proofread your mystery for spelling, punctuation, and capitalization.

Publishing Get Ready to Share Your Mystery

▶ **Presentation** Neatly type or rewrite your final copy.

▶ **Presentation** Consider illustrating your mystery.

Adventure Stories

An **adventure** is an exciting fictional story with characters, places, and events that seem real. Suspense, action, and danger are the important features in adventure stories.

One of the most famous adventure stories of all time is *Treasure Island.* It is told through the eyes of Jim Hawkins, a boy who finds a treasure map in the sea chest of a man who is murdered. Jim goes on a sea voyage to an island with two trusted men from his village to find the buried treasure. After learning that most of their crew are pirates planning to steal the treasure, Jim gets into one dangerous situation after another while trying to save his partners' lives and escape with the treasure.

Survival Stories

Some adventure stories deal with survival. One or more main characters find themselves isolated from other people, sometimes in a place where they must use survival skills to get such basics as food, water, and shelter in order to live.

In *The Cay*, set in the Caribbean, a boy named Phillip becomes blind after the ship he is on is torpedoed during World War II. He ends up in a life raft with an older man named Timothy who knows what to do to keep them alive. Timothy knows that fresh, raw fish will provide them with both nutrition and much-needed water. After landing on a small island, he builds a hut from palm fronds, makes a trough to catch rainwater, and creates fishing lines from unraveled boat lines, using rusty bolts for sinkers.

Adventure stories contain the basic features of fiction: setting, plot, and characters.

Setting

The setting of an adventure story is very important and may even determine the action of the story. For example, an adventure could take place on a mountain during an avalanche. A survival story might occur near a river full of crocodiles in the Australian outback. The animals, natural landscape, and presence or lack of water in a location present a range of possibilities for challenge and suspense. To make your story realistic, you may need to do research to write accurately about the time and place that you choose.

Plot

The events of an adventure story are not real but must seem as if they could actually happen. Action, danger, and suspense are the main ingredients. Races, chases, and trying to find an object or reach a specific goal are common in adventure plots. The adventure should have some sort of conflict. To build suspense, use precise action verbs and colorful adjectives. Tell why a situation is dangerous and suggest what might happen if things do not work out. Delay telling the outcome. As with all plots, events should have an outcome or resolution.

Characters

The characters of an adventure story are fictional. In order for readers to identify with them, however, they should be well-developed and should seem real. Readers will care much more about the action and suspense in the story if they identify with the main characters.

The Lost Lake

Setting ▶ Melanie and Jake will never forget the time they talked their mother into taking the dirt road. The dirt road was near the cottage the family rented every August on Hamlin Lake.

Near Lake Michigan, Hamlin Lake is surrounded by giant sand dunes, tall grasses, and beech and pine trees. There are lots of places to explore. There are not many places to shop, however. When they needed eggs, milk, sunscreen, or anything else, they had to drive all the way around a large section of dunes to get to Jaeger's Corner Store. One time they noticed a dirt road just to the right of the store. On their side of the dunes, there was another dirt road. They never saw anyone drive down either road, but they wondered if the two roads were connected and could provide a shortcut to the store.

Suspense ▶ One afternoon, they started out to the store when they spotted the first dirt road. They begged their mother to slow down so they could take a look. The road snaked down into the trees and disappeared. They couldn't see where it went, so they asked their mother to drive farther. When the car plunged forward, Jake and Melanie looked at each other in amazement. Mom seemed up for an adventure.

The road was surprisingly smooth, and the three of them laughed carelessly as they dipped up and down its hills. It began to flatten near a clearing. They slowed down and were surprised to see a small lake. They had no idea that a lake was hidden behind the dunes. They wondered if it was one of the lost lakes

Setting ▶ whispered about by old-timers. They got out of the car and decided to explore. There was no sign of people. As they walked through mud and tall grass to get to the other side, they noticed the sky filling up with shrouds of billowing thunderclouds.

Suddenly everything went dark and it began to rain buckets. They headed for the car, taking giant steps trying to cover the marshy ground as fast as possible without getting stuck. They jumped into the car and took off in what they hoped was the direction of the store.

The car struggled to climb the first hill. The second hill was impossible. The car spun its wheels in the thick mud and went nowhere. "Melanie and Jake, you're going to have to get out and push," said their mom.

Danger ▶
Struggle ▶

They began pushing, but the wheels just spun and splattered mud. When it looked like they were getting somewhere, Jake stepped sideways onto an underground bees' nest. Before they had time to think, angry bees swarmed them. Jake and Melanie scrambled frantically to get back into the car, but the bees followed. They grabbed newspapers from the floor and tried to swat them, but the bees only became angrier. When they were finally rid of them, Jake discovered he had five bee stings, Melanie saw she had four, and Mom had two. The swelling bee stings hurt. After everyone calmed down, they talked about what to do.

Action ▶

They reasoned that they were not that stuck, because pushing helped. If they avoided the bees' nest, they could place the newspapers under the car wheels for traction. They tried it, and when Mom hit the gas, the car moved forward. A few enraged bees darted from the nest again, and Jake and Melanie dove back into the car. Mom gunned the engine, and the car went right over the hill, never stopping until they came to the end of the road—at Jaeger's Corner Store.

Resolution ▶

It was fun telling people about the shortcut and the hidden lake, but after that experience, Melanie and Jake never minded taking the long way around.

Try It

Can you think of a good plot for an adventure story? You may even be able to base your story on something that happened in your own life!

Analyzing the Model

Organization

The story tells about the events in the order that they happened. The first paragraph introduces the setting and characters. The conclusion briefly describes the characters after their experience and, in a humorous way, reminds readers of an earlier issue—the shortcut.

Setting

The muddy, deserted road creates a challenging environment. The characters must figure out how to get unstuck from the mud. They are also isolated from other people and can't call anyone for help.

Plot

The model contains the important adventure story features of suspense, action, and danger. Did you wonder with the characters what was down the road? If you did, you felt suspense. Driving down the path, running in the rain, fighting bees, and struggling to free the car provided action. Swarming bees suggested danger.

Do the events seem like they could have happened? Because everything that happened was part of the natural environment, the story seemed real. The conflict or struggle has to do with getting away from the lost lake. The story gains its resolution when the three make it to the store.

Characters

The story attempts some character development. We learn that Mom can be adventurous, and we may also identify with Jake and Melanie when we learn that they dislike the long trip to the store.

Reading Your Writing

An adventure is a thrilling fictional story that has characters, places, and events that seem real. It is easy to focus on the plot of an adventure, but don't forget your characters. Good character development will make your reader care about the people in the story.

Tips for Writing an Adventure Story

Prewriting Make a Plan

▶ Think of a setting that interests you and an adventure that could happen there. Do research if necessary in order to describe your setting.

▶ Develop the characters and figure out what will be their struggle.

▶ You can use a story map to plan your story.

Drafting Get Your Ideas on Paper

▶ Refer to your story map and other notes to write your story.

Revising Be Sure It Makes Sense

▶ **Ideas** Do the events seem like they could really happen? Does your story have action, suspense, and danger?

▶ **Organization** Is the action described in a logical way? Are events ordered in a way that will create the most suspense?

▶ **Organization** Is there an obvious conflict with a resolution at the end?

▶ **Word Choice** Do you use precise verbs and colorful adjectives?

▶ **Sentence Fluency** Are sentences put together well? Do they have rhythm, variety, and flow?

Editing/Proofreading Look Over the Details

▶ **Conventions** Proofread your adventure story for spelling, punctuation, and capitalization.

Publishing Get Ready to Share Your Adventure

▶ **Presentation** Neatly type or rewrite your final copy.

▶ **Presentation** Think about illustrating your story.

Historical Fiction

Historical fiction is a story that takes place in an actual time and place in the past. When you write historical fiction, you give lots of details about the period in which your events take place.

Like other fiction, historical fiction must have a setting, a plot, and characters. However, in historical fiction, the specific time and place in which the story takes place play a major role in the events and in some ways control what the characters think, say, and do.

Setting

When you write historical fiction, you will need to include plenty of detail about the time and place. This often requires research. Information about the way that people talked, their points of view, the tools they used, what they ate, drank, wore, and did for fun all help make the story accurate and seem real. This information should be included in a way that fits with the telling of the story.

Elizabeth George Speare's *The Sign of the Beaver* is set in Maine in the 1700s. When Matt, the main character, meets the other central character, Attean, we learn some of the language of the native people of the area, the Penobscot. We find out what Attean and some other Penobscot think—that white people have taken over their hunting grounds. We also learn about Penobscot foods such as corncakes, nuts, and cakes of maple sugar when Matt receives them as gifts. When Attean teaches Matt native ways to trap and fish, we learn about Penobscot tools and also the plants and animals of the Maine woods in the 1700s.

Plot

The problems that characters face and their decisions and actions have to do with actual historical events. In *Number the Stars*, a novel by Lois Lowry that takes place during World War II, a Danish family copes with food shortages and the constant presence of soldiers. The action and suspense have to do with hiding Ellen, a Danish Jew, and the resolution of the book is safely getting Ellen's family to Sweden.

Number the Stars bases its fictional storyline on actual events. The Danish people really did smuggle most of the Jews out of their country to safety in Sweden.

Characters

Just as the plots may include actual events, some of the characters in historical fiction may be actual people. When famous people from the past are used, it is especially important to do careful research so that the thoughts and actions you create for them do not contradict what is known about them. You may find it easier and less limiting to write about minor historical figures or made-up characters whose everyday lives are affected by the events of the time.

Anachronisms

An anachronism is a person, thing, or event that is chronologically out of place. To avoid anachronisms in your story, it is important to have the characters in historical fiction act the way that people of the time would act. Don't make the mistake of including things that do not belong to the time. For example, a story that takes place during the Middle Ages should not have characters bathing every day or using contemporary slang.

Golden Mountain

We were really scared. One of them had a shotgun, and it didn't look like they would see it our way. The five bearded men were searching for gold on the claim next to ours, and one afternoon they came with their picks and shovels to our side of the boundary. When we showed them our claim rights, they gruffly shoved us aside and laughed, saying California was their country and that we should go back to China. Believe me, I had thought of that plenty of times.

My name is Chang Hong. The year was 1853, and I was sixteen years old. My uncle, cousins, and I had been working our claim for four months without any luck. We had heard about Gaam San, which in Cantonese means "golden mountain," from relatives in China who said California was covered with gold. When we got here, we

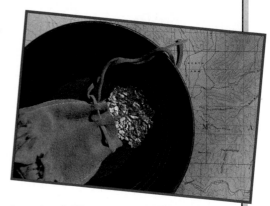

discovered that it was not what we imagined. We saw shacks and shanties everywhere. Back in our province in China, things were not much better, so we had no choice but to carry through with our plan to mine gold. We hoped to send for our families or at least bring some wealth home.

The tools needed for mining gold were very expensive, so we pooled what money we had and bought only what we really needed. Then we had to bargain for our mining claim.

Every day we dug in the hard earth and panned in a nearby stream. We saw only mud and rocks—no gold. When our bellies weren't twisting in pain from eating salt pork, beans, and other strange foods, they ached from hunger. It was hard to find the fresh vegetables and rice that we were used to eating. At least we had our tea. Sometimes we could buy rice and vegetables from other Cantonese carrying these provisions on bamboo poles. They traveled from mine to mine selling to Chinese and other hungry miners. We began to wonder if they were the ones striking it rich. As we spent our savings on food, we did not find the gold that would bring us more money. So when the five

Setting ▶

Character ▶

Plot ▶

bearded men threatened to take over our claim, instead of fighting back, we packed up and left.

We had heard of other Cantonese setting up "chow chows" similar to the eating places in China, and we wanted to open one. We pitched our tent on the edge of San Francisco near where others from our province had settled in a village made of shanties and tents. We were able to buy just enough chickens and pigs to get started. Some villagers gave us seeds so we could plant a vegetable garden, and we soon had enough food to start our own "chow chow."

We chose a spot near the center of town that would attract Chinese and non-Chinese. We flew a triangular yellow flag so people would see that we were a "chow chow." Our prices were very low, and word got around that our food was good, so we quickly became busy. As long as we were making food (not competing for gold or other jobs), the non-Chinese left us alone.

Point of View ▶ Tending a garden, taking care of animals, and making and selling food is very hard work. It isn't why we came here, but it is a lot better than coming up empty-handed in the gold mines. At the end of the day, my belly is content, filled with rice, vegetables, and sometimes chicken or pork. I could do worse!

Try It

If you were writing a historical fiction piece, what setting would you use? Would you include a real person from history or a fictional person who might have lived during that time?

Analyzing the Model

Point of View

Sometimes historical fiction is written as if it were someone's diary or journal. It takes this approach to encourage the reader to identify with Chang Hong and to provide a more personal view of what it may have been like to be a Chinese miner.

Setting

The story takes place in 1853, five years after gold was first found in California. Many Chinese did go to California searching for gold. The story includes many facts about the time and place, such as San Francisco being filled with the tents and shanties of miners. The Chinese did receive supplies from traveling Chinese carrying food from bamboo poles. The story includes these details in a way that fits with the telling of the story.

Plot

The main struggles of facing prejudice, searching for gold without results, and surviving with little food are historically based. The details such as the five bearded men are fictional. The resolution is realistic. Selling food was a way for many Chinese, unwelcome in the mines, to make a living.

Characters

Chang Hong is a fictional character based on an actual person, Chang De-ming. Information about Chang De-ming is scarce. The author wrote about a fictional Chang Hong with whom it is easier to identify and match historical information.

Fun Fact

By 1860, of the roughly 83,000 men in the California gold mines, 24,000 were Chinese.

Reading Your Writing

Historical fiction is a story that takes place in an actual time in the past. Don't make the mistake of putting a modern convenience in a story about the Old West or your reader will not believe your story.

Tips for Writing Historical Fiction

Prewriting Make a Plan

▶ Think of historical events or characters that interest you. Draw from social studies or other school subjects.

▶ Research historical details such as food, tools, and language that will make your story interesting and accurate.

▶ Consider using a story map to plan your story.

Drafting Get Your Ideas on Paper

▶ Refer to your story map or other notes to write your historical fiction story.

▶ Focus on the struggle in the plot and the historical details.

Revising Be Sure It Makes Sense

▶ **Ideas** Are the events of your story interesting? Does it have plenty of historical detail, described in a way that fits with the story?

▶ **Word Choice** Did you choose just the right words to describe the time and place? Will your reader understand, through context or explanation, the words you used?

Editing/Proofreading Look Over the Details

▶ **Conventions** Be sure to capitalize the names of historical events, characters, and any other proper nouns. Check punctuation and spelling.

Publishing Get Ready to Share Your Historical Fiction Story

▶ **Presentation** Neatly type or rewrite your final copy.

▶ **Presentation** Consider illustrating your story.

Fantasies

A **fantasy** is any story containing things that do not exist or cannot happen in the real world. Fantasy stories allow writers and readers to use their imaginations. A fantasy has a setting, a plot, and characters just as in other kinds of fiction—but in fantasy, one or more of the elements are not realistic.

Setting

The setting of the story may be a world or place that does not exist. In *The Phantom Tollbooth,* by Norton Juster, Milo travels in the Lands Beyond to one impossible place after another. Two examples are the Doldrums where no one is allowed to think and Dictionopolis where words grow on trees and are sold in cases in the "word market."

Plot

A fantasy story has a beginning, a middle, and an end just like other stories, but in a fantasy, impossible events occur. In addition, the conflict or struggle may involve a problem that would not exist in the real world. In *Heartlight,* by T.A. Barron, the main character, Kate, and her grandfather travel to alternate worlds to discover why the sun is losing its pure condensed light. Neither the problem nor the way it is solved in a fantasy reflects reality, but it makes for fun writing and reading.

Characters

Some fantasies have characters that do impossible things or simply could not exist, such as dragons, ogres, talking animals, or tiny people. In *The Indian in the Cupboard,* by Lynne Reid Banks, Omri is amazed when a plastic toy comes to life as a miniature, but very real, Iroquois brave when placed in a cupboard that has magic powers.

Things to Keep in Mind

Your story does not need to have every single feature of a fantasy. When you write a fantasy, you may wish to have only one unrealistic character or event.

Also keep in mind such things as character development and action. Even if your main characters are totally fantasy, you will want to develop their personalities so readers can identify with them. To make events interesting, you will want to add action, suspense, and surprise. Use your imagination and the tools of all good fiction writing to create a fantasy story that involves readers and makes them want to pretend the story is real.

Coming Up with Ideas

You may wish to keep a folder or journal with ideas for fantasy writing. You could create a chart like this. Title it *Wild Ideas*.

Wild Ideas

Setting: *An old barn in a new housing development.*

Characters: *A bat family. Two human girls named Iesha and Sandra.*

Plot: *A family of talking bats lives in the barn. The developers want to tear down the barn. The bats befriend Iesha and Sandra, who help the bats save their home.*

Setting: *The fifth grade section of an elementary school.*

Characters: *Two boys named Ashish and Rob.*

Plot: *Ashish and Rob find a secret locker. When they climb into it, they become someone else.*

Setting: *My house.*

Characters: *The pixies and me.*

Plot: *A family of tiny pixies lives in my house. Only I know about them. They create mischief such as scattering papers and spilling people's drinks. I often get the blame.*

The Secret Locker

It was really strange. They had never noticed it before. Toward the end of their row of lockers, between locker 97 and locker 98, was one more locker. The number on it was 97.6. Ashish and Rob agreed that they had never heard of lockers having numbers with decimals. They watched the locker carefully for the rest of the week. Nobody seemed to be using it. They talked about it by telephone over the weekend and decided that on Monday they would look inside.

The weekend finally ended, and they went back to school. Kids always seemed to be around so there was never a good time to look. Because neither Ashish nor Rob rode the bus, they were able to hang around at the end of the day. When the last locker banged shut and the hallway was empty, they walked over to the mysterious locker and opened it very slowly.

They looked inside and saw a strange glowing light. Ashish stepped in, and before he could say anything, he was sucked down a tube. He felt rushing air, darkness, and then a plop. He was watching a wide broom sweeping a floor. It looked just like the school hallway except that Rob was nowhere in sight.

He heard someone whistling, and it sounded like it was coming from his own mouth. He didn't feel like himself. When he looked down at his hands, they were large, muscular, and very hairy. Then he heard a voice much deeper than his own saying to a janitor, "I'm almost finished with this hall. Let me

know if you need help with the bathrooms." That was it. He was inside the body of the other janitor. He wished he could tell Rob. Then he wondered how he would get back, and he began to worry. He didn't have to worry long because the janitor sneezed. He felt rushing air and darkness, and he was back in locker 97.6. He stumbled backwards and fell out of the locker.

Rob was waiting. When Ashish told Rob about what happened, Rob wanted to try it, but then they saw someone coming. They decided to try the locker during recess the next day.

Unrealistic problem ▶ Recess finally came. After everyone went outside, Rob and Ashish met at locker 97.6. Rob was nervous. He was worried about getting back. Ashish assured him that a simple sneeze would bring him back. Still, what if whoever's body he was in didn't sneeze? Rob knew that if he wanted the experience, he would have to take his chances.

He stepped into the locker and was swept away. After the darkness and rushing air, he saw and felt his hand dribbling a basketball and shooting. He scored. Two minutes later he made another basket. Wow, he never knew what it was like to be this good at basketball! He heard someone yell, "Tony, I'm open." He was inside Tony Rivera, the best basketball player in fifth grade, and it was pretty great. Recess was almost over and Tony still hadn't sneezed.

Unrealistic power ▶ Rob worried about getting back to class on time. Then the playground aide blew the whistle, and Tony headed back with all the other kids. How could he get Tony to sneeze? Tony approached the building—and still no sneeze. Rob concentrated very hard on getting Tony to kick up some fine dirt near the corner of the school. Then Tony started kicking up the dust, and Rob heard him say, "This is really weird. What is going on?" Finally, Rob heard "Achoo," felt rushing dark air, and smelled the metal of locker 97.6. He stumbled out and saw Ashish waiting. The two of them made it to class just in time.

They decided to take a break from locker 97.6 for a while. Apparently the decision wasn't theirs to make, however. After school, locker 97.6 had a large brass lock hanging from its door.

Analyzing the Model

Fun Fact

The word fantasy comes from a Middle English word spelled fantasie, which also means "fancy," the free play of the creative imagination.

Setting

The setting of "The Secret Locker", a typical school, is mostly realistic. The locker with the unusual number suggests that something is different. Schools do not normally have lockers with decimal numbers. "The Secret Locker" is an example of a fantasy story set in the real world with one unusual feature.

Characters

The main characters are also realistic. Ashish and Rob are normal boys who have something very unusual happen to them. The story does suggest that Rob is able to use a special power when he gets Tony to kick up dust and sneeze. The characters in "The Secret Locker" could exist in the real world.

Plot

The story's plot contains much more fantasy. The impossible happens when Ashish and Rob are sucked down the tube into another person's body. These events cannot happen in the real world. The plot contains a problem—getting back to one's own body. But the problem would not exist in the real world. The main events, the problem, and the way the problem is solved are what make this story a fantasy.

Try It

Go back to the Wild Ideas chart on page 183 and see if you can pick out the fantasy elements for the other story ideas.

▶ Which ideas have unrealistic characters?

▶ Which ideas have events that could not happen in the real world?

Reading Your Writing

Remember to develop the characters in your fantasy so that your reader will care about what happens to them.

Tips for Writing a Fantasy

Prewriting Make a Plan

▶ Think of how you could write about any of your own fantasies such as having special powers, visiting an imaginary world, watching toys come to life, or seeing and talking to fantastic creatures.

▶ Look in your folder or journal for possible fantasy story ideas.

▶ Use a story map to plan the parts of your story that will have fantasy elements. Plan the problem, resolution, and any events containing fantasy.

Drafting Get Your Thoughts on Paper

▶ Refer to your story map and other notes to write your fantasy story.

▶ Let your imagination run free as you write.

Revising Be Sure It Makes Sense

▶ **Ideas** Are your ideas original? Will readers find them interesting?

▶ **Organization** Do the story events make sense and fit together? Does your story have a problem or conflict that is solved?

Editing/Proofreading Look Over the Details

▶ **Conventions** Proofread your fantasy for mistakes in spelling, punctuation, and capitalization.

Publishing Get Ready to Share Your Fantasy

▶ **Presentation** Neatly type or rewrite your final copy.

▶ **Presentation** Consider illustrating your fantasy.

Plays

A **play** is a story that is written to be acted out before an audience. What the characters say and do tells the story in a play. People called actors memorize and perform their parts, which are the words and actions written for their character.

Plays have the basic elements of other forms of literature. When you write a play, you will want to include setting(s), a plot, and characters.

Setting

The **setting** refers to the time and place where events occur. Plays often have more than one setting. These different settings are called **scenes.** Scenes are like chapters in a book. For example, a play based on *The Princess and the Pea* might have its first scene in the late afternoon at the castle gate where the princess appears during a storm. The next scene might be in the evening in the bedroom where the queen tests the princess by placing a pea under twenty mattresses. When describing the settings and scenes in a play, be sure to tell when and where the action takes place.

Plot

Plot refers to what happens in the play. It should include not only a beginning, a middle, and an end but also conflict and resolution. The audience finds out about the play's conflict or struggle through what the characters say and do. For example, in a play based on *Charlotte's Web*, you discover the central struggle in dialogue between the old sheep and Wilbur, the pig, when the old sheep tells Wilbur he is being fed so that he can be slaughtered for ham. The events and the resolution that follow (the actions of Charlotte, the spider) are based on the struggle to save Wilbur's life. When writing a play, be sure to include a conflict and a resolution.

Characters

Characters refer to the figures that act and speak in the play. They are listed at the play's beginning as the **cast of characters.** For example, a play based on *Alice's Adventures in Wonderland* might list Alice, White Rabbit, Cheshire Cat, and Queen of Hearts as its cast. A character in a play may be a person, an animal, or even an object such as a car or a tree.

Other Elements That Belong to Plays

Dialogue

Dialogue refers to the words or lines spoken by the characters. In plays, words spoken by characters are not put in quotation marks as they are in other forms of writing. Instead, the character's name followed by a colon marks the lines or dialogue. This is how dialogue in a play based on *The Princess and the Pea* might look.

> **Queen:** How did you sleep, dear?
> **Princess:** Not very well. Something round and hard poked my back all night.

Stage Directions

Stage directions describe just about everything going on in the play that isn't dialogue. They include where characters move, how they should express themselves, and also directions on how to use props, sound effects, costumes, and lighting. Place stage directions in parentheses or in brackets. You may also wish to underline them or use italic type. See these stage directions for a play based on *Charlotte's Web*.

> **Charlotte:** (*talking in a quiet, soothing voice from a dark corner of the barn*) I'll be your friend, Wilbur.
> **Wilbur:** (*jumping to his feet*) But I can't see you. Where are you?

Play Model

This student-written play was adapted from a book. Look for the features of a play such as stage direction and setting.

When Shlemiel Went to Warsaw

Based on the book by Isaac Bashevis Singer

Cast of Characters ▶

Shlemiel (a peasant man, married to Mrs. Shlemiel)

Mrs. Shlemiel (married to Shlemiel, runs the household)

Shlemiel children (two older boys, three younger girls, and a baby boy)

Villager and Neighbors 1, 2, and 3 (live near the Shlemiels)

Blacksmith (a prankster, lives outside the village)

Setting ▶ Hundreds of years ago in a small Polish village named Chelm.

Scene I (one morning at the Shlemiels' house)

Narrator: In a Polish village named Chelm there once lived a man called Shlemiel. He was married to Mrs. Shlemiel, who did most of the work running their household of six children. Shlemiel spent most of his time sleeping and daydreaming. One morning the two had a conversation.

Dialogue ▶ **Shlemiel:** I would like to go on a long journey and see the world someday.

Mrs. Shlemiel: Long journeys are not for a Shlemiel. I need you to stay home and mind the children while I go to the market to sell my vegetables.

Shlemiel: A visitor from Warsaw told me the big city has beautiful streets, high buildings, and luxurious stores.

Mrs. Shlemiel: Stop daydreaming, Shlemiel. We can't afford to travel.

Narrator: Shlemiel could not stop wondering about Warsaw. He had to see it for himself. One morning, after Mrs. Shlemiel left for the market, he gathered his two older boys.

Shlemiel: (to his older sons while the younger children play nearby) I'm going on a journey and may not be back for a while. Please take good care of the children and tell your mother when she returns.

Stage Directions ▶ (Shlemiel wraps bread and an onion into a scarf that he attaches to a long pole. He carries this on his shoulder as he walks out of the house.)

Scene II ▶ (late afternoon on the road to Warsaw)

Shlemiel: (After walking a distance, he acts very tired.)

This journey makes me tired. A nap would be nice. (He settles down on the grass near the road then looks puzzled.) When I wake up, I may not remember which way leads to Warsaw and which way leads back to Chelm. (face brightening) Aha! (He takes off his boots and points them toward Warsaw.) That'll show me the right way.

(While Shlemiel naps, the blacksmith appears. The blacksmith studies Shlemiel, chuckles, and turns his boots in the opposite direction. He leaves.)

Shlemiel: (yawning and stretching) Not a bad nap. I am a little hungry, though. (chomps on his onion) Well, I'd better be on my way. (pulls on his boots and walks in the wrong direction)

Shlemiel: (begins looking puzzled) This is strange. It looks just like the countryside near Chelm. (As he gets closer, he is even more puzzled.) These houses look just like my neighbors' houses. (stopping a villager) What is the name of this town?

Villager: Chelm.

Shlemiel: (rubbing his forehead, talking to himself) I guess there is another Chelm on the way to Warsaw. I've heard Earth is the same everywhere, so why shouldn't a second Chelm be the same as the first? Still, it is strange how much alike they are. I wonder if there is a street and a house just like mine.

Scene III ▶ (evening, the Shlemiel house)
(Shlemiel walks toward his house and knocks on the door.)

Mrs. Shlemiel: Where in the world have you been? Why did you leave the children and what are you carrying?

Children: Papa, where have you been?

Shlemiel: (pausing) Mrs. Shlemiel, I'm not your husband. Children, I'm not your papa.

Mrs. Shlemiel: (shouting) Have you lost your mind?

Shlemiel: I am Shlemiel of Chelm One. This is Chelm Two.

Mrs. Shlemiel: Children, your father has gone crazy!

(The neighbors hear the noise and crowd into the house.)

Neighbor 1: Shlemiel, what's the matter with you? You are in your own house, with your own wife and children, your own neighbors and friends.

Shlemiel: No, you don't understand. I come from Chelm One. I was on my way to Warsaw, and between Chelm One and Warsaw there is a Chelm Two. That is where I am.

Neighbor 2: What are you talking about? We all know you, and you know us.

Shlemiel: No, I'm not in my town.

Mrs. Shlemiel: (clasping her hands) This is crazy.

Neighbor 3: Let's take him to the town elders. They'll know what to do.

Scene IV ▶ (the next day, the village square)

Narrator: So the neighbors took Shlemiel to the elders, who believed Shlemiel when he said he was a different Shlemiel. At first they decided he should live in the poorhouse because he was not Mrs. Shlemiel's husband. Then Mrs. Shlemiel moaned about not having someone to watch her children, so they decided to let Shlemiel stay with her. They even paid him to watch the children. Of course he turned the money over to Mrs. Shlemiel, who provided him with food and did all the work at the house anyway.

Shlemiel: (sitting on a bench in the village square with a single spotlight shining on him, thinking aloud) I wonder where the other Shlemiel is. When will he come home? What is my real wife doing? Is she waiting for me, or has she got herself another Shlemiel?

Narrator: These were questions Shlemiel could never answer.

Analyzing the Model

Setting

Information at the beginning of the play and at the beginning of each scene should tell you when and where the action takes place. In this play, it is given at the very beginning after the setting and also after the heading for each scene.

Plot

How would you describe the plot? What is the conflict? How is it resolved? Through the character's words, we learn that the conflict or problem has to do with Shlemiel believing he is in another village by the same name as the one from which he came. Mrs. Shlemiel thinks he is crazy but wants him to stay with her to watch the children. At the end of the play, the narrator describes the solution, which is that the village pays Shlemiel to watch the "other" Shlemiel's children.

Character

How are characters developed? The play develops personalities through dialogue and action (described by stage direction). Through Mrs. Shlemiel's dialogue, we learn that Shlemiel is a dreamer. When he naps and gets turned around on his journey (stage direction), we learn that he is somewhat lazy and confused. Stage directions also tell us that Shlemiel often looks puzzled and that Mrs. Shlemiel shouts and moans. She is more dramatic than Shlemiel.

Who Is the Narrator?

Plays often use narrators to provide the audience with background information and to summarize events. Narrators usually stand out of sight or off to the side. They are not part of a play's action. Because this play is based on a much longer book, the narrator summarizes the resolution and ending.

Try It

Can you think of any stories or books that you would like to make into a play? What would be the setting of the play? Who would be the characters? What kind of stage direction might you add?

Reading Your Writing

A play is a story that is written to be performed for an audience. When writing your play, include good stage directions so the actors can understand what their characters should do.

Fun Fact

When Shakespeare's plays were first performed, men played the roles of women. In *Romeo and Juliet,* a young man played the part of Juliet.

Tips for Writing a Play

Prewriting Make a Plan

▶ Plan your setting and plot. You could make a chart listing *when* and *where* each scene occurs and *what* happens.

▶ Develop your characters. Plan what they will say and do.

Drafting Get Your Ideas on Paper

▶ Refer to your prewriting plan to write your play.

Revising Be Sure It Makes Sense

▶ **Ideas** Do your dialogue and stage direction show clearly what happens in your play?

▶ **Organization** Does your play have a beginning, a middle, and an end?

▶ **Word Choice** Do you have characters using words and language in a way that develops individual personalities?

Editing/Proofreading Look Over the Details

▶ **Conventions** Check to make sure character names and other proper nouns are capitalized. Check punctuation and spelling.

Publishing Get Ready to Share Your Play

▶ **Presentation** Make neat final copies for each cast member to read and memorize.

▶ **Presentation** Present your play to an audience.

Descriptive Writing

Descriptive writing provides the reader with a clear, vivid picture of something or someone. Think about the best place you ever visited. What do you remember about the way it looked, sounded, and smelled? When you use those kinds of details in your writing, you help your readers see what you see, hear what you hear, and feel what you feel. The following lessons will give you tips on writing good descriptions.

▶ Writing Descriptions **200**

▶ Observation Reports **206**

Writing a Description

Descriptions tell about how things and events look, sound, feel, smell, and even taste. If you write good descriptions, your readers can almost experience the things about which you are writing.

Descriptive Writing

Writing that is descriptive uses details to create a clear and interesting picture in the reader's mind. Unlike a story, descriptive writing does not usually contain events with a beginning, a middle, and an end. Descriptive writing, in the form of sentences or paragraphs, is usually found *within* another type of writing. Descriptive writing is used in many different kinds of writing, both fiction and nonfiction.

In your own writing, you might choose to write a paragraph to describe a setting, a character, an action, or an object. Descriptive paragraphs help readers create detailed mental pictures that make the descriptions seem real.

Good Description Is in the Details

Sensory writing tells how something smells, tastes, feels, and sounds as well as how it looks. The sentences below engage the reader's memories of taste and smell.

As I blew up the rubber raft, I could taste the salt of last year's trip to the ocean. The raft smelled like the moldy garden hose stored in our basement.

Try It

Which senses do these sentences rely on for sensory description?

▶ The aroma of banana and peanut butter sandwiches floated toward me.

▶ Drills whirred and hammers clanged as sawdust filled the air.

Select the Right Word

Colorful adjectives such as *bumpy, spongy,* and *shrill* are an obvious choice for descriptive writing. Specific nouns such as *Big Ben, cicada,* and *No. 2 pencil* add interest, also. Precise action verbs such as *plunge, saunter,* and *singe* add energy and interest to your writing. Be creative and exact with your words. For example, the narrative sentence *My boots were getting stuck in the mud* becomes much more interesting when you add descriptive adjectives and verbs: *The brown-green mud sucked at my favorite boots as I wrestled to free myself.*

Tell How

Don't just tell *what*; tell *how* something looks or sounds. Similes and metaphors are great for describing *how.* For examples of similes and metaphors, see pages 286–287.

Organizing Your Descriptions

When writing a description, you will want to present the details in a way that makes sense to your reader. Avoid jumping from one unrelated detail to the next. Descriptions may be organized in any number of ways: from top to bottom, left to right, near to far, most recent to least recent, or any way that makes sense for what you are describing.

The three descriptive models on these pages are each part of a longer piece of fiction. *Up on a Roof* describes the planets and the place where a girl sets up her telescope. The details are arranged from the nearest details to the ones farthest away. *Under the Sea* describes what a group of snorkelers sees under the water. The details are organized from top to bottom. *In the Gym* describes what the writer sees while looking for his friends. The details are organized from left to right.

Up on a Roof

Old newspapers, aluminum cans, and discarded rags littered the rooftop. A pungent tar odor from the roof filled Luisa's nose. The roof had been baking in the hot sun all day, and she could feel the warmth under the soles of her shoes. A soft, warm breeze fluttered the laundry hanging on nearby apartment balconies.

Farther out, a few wispy clouds floated by the silver glow of the moon. Overall, it looked like a clear evening, perfect for viewing the night sky. Luisa's grandfather had told her that four planets should be visible with her telescope that evening. Venus was the easiest to spot. Low in the sky, looking close enough to touch, it shone brighter than anything else. Jupiter was also easy to find. It appeared much higher, but it, too, was bright. Luisa scanned the sky for Mars and trained her telescope on a pinkish star. When she increased the magnification, she saw the object's roundness and knew it was the planet Mars. Last she searched for Saturn. She finally spotted something far away that did not seem to belong to the nearby constellation. It was Saturn. When she focused the lenses, she saw the spectacular rings circling the planet like a silver disk.

Under the Sea

A gentle breeze rippled the top of the water. Just under the surface, bubbles from other snorkelers floated to the top. The turquoise blue of the Caribbean deepened to a sapphire when we looked down. Tiny silver fish swam in schools just five feet below. Beneath them we saw striped fish, royal blue fish with black and yellow markings, and one silvery bronze fish with black spots.

As we dove toward the coral at the bottom, colder water surrounded our bodies. Shades of pink, orange, green, and purple tinted the vast array of coral on the seafloor. Small orange and white clown fish swam in and out of the formations. What was that in the sand? A large manta ray emerged from its spot and moved on, leaving us to our underwater exploration.

In the Gym

As I entered the hall to the gym, I heard the loud buzzer announcing halftime. I wanted to find my friends. To the left of the bleachers was the drinking fountain with its usual small puddle of water on the floor in front of it.

Even though it was halftime, the bleachers were almost full. I could feel the heat of the crowd. On the left side of the bleachers sat a group of sixth graders. They were wearing red T-shirts that said, "Go Eagles." I saw some kids from my fifth-grade class sitting to the right of them and, farther to the right, lots of parents. Closer to the center, on an empty bleacher at the bottom, were water bottles and towels. A net bag held the extra basketballs. To the right of the bench was the scoring table, then the speaker's stand. On the right end of the bleachers, I saw fans from the other team waving their green banners.

Analyzing the Models

Up on a Roof

What do you notice about the first model? Do you see how the author first describes what is nearby and then describes what is farther away? Details in this description are organized from near to far. The description uses location words such as "near," "nearby," "close," "farther," and "farther out." Luisa first senses her immediate environment. She sees the litter, she smells the tar, and she feels the heat under her feet. The author tells about the laundry hanging "nearby" in Luisa's neighborhood. Next, the description moves "farther out" to the clouds, then to the moon, and finally to the planets farther out in the solar system. Saturn is described last as being "far away."

Under the Sea

The details in this piece are organized from top to bottom. Location words such as "top," "under," "down," "below," "beneath," "bottom," and "seafloor" guide the reader from the top to the bottom of the underwater scene. Organizing the description from top to bottom allows the reader to follow the snorkelers to the bottom of the sea.

In the Gym

This model describes a scene from left to right. Location words and phrases include "to the left," "left side," "to the right," and "the center." These words take the readers along with the speaker as they scan the bleachers from left to right.

Reading Your Writing

Descriptions use details to tell about objects, people, places, and things that happen. Organized descriptions help readers see a picture in their heads.

Tips for Descriptive Writing

Prewriting — Make a Plan

▶ Figure out how you want to organize the details of your description, whether from top to bottom, near to far, or left to right.

Drafting — Get Your Ideas on Paper

▶ Use your notes from prewriting to write your descriptive piece.

Revising — Make Sure It Makes Sense

▶ **Word Choice** Have you provided a lot of detail to make the scene real? If not, add more detail to your description.

▶ **Word Choice** Have you chosen descriptive words that are precise and have sensory appeal?

▶ **Organization** Is your piece written in an organized way that helps the reader understand what is described? Did you use location words?

Editing/Proofreading — Look Closely at the Details

▶ **Conventions** Proofread your descriptive writing to check for spelling mistakes. Check capitalization and punctuation, and make any corrections.

Publishing — Get It Ready to Go

▶ **Presentation** Revise your original story or nonfiction piece to include your description.

Observation Reports

An **observation report** is written
with information collected by the senses.
Your five senses—seeing, hearing,
smelling, touching, and tasting—allow
you to experience what you are
describing so that you can write an
observation report.

Observing an Experiment

You will have a specific reason for
writing an observation report. For example, an observation report
could be a lab report, describing how an experiment was put
together and its results. When scientists do experiments, they don't
go to a library to test their **hypotheses,** or ideas about how
something works. They watch, pay attention, and take note of
changes they observe with their senses. Scientists include these
data, the details they observe, in their reports.

Observing a Scene

Another kind of observation report requires taking notes and
writing about what you observe in a scene. Imagine being near
the start of a forest fire. What if a forest ranger wanted you to
describe what happened? If you took notes right after it started,
you could use what your five senses told you to describe the
scene. Did you see or hear anything unusual? When did you
smell smoke?

Try It
Imagine that you are in the following places with the assignment
of writing an observation report. Shut your eyes and use your
other four senses to take in the information.
▶ The school cafeteria
▶ An open window in your classroom

Here's the process a student went through when she wrote an observation report for her science project.

Ant Investigation

Constance chose to do an ant investigation for her science project. Her grandmother had told her that the mint growing around her porch keeps away ants. She decided to test her hypothesis that ants avoid different types of mint.

First she made a chart to record her data. Next, she gathered leaves from three types of mint and from dandelions. Because Constance knew that ants do not avoid dandelions, she used them as a control group. She would compare how the ants reacted to the mint leaves with how they reacted to the dandelion leaves. Then she gathered 16 black ants and put them in a plastic container with breathing holes. She crushed the leaves of the four plants and took notes about the leaves' smell. Constance recorded every step of her procedure. She made four 10-inch-diameter circles with the four different types of leaves. Then she placed ants in each one of the leaf circles and observed their behavior. She recorded the results in her chart. Notice how her description helps the reader visualize the behavior of the ants.

Horsemint: Ants run toward the leaves but stop 1 centimeter before getting to the edge. They will not leave the circle.

Peppermint: Ants run all around the inside of the circle; most stay 2 centimeters from the edge. Two go closer, but not outside.

Spearmint: Ants run around the inside again, but most stay within 1 centimeter of the edge. One large ant stops near the leaf line and then scurries over it. Ants run all around the inside of the circle.

Dandelion: Many of them pause near the dandelion leaf line and then continue over it.

When Constance wrote her observation report, she tried to use as much detail from her chart as possible. Through careful observation, she was able to interpret her data and come to a conclusion.

Observing Ant Behavior

Hypothesis: Ants avoid different kinds of mint leaves.

Procedure: I gathered four types of leaves for the experiment. I used horsemint, peppermint, spearmint, and dandelion. The dandelion leaves were my control group.

I lightly crushed the four types of leaves with my fingers. I washed my hands in between crushing the leaves so I did not mix leaf juices. The three mint plants gave off a stronger mint smell when crushed. I made four 10-inch-diameter circles with each of the different crushed leaf types. I used 16 black ants.

Observation: First I placed the 16 ants in the horsemint circle. They ran around the inside of the circle and stopped 1 centimeter away from the line. Next I placed ants in the peppermint circle, and all but two stayed at least 2 centimeters away from the leaves. When I placed the ants in the spearmint circle, all but one ant stopped at least 1 centimeter inside the leaf border. That particular ant paused and then scrambled over the spearmint leaves. Last I placed the ants inside the dandelion circle. Most of them scurried around the inside, paused near the leaf line, and then continued over it.

Conclusions: Black ants appear to dislike or avoid mint. The one ant that made it over the spearmint leaves was an exception, but I think I used enough ants and enough different types of mint to prove my hypothesis. I came to the conclusion that black ants do not like different types of mint and will avoid it even when it blocks their path.

Tips for Writing a Science Observation Report

Prewriting ▶ Make a Plan

▶ Brainstorm ideas for an experiment or scientific investigation.

▶ Form your hypothesis.

▶ Plan your procedure and create a chart for entering data.

▶ Perform the experiment.

▶ Take detailed notes and enter your data in the chart.

Drafting ▶ Get Your Data and Conclusions on Paper

▶ Write down your hypothesis and procedure.

▶ Use your senses to record and interpret the data for your observations and conclusion. Be as detailed as possible.

▶ Use exact measurements and precise numbers.

Revising ▶ Make Sure It Makes Sense

▶ **Word Choice** Are your descriptions detailed and clear? If not, change the writing to better describe your observations.

▶ **Word Choice** Are your words accurate and precise? Did you list specific measurements and key sensory details?

▶ **Organization** Does your report include a hypothesis, a procedure, observations, and a conclusion? Do these elements make the process of your investigation clear to the reader?

Editing/Proofreading ▶ Check the Details

▶ **Conventions** Proofread each section of your observation report to check for spelling mistakes. Check capitalization and punctuation.

Publishing ▶ Present your work

▶ **Presentation** Neatly type or write your final copy.

▶ **Presentation** Share and discuss the report with your teacher and/or classmates. Add diagrams, drawings, or charts.

Persuasive Writing

Persuasive writing encourages readers to think or feel a certain way or to see the writer's point of view. It can also motivate readers to take action. Sometimes persuasive writing can do all of these things at the same time. To do this, you, the writer, must get and keep the attention of your readers. The following lessons will show you how.

▶ Persuasive Writing **212**

▶ Persuasion in Advertising **214**

▶ Letters to the Editor **216**

▶ Persuasive Reports **220**

Persuasive Writing

The purpose of persuasive writing is to change the way readers think or feel about a topic. A second purpose of persuasive writing may be to inspire action.

Persuasive writing is different from writing to inform or entertain. Persuasive writing provides information mainly for the purpose of getting readers to accept the writer's point of view as reasonable.

Organizing Your Writing

▶ **Start out a piece of persuasive writing by stating your opinion or goal.**

The YMCA should convert two of its tennis courts into a skate park.

▶ **Next, give reasons in the form of facts, examples, and/or expert opinions to support your opinion or goal.**

Facts:

1. All four tennis courts are almost never used at once.

2. Lots of kids love skateboarding and in-line skating.

3. It would meet a need. Three nearby parks have tennis courts, but there are no skate parks anywhere in town.

4. Using the existing surface of the courts to skate on would save the cost of making a new surface.

Example: The YMCA in Lionburg changed two of its courts into a skate park, and the skate park is in constant use.

Expert Opinion: Mr. Kidon, my guidance counselor, said it's really healthy for kids to do something active with their free time. He likes skateboarding because it allows for play and creativity. He said helmets, knee pads, and elbow pads should be worn at all times.

▶ **Last, restate your opinion, summarize your reasons, and, if appropriate, urge action.**

A skate park should be created from two of the YMCA tennis courts. It could be inexpensive, would meet a need, and would give kids a place to do a healthful and popular activity. I urge the YMCA board to approve the project so work can begin.

Who Is Your Audience?

It's important to consider your readers, or **audience,** for persuasive writing. Whom are you trying to persuade? You will want to give reasons that appeal to them. The skate park example appeals to the YMCA board by suggesting how to save money. It also provides an example of a successful park at another YMCA, a point that may add to the YMCA board's acceptance of the idea.

Different readers have different interests. It's important to tailor your reasons to what you know about your audience.

Try It

What types of reasons would you give each of these audiences?

▶ You write to your parents for permission to have a slumber party.

▶ You write an article for your school newspaper persuading students to recycle paper by using both sides of sheets.

Reading Your Writing

Persuasive writing attempts to get readers to change their points of view about a topic. Before you write, it's important to figure out how much your audience knows about the topic you have chosen and how they feel about it.

Persuasion in Advertising

An **advertisement,** or **ad,** is a public announcement placed in print, on television, on the radio, or in other media to sell a product or service. Most advertising is paid for by a business wishing to create interest in a product or service that it sells. Some advertising creates interest simply by being clever and getting the audience's attention. Traditional ads use persuasive writing.

Appealing to the Interests of the Audience

Persuasive writing in advertising, called ad copy, aims to convince its audience that a product or service will improve their lives. As with persuasive writing in general, ad copy may appeal to the interests of its audience by using facts, examples, and expert opinions to change the way people think.

An advertisement for sunscreen might provide facts. *"One out of five people will develop skin cancer in their lives. You deserve maximum protection."* A shampoo advertisement using an example might show beautiful hair on a model with this copy: *"Would you like to have hair like this?"* A dog-food advertisement relying on expert opinion might say, *"Four out of five veterinarians recommend Healthydog."* Notice how the type of approach used each time depends on the interests of the audience.

Appealing to the Senses

An advertisement for chocolate might appeal to our sense of taste by showing a rich swirl of chocolate with the words *"Taste the richness."*

Appealing to Emotion

An ad that says, *"Pennsylvania Memories Last a Lifetime,"* may give you a warm feeling about a family vacation next summer. Advertisements may also try to sell a product or service by talking about a concern: *"The Family Truckster is the safest car on the road."*

Businesses are not the only organizations that advertise. Nonprofit organizations such as tourist bureaus may place ads in travel magazines to increase tourism in their state or city.

Public Service Advertisement

A **public service ad** promotes a specific stance on an issue. Public service ads may encourage kids to stay in school, tell parents to read with their children, or encourage people to ride public transportation. Like other advertising that uses persuasive writing, the ads appeal to people's sense of reason, their emotions, and their senses.

You may be able to think of public service ads you have seen that warn against dangerous activities. A television commercial created several years ago shows a pan with two eggs frying in it. The voice in the ad says, "This is your brain on drugs."

Developing a Public Service Ad

Suppose that a statewide bicycle club wanted to develop a public service ad about using bicycles for transportation to save fuel and reduce pollution. The club might want to persuade people to drive a short distance in their cars each week (and they suggest riding a bicycle to work or school the rest of the way). They could create a billboard with a slogan that says:

"Ride five miles."

The copy might tell how long it took to create the fossil fuel needed for the average car to travel just five miles.

Try It

Think of an issue that means a lot to you. What kind of public service ad would you develop for it? Who would be your audience? How would your copy persuade?

Letters to the Editor

A **letter to the editor** is written to a newspaper or magazine for a specific purpose. Letters to the editor are meant to influence the way readers think, act, or feel about a problem or issue.

When you write a letter to the editor, you do not write to one individual. You write with the goal of getting your letter printed so you can influence anyone who reads it.

Tools of Persuasion

In a letter to the editor, state your viewpoint and support it with one or any combination of these three techniques:

▶ Appeal to your reader's sense of reason by providing **facts and reasons** that support your opinion.

▶ Use **examples** to prove your point.

▶ Provide a **solution** to a problem.

Other Things to Keep in Mind

If you are responding to an article or letter to the editor that was printed earlier, give the date it was printed. Keep your letter brief and to the point. Look for instructions and the mailing address on the editorial page of the magazine or newspaper.

Format: Follow this format for letters to the editor.

▶ Be sure to type the **heading** (your address) and the date in the upper left corner.

▶ Include the **inside address** next to the left margin.

▶ Leave two spaces and type the **salutation** followed by a colon.

▶ Leave two spaces and begin the **body.** Do not indent.

▶ Add the **closing** by the left margin.

▶ Leave four spaces, and type your full name. Write your **signature.**

Zev Norris wrote a letter to the editor of a magazine after he read a letter that the magazine printed on trampolining. Find the examples he uses. How does his choice of technique help make his point?

Letters to the Editor

Dear Editor:

This is in response to a letter to the editor written by Elise VanDermark that appeared in the November 24 issue. In that letter, she said that trampolining should not be considered a sport. I disagree with her.

The dictionary says that a sport is "an athletic game or contest that requires physical activity and skill." Trampolining is a difficult activity that includes many of the same skills as gymnastics. The event was even included in the Sydney Olympics! The judges score the athletes on two routines that include ten moves. The competitors must master moves like full twisting back somersaults. If that doesn't meet the definition of *sport,* I don't know what does.

Yours truly,

Zev Norris

Sometimes, emphasizing the solution may help change people's minds. Lindsay Diaz wrote to her school newspaper about getting too much homework. Look for her solution.

Dear Editor:

Kids have been writing to the school newspaper about getting too much homework. I've noticed that we are now getting weekend homework as well. Could we fix this problem by making a school-wide policy of not assigning homework on Fridays? If there is an extra project we have to do, assign it during the week. Let us have our weekends free.

Lindsay Diaz
Mr. Wilson's Fifth-Grade Class

Derek Riley wrote a letter to the editor of his local newspaper to state an opinion about the hours of the local library. Locate the facts and reasons he uses to support his view.

Dear Editor:

The Silverton Public Library should stay open later. Many kids would like to use the library to do research for school projects, but they have a problem getting there during the week. It is open only from 10 A.M. until 5 P.M. through the week and on Saturdays until 3:00 P.M. During the week, kids have activities after school. Some kids go to the community center after school because both parents work. On Saturdays, some of them have soccer or basketball. It would help kids and their parents if the library would stay open later on weekdays and Saturdays.

Sincerely,
Derek Riley

Notice how the letters on this and the previous page look different from the business letter models on pages 86–91. When newspapers and magazines publish letters to the editor, they do not include the heading, inside address, or signature.

Reading Your Writing

A letter to the editor is written to a publication with the goal of influencing how people think, feel, or act. Remember to check the facts in your letter to make sure they back up your point.

Tips for Writing a Letter to the Editor

Prewriting **Plan What You Want to Say**

▶ Select an issue you care enough about to write a letter to the editor.

▶ Choose a persuasion technique that works best for your issue.

▶ Go to the editorial page of the publication for instructions and a mailing address.

Drafting **Get Your Ideas on Paper**

▶ State your viewpoint and use a technique to persuade your audience, such as giving examples or stating facts.

▶ Add the heading, inside address, salutation, closing, and signature.

Revising **Make Sure It Makes Sense**

▶ **Organization** Is your letter organized in a logical sequence with a technique that strengthens your central idea or opinion?

▶ **Organization** Do you restate your opinion or offer a solution in the conclusion?

▶ **Voice** Does the writing grab your reader's attention, encourage audience involvement, and inspire a change in thinking or action?

Editing/Proofreading **Check the Details**

▶ **Conventions** Proofread your letter to check for spelling mistakes.

▶ **Conventions** Check to make sure the name of the publication and any other proper names are capitalized. Check all punctuation.

Publishing **Get It Ready to Go**

▶ **Presentation** Neatly type your final copy and then mail it.

Persuasive Reports

Write a persuasive report to change the thinking, feeling, or action of your readers about a specific issue. A persuasive report requires the research, planning, and formatting of a regular research report. It is different from a research report because you use your research to influence your audience.

Choose Your Topic

Choose a topic that you care about and want others to care about as well. Make sure it isn't so broad that you would have too much to cover.

> The environment is suffering because people abuse it.

On the other hand, a topic that is too narrow may make finding information difficult.

> The U.S. should stop exporting a chemical that poisons the Swainson's hawk of Argentina.

Begin the Research

Use any of the following resources to research your topic: almanacs, encyclopedias, dictionaries, nonfiction books, magazines, brochures, video- and audiotapes, the Internet, and experts such as a relative or someone in your community.

Decide How to Use the Information

As you take notes, focus on things that will support your view.

Facts and reasons: Look for the facts and reasons that you believe will persuade your audience.

Examples: Find examples in your research or from personal experience that strengthen your position.

Expert opinions: You may interview community members or find opinions in outside resources. Opinions are most persuasive when they come from an expert.

Write to Your Audience

The approach you use will depend on your audience. Select the information and approach that you believe will best persuade your readers by appealing to their interests and experiences. You may choose one or any combination of the approaches below, but make sure the technique also provides organization and structure.

Select a Technique

Organize your report in one or more of the following ways:

▶ State a viewpoint and use **facts and reasons** to support it.

▶ State a viewpoint and provide **examples.**

▶ State a viewpoint supported by **expert opinions.**

▶ State a **problem** and describe one or more **solutions.**

Take a Look

See how these topics vary in audience and choice of technique.

▶ You think that it's important to wear helmets and safety pads when bike riding, so you write a persuasive report giving reasons that your class should wear safety gear while riding. Your class is the audience.

▶ You believe sharks are disappearing, so you write a report to explain the problem to a general audience and provide a combination of facts and reasons to arrive at some possible conclusions. (See the model on pages 223–224.)

Opening and Concluding Paragraphs

Be sure to include opening and concluding paragraphs in your persuasive report. The opening paragraph(s) should introduce readers to the purpose of your report. The closing paragraph(s) should summarize the reasons or solutions and restate the purpose.

Use a Graphic Organizer

For help with choosing the key points use a graphic organizer. This chart helped the writer decide which solutions, facts, or opinions to include in a report about disappearing sharks. The problem appears in the top rectangle. The solutions, facts, or opinions appear in the order they will be presented, with the strongest one saved for last.

Topic

Many species of sharks are disappearing.

Subtopic

Educate people

1. Not a major threat to people
2. Play valuable role in the food chain

Subtopic

Limit shark fishing worldwide

1. Sharks can't reproduce fast enough

Subtopic

Boycott shark products

1. Not needed for human survival

Conclusion

We need to do something new so sharks will be around later.

Here's the report written using the graphic organizer on page 222.

Attack of the Shark Killers

Introduction ▶ Many species of sharks are starting to disappear. The demand for shark meat and products increases every year. As human numbers grow, the number of sharks shrinks. Four hundred species may be threatened beyond recovery. There are several ways to solve this problem.

Solution 1 ▶ One solution to the problem would be to educate people about sharks. People would care more about sharks if they knew more about them. Sharks rarely kill people. Although they kill humans once in a while, many more people die from lightning and bee stings. Great white sharks sometimes mistake humans for sea lions, but humans are not their natural prey. Most shark species are completely harmless. If people did not see sharks as threats, they might care about protecting them.

Sharks have an important role at the top of the ocean food chain. They help keep nature in balance. Biologists observe that when sharks disappear, their prey—seals and walruses—multiply to the point of becoming an unhealthy burden on their own environment. If people understood the importance of sharks, they might care about what is happening to them.

Solution 2 ▶ Another way to solve this problem would be to limit shark fishing in all countries. The United States is one of the few countries that controls shark fishing, but that doesn't help the many sharks that travel long distances during their lives. A shark may spend its early years off the coast of California only to be killed later in the South Pacific. Sharks replace themselves very slowly. Many don't give birth until they are ten years old. Scientists believe that sharks in eastern U.S. coastal waters have been killed off twice as fast as they can reproduce. Until we know what species are stable, shark fishing should be strictly limited worldwide.

Solution 3 ▶   Perhaps the best way to solve the problem would be to boycott, or stop buying, all shark products. Even though shark fishing is sometimes controlled, most products made from sharks are not. Shark fins bring a high price, so some fishermen illegally slice the fins off living sharks and throw the sharks back into the ocean to die. In addition to reducing demand, a worldwide boycott would send a message to those in the business of slaughtering sharks. It would tell them to figure out a way to make their products so that they are not harmful to the environment.

    Shark products are not needed for human survival. Shark meat is high in protein, but there are many other ways to get protein. There is also shark-tooth jewelry and some lubricants and cosmetics that contain shark liver. We can do without these products. If we did, the demand for shark products would stop.

Conclusion ▶   Sharks are disappearing. To solve this problem, people should learn that sharks do not pose a threat to their safety and that shark products are not necessary for their survival. Further, shark fishing everywhere should be strictly limited. In addition, if people increased their awareness of sharks' role in the environment, they might be motivated to protect them. Finally, a worldwide boycott would decrease the demand for shark products. It is important to take action now to help preserve the shark population for the future.

Try It

Answer these questions about the persuasive report about sharks.

▶ Did the way the solutions were presented help you organize the ideas as you read? How else could the report have been organized?

Reading Your Writing

A persuasive report is written to change a reader's thinking on an issue. A graphic organizer can help you put your research and ideas in order.

Tips for Writing a Persuasive Report

Prewriting Plan What You Want to Say

▶ Research with your audience in mind. As you take notes, write down the information that will most influence them.

▶ Use a graphic organizer to organize your ideas and plan your draft.

Drafting Get Your Ideas on Paper

▶ State the problem and write about the solutions. You could also give your viewpoint with the facts, reasons, and examples to support it.

▶ Put the ideas you get from other sources in your own words.

Revising Make Sure It Makes Sense

▶ **Organization** Is your paper organized logically and persuasively? Is the strongest solution or point saved for last?

▶ **Organization** Do ideas connect? Does your introduction grab the audience's attention and state the problem or issue? Does your conclusion restate the problem or issue and summarize reasons or solutions?

▶ **Voice** Does your writing show that you know your audience?

Editing/Proofreading Check the Details

▶ **Conventions** Proofread your report to check for spelling and punctuation mistakes and make sure that all proper names are capitalized.

Publishing Get It Ready to Go

▶ **Presentation** Neatly type or write the final copy.

Poetry

Poetry is very different from other forms of writing. For one thing, it looks different. Think of some poems you have read. They look very different from stories or articles. The capitalization and punctuation are different. The familiar patterns of sentences and paragraphs are not present in poetry.

There is something else about poetry. It can describe things in a way that you may never have considered. Poetry often contains thoughts and feelings of the writer. It also contains images, or word pictures, that can make a deep impression on readers. The following lessons will give you a chance to explore some different kinds of poetry.

▶ Rhyming Poetry **228**

▶ Nonrhyming Poetry **232**

▶ Pattern Poetry **236**

Rhyming Poetry

Up until now, all of the writing in this book has been prose. Prose is defined as all types of writing that are not considered poetry. *Poetry* combines the sounds and meanings of words to create ideas and feelings. What are some differences between prose and poetry?

Take a Look

PROSE	POETRY
▶ complete sentences	▶ fragments allowed
▶ capitalization necessary	▶ capitalization optional
▶ punctuation necessary	▶ punctuation optional
▶ nonrhyming	▶ rhyming and nonrhyming
▶ paragraphs	▶ stanzas (groups of lines)
▶ rhythm *sometimes* matters	▶ rhythm *usually* matters
▶ sound patterns *sometimes* matter	▶ sounds patterns *always* matter
▶ images *sometimes* present	▶ images *usually* present

Try It

Think about how poetry and prose look. How would you explain the differences to someone?

Common Forms of Rhyming Poetry

Let's take a look at some of the more common forms of rhyming poetry.

Couplet

A couplet is a two-line poem or a two-line verse of a longer poem. Both lines usually rhyme, are of equal length and meter, or rhythm, and express one thought.

Take a Look

On a branch the birdie sat,
Or, oh my gosh, is that a bat?

Down and down and down and down
Escalator underground.

Triplet

A triplet is a three-line poem or three-line verse of a longer poem. All three lines usually rhyme and are of equal length and meter, or rhythm. They all express one thought.

Take a Look

My heart skips a beat as you tell me the news
Of your moving away and the path that you choose.
As for me it is clear I'm the one who will lose.

A quatrain is a four-line poem or a stanza of a longer poem. It expresses one thought and has a variety of rhyming patterns. In one pattern, the first two lines and the last two lines may rhyme. In another pattern, the first and third lines and the second and fourth lines could rhyme. A third pattern could have only the second and fourth lines rhyme.

Take a Look

▶ First two lines rhyme; last two lines rhyme:

> *Everyone remembers old Rodeo Bill,*
> *How he roped his steer with cunning skill.*
> *But now he just sits in the bleachers and grins*
> *While the feisty crowd cheers and the show begins.*

▶ First and third lines rhyme; second and fourth lines rhyme:

> *Coaster rolling on the track,*
> *Climbing to its height*
> *Reach the top, we all lean back*
> *Ready for the fright.*

▶ Only the second and fourth lines rhyme:

> *Cold winds blow and snowflakes fly;*
> *Branches mourn their fallen leaves.*
> *An icy chill crawls up the oak*
> *As Old Man Winter puffs and breathes.*

A lyric is a type of poem that expresses strong personal emotions, often using details of the five senses.

Take a Look

> *Over, under, round, and through*
> *These woods fill me with such delight,*
> *Whether wading through the winding creek*
> *Or gazing at a star-filled night.*
>
> *I uncover treasures of rubies and gold,*
> *Defend fortresses high and mighty,*
> *Slay towering dragons—a sight to behold!*
> *A new adventure waits at every turn.*

Try It

Try writing a rhyming poem. First think of an idea that includes vivid images. Then choose a poetry form and a rhyming pattern. You can use a rhyming dictionary to help you create a list of rhyming words for your poem.

Reading Your Writing

There are many forms of rhyming poetry, but they all usually have specific rhyme and rhythm patterns. When you write your own poems, make sure you follow the pattern for the form you have chosen.

Nonrhyming Poetry

Poetry has many forms. Here's a sampling of some of the forms of nonrhyming poetry.

Diamante

A diamante is a seven-line poem that has specific information in each line and an exact number of words. This form can also appear in various patterns.

Line 1	one word	subject, noun
Line 2	two words	adjectives
Line 3	three words	participles
Line 4	four words	nouns
Line 5	three words	participles
Line 6	two words	adjectives
Line 7	two words	nouns

Scooters
Speedy, smooth
Careening, turning, braking
Taxi, rickshaw, soapbox, bike
Transporting, energizing, relaxing
Funny, fantastic
Travel, plans

Cinquain

A cinquain is a five-line poem that has specific information in each line. This form of poetry has an exact number of words or syllables per line and can appear in a variety of patterns.

Line 1	one word	title
Line 2	two words	describing title
Line 3	three words	an action
Line 4	four words	a feeling
Line 5	one word	refers to title

Take a Look

	Planets
	Heavenly bodies
	Rotating, revolving, renewing
	Others are out there
	Magnificent

Haiku

A haiku is a three-line poem about nature. There is an exact number of syllables for each line. The first line has five syllables, the second has seven, and the third has five.

Fun Fact

Haiku originated from Japan. Japanese haiku are usually written in a single vertical line.

Take a Look

Wind whips my window,
Pounding hail pelts my rooftop,
Skies clear for rainbows.

Little yellow leaves,
Floating on top of the stream,
Autumn is ending.

Free verse is just what it sounds like—poetry without rhyme or rhythm (meter). Rather than emphasizing the matching sounds of words, free verse *frees* you to concentrate on ideas and images.

Free verse has no specific form and can be any length. It does not always rhyme, because the ideas and image it expresses are most important. This form of poetry can be used to create different line shapes with word and line placement.

Take a Look

Inky

Hanging.   Dangling.
By   a   thread.
C r e e p i n g   W e a v i n g
Leaving   its   web.

And then .... whoosh!
The end.

Forget It

Music's in my brain.
Can't
    Get
        It
            Out.

Try a vacuum. Try floss. Try some tweezers.
Forget it.
    Just
        Leave
          It
            In.

Try It

Try writing a nonrhyming poem. Choose an idea with vivid images. Don't worry about rhyming or rhythm patterns. Instead, concentrate on creating visual patterns with your word and line placement.

Reading Your Writing

Many forms of nonrhyming poetry have a specific structure. Make sure that your poem follows the correct format.

Pattern Poetry

Pattern poetry is created from an existing form, often a familiar song. Do you remember this one?

I've been working on the railroad	**(8 syllables)**
All the live long day.	**(5)**
I've been working on the railroad	**(8)**
Just to pass the time away.	**(7)**
Can't you hear the whistle blowing,	**(8)**
Rise up so early in the morn?	**(8)**
Can't you hear the captain shouting,	**(8)**
"Dinah blow your horn!"	**(5)**

Take a Look

Suppose your class needed a field-day spirit song and you were chosen to give this tune new lyrics. You might write something like the lyrics below. Sing it to the tune of "I've Been Working on the Railroad." Notice the matching patterns of rhyme and syllables.

We're the Jaguars of Ms. Smith's class	**(8 syllables)**
Ready for the race	**(5)**
We are fast and strong and agile	**(8)**
And we'll put you to the pace	**(7)**
Try to understand our message	**(8)**
We are the best class in the school	**(8)**
Don't forget our simple motto	**(8)**
We are smart and cool.	**(5)**

Let's try another one. Remember this song?

> Yankee Doodle went to town   (7 syllables)
> A – ridin' on a pony.   (7)
> He stuck a feather in his hat   (8)
> And called it macaroni.   (7)
> Yankee Doodle keep it up,   (7)
> Yankee Doodle Dandy,   (6)
> Mind the music and the steps   (7)
> And with the girls be handy.   (7)

Take a Look

Using the same melody, here's a student government campaign song.

> Amy Edwards came to school   (7 syllables)
> To help improve conditions.   (7)
> She'll try to get some uniforms   (8)
> For all the band's musicians.   (7)
> Amy Edwards gets our vote,   (7)
> Amy Edwards "Do it!"   (6)
> Vote for her this Tuesday morn   (7)
> There's nothing really to it!   (7)

Try It

Make up a song of your own using one of the patterns in this lesson.

Reading Your Writing

Pattern poetry often uses the melody of a favorite song as a format. When writing this type of poetry, choose a melody that you are sure your readers will recognize.

Structures of Writing

Words, sentences, and paragraphs are the building blocks of writing. Think about what you do when you write. You use words to build sentences. You use sentences to build paragraphs. You use paragraphs to build reports, stories, and other kinds of writing.

In this unit, you will find out how sentences and paragraphs are constructed. You will also learn how to combine short, choppy sentences into one flowing sentence. You can use what you learn in these lessons in many different kinds of writing.

▶ Writing Sentences **240**

▶ Sentence Problems **246**

▶ Paragraphs **248**

▶ Types of Paragraphs **252**

▶ Graphic Organizers **256**

Writing Sentences

Sentences are the building blocks of writing. Learning how to construct good sentences is part of becoming a good writer. There are different kinds of sentences, but they all have some things in common.

It is difficult to precisely define a **sentence.** One definition is that a sentence is a group of words that has a subject and predicate and expresses a complete thought. Every sentence begins with a capital letter and ends with a punctuation mark. A complete sentence includes a subject and a predicate. The **subject** tells who or what the sentence is about, and the **predicate** tells more, including what the subject is or does.

Take a Look

In the sentences below, the subject is in **bold** and the predicate is in *italics*.

The first telescope *was a refracting telescope.*
Isaac Newton *built a reflecting telescope.*

Kinds of Sentences

Different kinds of sentences give different kinds of information to readers. The four kinds of sentences are declarative, interrogative, imperative, and exclamatory.

A **declarative sentence** makes a statement. Declarative sentences end with a period.

Germs cause many kinds of illnesses.
Sneezing sprays germs into the air.

An **interrogative sentence** asks a question. Interrogative sentences end with a question mark.

> Do you have a cold?
> Would you like this cough drop?

An **imperative** sentence gives a command or makes a request. An imperative sentence ends with either an exclamation point or a period. If the sentence expresses a strong emotion, it ends with an exclamation point. All other imperative sentences end with a period.

Note that the subject of an imperative sentence is not stated. Instead, the subject is understood to be the pronoun *you*.

> Cover your mouth!
> Get plenty of rest.

An **exclamatory sentence** expresses strong emotion, such as surprise, fear, or excitement. Exclamatory sentences end with an exclamation point.

> I used a whole box of tissues!
> This virus won't go away!

Try It

What kind of punctuation should be used at the end of this sentence?

▶ Please fix me some soup

Combining Sentences

When two sentences contain many of the same words, you can combine them. You might combine parts of sentences or whole sentences to make your writing more interesting and easier to read.

Combining Subjects, Objects, Verbs, and Modifiers

You can combine parts of two shorter sentences to make one sentence that reads more smoothly. Use the conjunctions *and*, *but*, and *or* to make compound subjects, objects, and verbs.

Rectangles are polygons. Hexagons are polygons.
Rectangles and hexagons are polygons.
(compound subject)

Did Jasmine draw a bar graph? Did Jasmine draw a line graph?
Did Jasmine draw a **bar graph or a line graph?**
(compound object)

Claudio checked his answer. Claudio erased his answer.
Claudio **checked and erased** his answer. (compound verb)

A **modifier** is a word or group of words that adds information to a sentence. A word that modifies a noun is an adjective. A word that modifies a verb is an adverb. Use a comma or a conjunction to combine modifiers from different sentences.

I drew a large triangle. I drew a right triangle.
I drew a **large, right** triangle.

Solve the problems quickly. Solve the problems carefully.
Solve the problems **quickly but carefully.**

Combining Phrases

Phrases from separate sentences can be combined to improve the flow of your writing. You might even be able to combine phrases from several sentences to avoid repeating words.

> The key is under the mat. The mat is on the porch.
> The key is **under the mat on the porch.**

> Sam found the key. Sam unlocked the door.
> Sam **found the key and unlocked the door.**

> The dog ran up the stairs. It ran to the front door.
> Then it jumped on Sam.
> The dog ran **up the stairs to the front door and jumped on Sam.**

When you combine words or phrases from different sentences, be sure the new sentence makes sense. Otherwise, you might confuse your readers.

Sam threw a ball to the dog. Sam threw a ball high in the air.

Sam threw a ball to the dog high in the air. (This sentence is confusing. The dog isn't high in the air.)

Sam threw a ball high in the air to the dog. (This sentence correctly combines the two original sentences.)

Creating Compound Sentences

Two simple sentences that are related can be combined to form a **compound sentence**. Both parts of a compound sentence express a complete thought. Use a conjunction such as *and, but,* or *or* between the two simple sentences, and place a comma before the conjunction.

Mariah loves to swim. She wants to be a lifeguard.
Mariah loves to swim, **and** she wants to be a lifeguard.

You can wear your swimsuit. You can change at the beach.
You can wear your swimsuit, **or** you can change at the beach.

Creating Complex Sentences

Another way to combine sentences is by creating complex sentences. A **complex sentence** is made of an independent clause and one or more dependent clauses. A **clause** is a group of words that has a subject and a verb. An **independent clause** can stand alone as a sentence, but a **dependent clause** cannot. A dependent clause begins with a subordinating conjunction such as *after, although, because,* or *when* or with a relative pronoun such as *that, which,* or *who*. To combine two sentences into a complex sentence, make the idea from one of the sentences into a dependent clause. Note that a comma is not always used between the independent and dependent clauses.

Mariah joined the swim team. She became the captain.
After Mariah joined the swim team, she became the captain.

These are Mariah's lucky goggles. She wears them at every meet.
These are the lucky goggles **that Mariah wears at every meet.**

Varying Sentence Beginnings

Beginning your sentences in different ways helps add variety to your writing. This not only keeps your readers interested but it also makes writing more fun.

The natural order of a sentence is for the subject to come first, followed by the predicate.

The roller coaster climbed toward the peak.

However, there are many other ways to organize your thoughts, such as moving part of the predicate to the beginning of the sentence.

Take a Look

Before: I checked the strap on my seat **nervously.**
After: **Nervously,** I checked the strap on my seat.

Before: I closed my eyes and screamed **at the top of the hill.**
After: **At the top of the hill,** I closed my eyes and screamed.

Before: My legs were shaking **when I got off the ride.**
After: **When I got off the ride,** my legs were shaking.

Try It

Rewrite the following sentence using a different beginning.

▶ I got in line because I wanted to ride again.

Reading Your Writing

A sentence expresses a complete thought as a statement, a question, a command, or an exclamation. You can combine sentences or parts of sentences to avoid repeating words and to make your writing read more smoothly. There are also different ways to begin a sentence. Use variety in your sentences to keep readers interested.

Sentence Problems

A good writer recognizes problem sentences and knows how to correct them. Sentence fragments, run-on sentences, and rambling sentences are three common mistakes to watch for in your writing.

Fragments

A **fragment** is a group of words that does not express a complete thought. A fragment is missing a subject, a predicate, or both.

> Meets in the cafeteria. (missing a subject)
> The doctors and nurses. (missing a predicate)
> Just in time. (missing a subject and a predicate)

These fragments confuse the reader with incomplete information. Adding the missing parts makes the messages clear.

> The student council meets in the cafeteria.
> The doctors and nurses prepared for surgery.
> Lucy arrived just in time.

Try It

Correct the following fragment to make a sentence.

▶ All the way home

Run-On Sentences

A **run-on sentence** contains more than one complete thought. To correct a run-on sentence, add a comma and a conjunction, or rewrite it as two separate sentences.

> *Run-on*: J. K. Rowling is my favorite author she wrote the books about Harry Potter.
> *Correct*: J. K. Rowling is my favorite author. She wrote the books about Harry Potter.

> *Run-on*: I own two of the books I borrowed the others from the library.
> *Correct*: I own two of the books, but I borrowed the others from the library.

Rambling Sentences

A **rambling sentence** contains too many thoughts connected by conjunctions. This problem can be corrected by writing a separate sentence for each thought. Some parts of a rambling sentence might really belong together. In this case, just add a comma before the conjunction.

Rambling: My family went to California last summer and there were so many things I wanted to see and we did drive across the Golden Gate Bridge and go to Disneyland but I didn't see the giant redwood trees and my parents said we will go back someday.

Correct: My family went to California last summer. There were so many things I wanted to see. We did drive across the Golden Gate Bridge and go to Disneyland, but I didn't see the giant redwood trees. My parents said we will go back someday.

Reading Your Writing

The most common sentence problems are fragments, run-on sentences, and rambling sentences. Learn to recognize and correct these mistakes so that your message will be clear to readers.

Paragraphs

A **paragraph** is made of two or more sentences about one idea or topic. Many paragraphs include a topic sentence, supporting sentences, and a closing sentence. All of these parts help make an organized paragraph.

A **topic sentence** states the paragraph's main idea. The first sentence of a paragraph is often the topic sentence; however, you might find it later in the paragraph, even at the end. Most paragraphs that inform or persuade have topic sentences. Most narrative paragraphs do not include a topic sentence.

Supporting sentences tell more about the paragraph's main idea. Sentences that do not support the main idea do not belong in the paragraph. Supporting sentences should be arranged in a logical order. For example, you might present information by order of time, location, or importance.

Some paragraphs have a **closing sentence.** A closing sentence provides a final thought about the main idea, a summary of the paragraph, or a smooth transition to the next paragraph.

Take a Look

Here is an example of an expository paragraph taken from *Buffalo Hunt* by Russell Freedman. Note that the first line of a paragraph is indented.

The topic sentence states the main idea of the paragraph.

To the Plains Indians, the buffalo, or American bison, was the most important animal on Earth. This snorting, lumbering beast provided almost everything the Indians needed to stay alive. The buffalo kept their bellies full and their bodies warm. It supplied raw materials for their weapons, tools, ornaments, and toys. The rhythm of their daily lives was ruled by the comings and goings of the great buffalo herds.

Supporting sentences tell more about the main idea.

The closing sentence provides a final thought about the main idea.

Staying on Topic

All of the sentences in a paragraph should relate to the main idea. If a writer includes information about a different topic, it is confusing to readers. The student who wrote the paragraph below realized that one of the sentences does not stay on topic.

Take a Look

A legend is a type of story that is passed down from one generation to the next. Legends are often repeated because they are important to a certain group of people. ~~Examples of culture can be found in people's behavior and beliefs.~~ Members of that group tell the legends again and again to help keep their culture alive. Many Native American people tell legends about their ancestors' beliefs and way of life. These stories can teach as well as entertain listeners.

A sentence that doesn't stay on topic in one paragraph might be a good main idea or supporting sentence in another paragraph. Try to include all of your interesting information in an organized way.

Try It
Does the following sentence belong in the sample paragraph above?
▶ There are many different kinds of legends.

Supporting the Main Idea

Writers use different kinds of information to support their ideas. Use examples, facts, and evidence to help you make your point.

Examples: In the sample paragraph on page 248, the writer used examples to support his main idea. The examples make it clear why the buffalo was important to the Plains Indians.

Facts: Writers may also support a main idea with facts. Using facts helps make your writing more believable.

Evidence: Sometimes, a writer uses evidence as support for a main idea. This happens most often in persuasive writing, such as a letter to the editor. A writer might express an opinion then use evidence to convince readers that the opinion is reasonable.

Starting a New Paragraph

Paragraphs give order to your writing. Knowing when to start a new paragraph is important for helping your readers stay focused.

Start a new paragraph when
- ▶ you start writing about a new idea
- ▶ you start writing about a new location
- ▶ you start writing about a different time
- ▶ a new character is speaking

In the following narrative paragraphs from "The Story of Jumping Mouse," you can see how John Steptoe organized his writing.

The far-off land sounded so wonderful that the young mouse began to dream about it. He knew he would never be content until he had been there. The old ones warned that the journey would be long and perilous, but the young mouse would not be swayed. He set off one morning before the sun had risen.

It was evening before he reached the edge of the brush. Before him was the river; on the other side was the desert. The young mouse peered into the deep water. "How will I ever get across?" he said in dismay.

"Don't you know how to swim?" called a gravelly voice.

Change of time and location

Change of speaker

Reading Your Writing

Many paragraphs that inform or persuade include a topic sentence, supporting sentences, and a closing sentence. Supporting sentences can include examples, facts, or evidence to support the main idea. Remember to start a new paragraph when you start a new idea. This will give order to your writing and help your readers stay focused.

Types of Paragraphs

You can use different types of writing for different purposes.

Narrative

Narrative writing is used for telling stories. When writing narrative paragraphs, use chronological order to show when events happen. Use signal words such as *then*, *next*, and *when* to show changes in time.

Keep in mind that most narrative paragraphs do not include topic sentences. Instead, they rely on dialogue and description to move the action along.

Take a Look

The following narrative paragraphs are from the story "Class President" by Johanna Hurwitz. Notice the signal words, dialogue, and description.

> "If you're going to run against Cricket, we've got to get to work," Julio told Lucas on their way home. Julio wasn't very good at making posters, as Cricket and Zoe were, but he was determined to help his friend.
>
> The next morning, a new poster appeared in Mr. Flores's classroom. It said, DON'T BUG ME. VOTE FOR LUCAS COTT. Julio had made it.

Descriptive

In descriptive paragraphs, writers use vivid words to create an image or experience for the reader. Good descriptions include words that appeal to the readers' five senses: sight, hearing, taste, touch, and smell.

Descriptive writing is often used within other types of writing. For example, you may use it in stories, information reports, and letters. You might also use it in a science report.

Take a Look

When writing a descriptive paragraph, organize by order. This can be front to back, left to right, top to bottom, or any other way that will make sense to the reader. Read this paragraph and note how the writer organized the description from top to bottom.

> We stopped in our tracks when we saw the gigantic moose. Its enormous antlers looked as if they could easily weigh 40 pounds. Its huge, bulging eyes seemed to bore right into us as we tried to stand perfectly still. The moose's body was wet from the lake it was wading through, and its legs disappeared into the murky green water.

Try It

Write two descriptive sentences about an animal. Remember to appeal to the readers' senses.

Expository

Expository writing is used for giving information or explaining. Most newspaper and magazine articles are expository. Textbooks and biographies are also expository. When you write to give information, remember to think about your audience. Ask yourself what they might already know and what they might want or need to know.

Expository paragraphs usually begin with a topic sentence that clearly states what will be discussed. Expository paragraphs can be developed by facts, reasons, examples, or a combination of these.

Take a Look

In this expository paragraph, the writer uses examples to support the main idea.

Minerals are in many things that we use every day. For example, quartz is a mineral used to make clocks and watches. The quartz helps them keep accurate time. You may not know it, but you even write with minerals. The mineral graphite is used to make pencils, and chalk is made from a mineral called gypsum. There are probably at least three minerals in your bathroom at home. Powder is made from a mineral called talc, and mirrors are made from the minerals silica and silver. Minerals start out deep in the ground, but they end up all around us.

Persuasive

In a persuasive paragraph, a writer tries to get readers to think, feel, or act a certain way. Knowing your audience is very important in persuasive writing. This will help you choose the best strategy for presenting your argument. For example, you might present your opinion as a problem then suggest a solution. Providing evidence to support your idea is another effective way to persuade. You might also present the points of your argument in order of their importance. This leaves readers with your most convincing point fresh in their minds.

Take a Look

Brandon wrote this persuasive paragraph for social studies class.

The legal voting age ought to be lowered from 18 to 10. By age 10, most people can read well enough to understand the ballots. Voting would also teach us to be responsible, which is something adults tell us is important. Many issues on the ballots relate to schools, so the people who go to school ought to have a vote. Voting decides what will happen in the future, and kids are affected by those decisions. If we are the future, then we should get to help create it by having the right to vote.

Try It

What strategy did Brandon use in his persuasive paragraph?

Reading Your Writing

Different kinds of writing are used to tell a story, describe, explain, or persuade. No matter what your purpose is for writing, it is important to include all the parts of a paragraph and to think about your audience. Write about something that will interest your readers and that they will understand.

Graphic Organizers

Graphic organizers are planning tools that writers can use to collect and organize information. There are many different kinds of graphic organizers. Choose one that works with the kind of writing you will be doing.

Web

A web can be used for many purposes. For example, you might use a web to list characteristics of a person or thing, to show how story characters are related, or to identify subtopics related to a main topic. The web below lists characteristics of the American barn owl.

Story Map

A story map is used to outline the events of a story, either fiction or nonfiction. You can also include information about the story's characters and setting. Below is a story map of an excerpt from Joseph Krumgold's book *And Now Miguel*. The excerpt is titled "The Search."

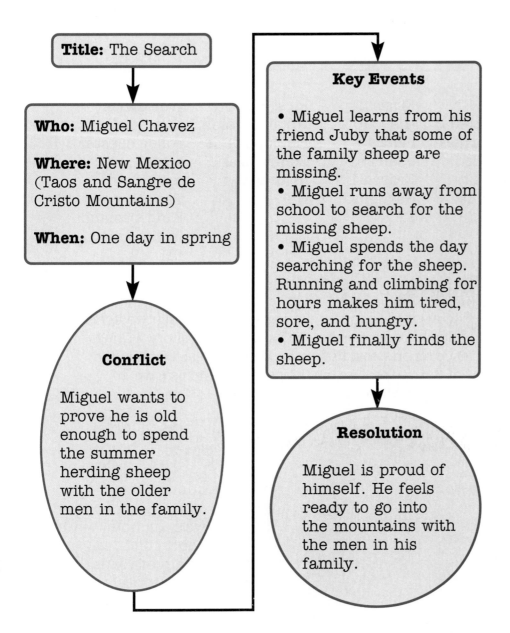

Title: The Search

Who: Miguel Chavez

Where: New Mexico (Taos and Sangre de Cristo Mountains)

When: One day in spring

Conflict

Miguel wants to prove he is old enough to spend the summer herding sheep with the older men in the family.

Key Events

- Miguel learns from his friend Juby that some of the family sheep are missing.
- Miguel runs away from school to search for the missing sheep.
- Miguel spends the day searching for the sheep. Running and climbing for hours makes him tired, sore, and hungry.
- Miguel finally finds the sheep.

Resolution

Miguel is proud of himself. He feels ready to go into the mountains with the men in his family.

Time Line

A time line is used to show a sequence of events. In addition to showing the order in which events occurred, a time line can show relationships among events. This kind of graphic organizer is especially useful if you are writing about people (a biography or autobiography) or historical events.

History of Roller Coasters

1400–1500	1846	1884	1972
First constructed gravity rides for public built in St. Petersburg, Russia	First loop-the-loop railway opens at Frascati Gardens, PA	First U.S. roller coaster ride opens at Coney Island in Brooklyn, NY	Worldwide interest in roller coaster begins with opening of The Racer at King's Island in Cincinnati, OH

Venn Diagram

A Venn diagram is used for comparing and contrasting two items. This kind of graphic organizer can be useful in expository writing, such as science reports. List the unique details of each item in the outer areas of the circles. List the things that the items have in common in the area where the circles overlap.

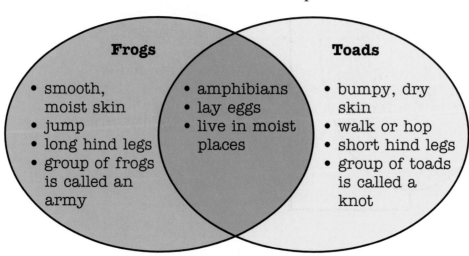

Frogs
- smooth, moist skin
- jump
- long hind legs
- group of frogs is called an army

- amphibians
- lay eggs
- live in moist places

Toads
- bumpy, dry skin
- walk or hop
- short hind legs
- group of toads is called a knot

Topics and Subtopics Chart

Writers often find it very useful to list their topics and subtopics when planning for expository writing. This kind of outline helps the writer create a thorough and well-organized report.

Topic

Tips for Parakeet Owners

Subtopic

The Birdcage

1. Should have two perches and a swing
2. Use plastic seed guards
3. Decorate with bells and colorful toys

Subtopic

Care and Feeding

1. Give quality seed and fresh water daily
2. Change paper towel at the bottom of cage every 3 days
3. Give "seed tree" treat occasionally

Subtopic

Training

1. Avoid sudden movements, which frighten bird
2. Training to talk: repeat word or phrase for 20 minutes daily—speak in gentle voice
3. Finger training: slowly and gently introduce your finger for bird to stand on

Conclusion

With proper care and training, parakeets can be very nice pets.

Cause and Effect Chart

Cause-and-effect relationships are important in many different kinds of writing. Science reports and papers about historical events might focus on cause-and-effect connections. You might also write a story in which several events cause a certain effect on a character or characters. Note that one cause might have several effects, or many causes could result in one effect.

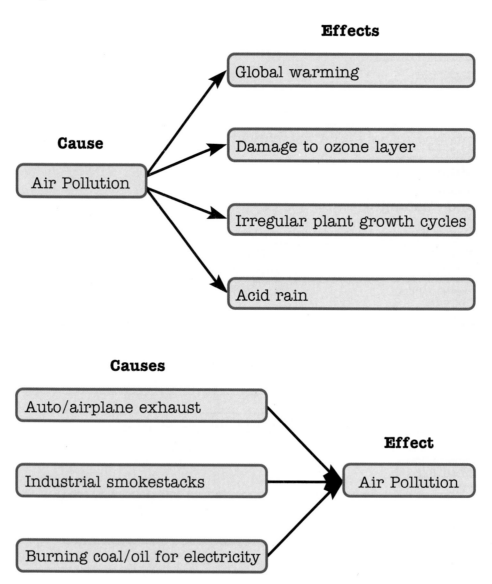

Effects

Global warming

Cause

Air Pollution

Damage to ozone layer

Irregular plant growth cycles

Acid rain

Causes

Auto/airplane exhaust

Industrial smokestacks

Effect

Air Pollution

Burning coal/oil for electricity

Collecting Grid

Use a collecting grid, or chart, to record information gathered from many different sources. Collecting grids are useful for preparing research papers or factual reports.

This collecting grid shows information that the writer has gathered about the history of pencils. The first column lists the questions the writer is researching. The first row across the top names the sources used. You should check facts in more than one source to make sure that they are accurate.

History of Pencils

	Pencil Points	The Pencil Pages	Kids Journal
made of?	wood and graphite (p. 6)		
famous users?		Leonardo da Vinci, Benjamin Franklin	
why yellow?		best graphite came from China; yellow stands for royalty and respect in China	lets people know they contain Chinese graphite
first mass-produced?	Nuremburg, Germany in 1662 (p. 9)		

Reading Your Writing

Writers can choose from many different graphic organizers to help them gather information and organize their ideas. Your stories and reports will be more organized and easier to read if you get your thoughts and facts in order before you start writing.

Writer's Craft

Like anything else that's worth doing, writing requires some skill and a lot of practice. The lessons in this unit will help you learn some of the skills that make good writing better. Just like athletes or musicians, writers learn the skills they need to improve, and then they practice, practice, practice. Look for new ways to improve your writing as you read these lessons.

▶ Audience and Purpose **264**

▶ Ordering Information **268**

▶ Transition Words **272**

▶ Effective Beginnings and Endings .. **276**

▶ Variety in Writing **280**

▶ Combining Sentences **282**

▶ Figurative Language **286**

▶ The Sound of Language **290**

▶ Ways to Develop
Expository Text **294**

▶ Ways to Develop
Persuasive Writing **300**

▶ Ingredients for Writing a Story ... **304**

▶ Using Dialogue **308**

Audience and Purpose

The goal of writing is to communicate with others. Your audience and purpose should guide how and what you write.

Audience

Audience refers to your readers, the people who will read what you write. Think about who they are. Are they old or young? Will certain information interest them more than other information? How and what you write should be influenced by what you know about your audience.

Take a Look

Audience: eight-year-olds
Before you get a pet, think about how it will fit into your house. If you live in an apartment, you may want to think about smaller animals. Gerbils, hamsters, and goldfish do not need a lot of room. Dogs and cats make great pets but need more room.

Audience: working adults
People should consider where they live and how much time they have before choosing a pet. Gerbils, hamsters, and goldfish take up little space and require less care than dogs and cats. Dogs, especially, require a greater time commitment.

Audience: older people who live alone
Pets are wonderful companions. They add life to a quiet house or apartment and may ease loneliness. Before getting a pet, consider the amount of space you have and your ability to care for it. Gerbils, hamsters, and goldfish take up little space and require less care than cats and dogs. Larger dogs require more space. If they are not well-trained, they may accidentally topple people who are unstable on their feet or in a weakened condition.

Purpose

Your **purpose** is your reason for writing. Whenever you write, you should be aware of *why* you are writing. Are you writing to inform? Are you writing to explain? Are you writing to entertain? Are you writing to persuade? Being aware of your purpose will help you stay clear and focused as you write.

Write to Inform

When you write a school report or an article, you are writing to inform and sometimes explain. For example, if you want to tell readers about a volcano that erupted in Mexico, you write to inform. You will want to include information such as time, exact location, how many people it affected, and other details.

Write to Explain

If you want to describe to readers why a volcano erupts and what leads to an eruption, you write to explain. It's like writing to inform, but it goes a step further by telling *how* something happens. Other reasons for writing to explain include giving directions or telling how to do something.

When writing to explain, it is especially important to present the ideas in an organized way. To tell about how and why a volcano erupts, you can use transition words (such as *first, second, third*) for each event that leads to the eruption so readers can easily follow the process.

Write to Entertain

When you write to entertain, you want to capture your readers' attention so they enjoy what they are reading. You could, for example, write an adventure story about a family who escapes from an erupting volcano. Instead of giving all the scientific reasons for eruptions, you would use descriptive language that appeals to your audience.

The purpose of most fiction is to entertain, but other types of writing can entertain as well. Knowing your purpose while you write will guide you and help you make what you are writing funnier, scarier, or more entertaining in another way.

Write to Persuade

When you write to persuade, you write with the purpose of getting your readers to change their minds about something or take some action. Think about the information that would most likely influence them. For example, if you want to persuade people to get more exercise, you could include one or more of the following: an emotional appeal for living longer and feeling better, facts about possible results of not exercising, the opinions from doctors and fitness experts who study the benefits of exercise, or examples of people who have improved their health through exercise. When you write persuasively, you should be clear about what you expect from your readers, whether it is help with a solution or simply a change in thinking.

Try It

Is your purpose, to **inform, explain, entertain,** or **persuade**, in each item below?

▶ You need to give a friend directions to get to your house.

▶ You want to tell a story about the time you ate turkey for breakfast.

Analyzing the Models

Do you see how the author chose simpler words such as *think* and *need* for the eight-year-olds and more difficult words such as *consider* and *require* for the working adults and older people? Your word choice will depend on the age and reading level of your audience.

What do you notice about the information in each example? The piece written for older people focuses on the things they may care about, such as companionship, the ability to care for a pet, and safety. The paragraph for working people discusses time commitment and the fact that the owners may be away during the day. The piece for eight-year-olds focuses on what size of pet is appropriate for where they live. Notice how the writing voice changes each time to show that the writer cares about each audience and wishes to make a connection. The things about which the author writes are also aimed at what is important to each audience.

Try It

See if you can come up with a purpose and audience for each of these topics.

▶ All pet goldfish should live in aquariums with air pumps.

▶ A story about two goldfish who become friends.

▶ Step-by step instructions on how to clean your tank while you are away.

Reading Your Writing

Knowing your purpose and audience guides you as you write by helping with word choice, writing voice, and the ideas you choose to emphasize.

Ordering Information

To communicate clearly, you must present your ideas in a logical order. There are a variety of ways to organize your ideas. Which one you choose depends upon your purpose for writing.

Organizing by Time

One way to organize your writing is chronologically, or in time order. When organizing by time, you place events in the order in which they happened. You may want to describe events from least to most recent or the other way around. Use transition words that indicate time such as *yesterday, this morning, tomorrow,* and *tomorrow evening* to tell when each event occurred or will occur. This kind of order is almost always used in biographies and autobiographies. It may also be used in writing stories.

Take a Look

__Two days ago__ I rode my bicycle to school, but __yesterday__ it rained so my mother drove me. __Today__ my friend and I had enough time to walk to school. We hope to walk again __tomorrow__.

Notice what happens when this same information is not organized by time and does not use transition words.

It rained so my mother drove me to school. I hope we can walk. Another day I rode my bicycle, and another day a neighbor and I walked.

Do you see how much clearer the first paragraph is than the second? The mixed-up order and lack of transition words that indicate time make it difficult to figure out when things happened and how they are related. The first paragraph not only lets the reader know exactly when each event occurred, it also shows how the events are connected.

Organizing by Order

Another way to present information chronologically is to organize your events by order of events. When you organize by order, you don't tell the exact time, but you tell when events happened in relationship to one another. Use transition words that indicate order such as *before*, *first*, *next*, *then*, and *later* to show order.

Take a Look

Before *the squirrel jumped onto our deck, it climbed the large holly tree.* **Next** *it scrambled out onto the end of a long branch and made a bold leap to the railing.* **Then** *it jumped onto a tomato plant, took one bite out of a ripe tomato and landed squarely on the deck.* **Last** *it stared into the window at us and swished its tail in a short, jerking motion.*

Try It

Try reading the paragraph above without transition words.

Do you see how ordering the events with transition words not only places the events in order but also makes the paragraph easier to read? When you don't take the time to order information, readers will be unsure about the relationship of points or descriptions, and they will have to struggle through choppy writing to figure out what you are trying to tell them.

Organizing by Order of Importance

A good way to organize ideas is to write about them in order of their importance. Writing that persuades orders ideas in importance from the least important reason to the most important. Newspaper stories order ideas the opposite way. When you write a news story, you order ideas and events from most to least important. Writing that informs or explains may order ideas either way, beginning with the most important or least important. Use transition words such as these—*first, second, third, most important,* and *finally*—to show order of importance.

Take a Look

We should be allowed to have a school newspaper. **First** a newspaper would keep students informed about what is happening in other grades. It could have a section for each grade and a calendar of events. **Second** a newspaper would give students a chance to be involved in a different kind of school activity. Some kids would like to participate in something besides sports or the other clubs we have at school now. **Finally, and most important,** working to put a newspaper together would help kids learn about responsibility and cooperation. The students putting the paper together would have to work as a team to make sure the deadline for publishing was met.

Did you see how this persuasive paragraph ordered its points from least to most important? Below, the paragraph from a news story opens with the most important information and follows with information that is less important.

Scientists have discovered what may be the largest dinosaur on record. The dinosaur is believed to be 27 feet longer than the 100-ton Argentinosaurus, which was until now considered the largest dinosaur. The bones from the new dinosaur were found in Patagonia, a remote area of Argentina. The new dinosaur has a small head and a long tail. It has not yet been named or classified.

Ordering by Location: Top to Bottom and Left to Right

Another way to organize information involves describing where things are located. When you write to explain or write to describe, you may find it useful to order details from **top to bottom** or from **left to right.** To cue your reader, use transition words such as *on top of, under, to the right of,* and *to the left of.* Take care not to jump around, but order your details in a way that is easy to read and easy for your reader to picture what you are describing.

Take a Look

The first description below moves from top to bottom. The next description moves from left to right.

> The set for the play *The Jungle Book* amazed us. Large trees formed a rain forest canopy. **Above** the canopy was the ceiling, painted to look like a bright blue sky. **On top** of the canopy, puppetlike birds flitted from tree to tree. **Beneath** the canopy were lots of hanging vines and **under** that were thick clumps of moss and ferns.

> We looked over the obstacle course. Ten large tires formed a path on **the far left. To the right** of the tires we saw a shallow pool filled with thick mud. **Next to** that was a sandbox filled with sawdust. **To the right** of the sandbox was a climbing wall and to the **far right** a large pile of shredded foam.

Reading Your Writing

Be sure to order your information in the way that makes the most sense for what is presented. Ordered writing is easier for readers to follow. If you do not order your long descriptions and explanations, readers will have a difficult time understanding your ideas.

Transition Words

When you have many different ideas to communicate to your readers, it's important to help them follow along. You can do this by using **transition words,** which connect ideas in a piece of writing. Transition words help your readers move smoothly from one idea to the next. They also make your writing clearer and more accurate.

Different kinds of transition words are used for different purposes. For example, transition words can signal a time or place, a comparison or contrast, or a summary.

Transition Words That Indicate Time

about	then	soon
after	until	later
at	meanwhile	finally
before	today	then
during	tomorrow	as soon as
first	tonight	now
second	yesterday	when
third	next	

Take a Look

> *This evening I used a page from my journal to write a fantasy story.*
>
> *This morning when Mr. Frazier gave us the assignment, I didn't have*
>
> *any ideas for a fantasy story. Then I remembered something I had*
>
> *written **yesterday** about talking turtles and was able to use my journal*
>
> *entry for the story.*

Transition Words to Show Location

above	by	on
across	down	on top of
against	in	outside
along	in back of	over
among	in front of	through
around	inside	throughout
behind	into	to the left
below	near	to the right
beneath	nearby	under
beside	next to	underneath
between	off	

Take a Look

We saw a boat tied to a dock on the **other side** of the river. **Across** the river were three men running toward the boat. They untied the boat, jumped **inside,** and rowed to the dock right **near** us. Then they began searching for something **underneath** the dock.

Words That Show More About Location

Location words may be used for school reports and for other nonfiction writing. The following paragraph shows how location words can help with the detailed descriptions required for an observation report.

Take a Look

I placed an ice cube **in** a bowl of water. I sprinkled salt **on top of** the ice cube, then I rested the **center** of a piece of string on the ice cube for 45 seconds. When I lifted the string **above** the water, the ice cube stuck to it.

Transition Words to Show Contrast

Use transition words to contrast things that are different. When you want to show readers how one or more things are different, transition words help signal a contrast.

although	however	still
but	on the other hand	yet
even though	otherwise	

Take a Look

Rocks that look like icicles that hang from the ceiling of a cave are called stalactites. Formed when water drips minerals from a cave's ceiling, they taper to thin, fragile points. Stalagmites, **on the other hand,** are formed on the floor of a cave. **Unlike** stalactites, they have broad bases that taper to thick, rounded domes.

Do you see how the transition words *on the other hand* and *unlike* signal the reader that the information that is about to follow will tell how stalagmites are different from stalactites?

Transition Words to Show Comparison

Sometimes you will need to show how two or more things are the same. Cue the reader with words that emphasize similarities.

also	in the same way	like	both
too	just as	similarly	likewise

Take a Look

Some caves have waterfalls in them that flow from underground streams. Most caves have formations called flowstones that look **like** waterfalls but are actually limestone. **Like** waterfalls, they **too** are formed by water. Flowstones appear **just as** an actual waterfall might appear if it were frozen.

Transition Words for Summarizing

as a result	last	lastly	in conclusion
finally	in summary	therefore	

These words alert readers to the points of a summary or a conclusion. Like most transition words, they help writers communicate effectively by providing organization and transitions.

Take a Look

Bats that sleep in caves during the day have been known to flee when they are disturbed. People who are afraid of bats sometimes swat at and injure them. Bats are usually harmless and can be very helpful by eating pesky insects. **In conclusion,** when you are doing activities near bats, take care not to disturb these creatures.

Effective Beginnings and Endings

A good beginning to your story or report makes your readers want to keep reading. A good ending helps them remember what you wrote.

Writing Effective Beginnings

A good beginning grabs the reader's attention. The type of beginning you use will depend on whether you are writing fiction or nonfiction. In both types of writing, however, the beginning should make them interested in your topic or story. Below are a few of the ways to begin your writing.

Tell About a Problem

Write about a problem in the opening paragraph to encourage your audience to think actively about your topic.

Take a Look

> Many of us are just too busy. We tape our favorite show so we won't miss it when we go out. We eat our dinner and listen to the radio while we finish our homework. All of the "important" things we do leave little time to spend with our family and friends.

Ask a Question

Begin with one or more questions to get readers thinking about your topic.

> When was the last time you were really nervous? Can you remember how you felt? I remember it well. I was a beginning debater. I sat across from the best debater in school. She looked calm and relaxed while I just couldn't stop sweating or keep my hands from shaking.

Tell an Interesting Fact

There is nothing like an interesting fact to capture a reader's attention. When readers see an interesting fact in the first sentence, they are likely to want to read more.

Take a Look

There were once billions of beautiful passenger pigeons in the United States and Canada. There were so many pigeons that when they flew they darkened the skies, completely shutting out the sunlight. Today, not a single passenger pigeon lives.

Describe an Experience

Start by writing about something that happened to you or another person. This is a great way to encourage readers to identify from the start with the person about whom you are writing. In writing fiction, you may wish to use dialogue to help describe your experience.

Take a Look

"Look what I found," my friend Lenny called to me as he stooped to pick something up from the street. "It's a five dollar bill. Isn't this great!"

"Yes, but maybe you should ask around to see if someone lost it," I answered. "If you can't find out who lost it, we can split it."

"What do you mean split it?" asked Lenny. "It's mine!"

Writing Effective Endings

Your ending is your conclusion. An effective ending consists of a single sentence or paragraph that does any of the following: 1) It may summarize your key points or the main idea. 2) It may bring the action of events to an end. 3) It may provide a reflection on how the outcome affects the world or life in general. 4) It may provide a reflection on how the outcome influences the individual reader. Take care not to introduce new ideas in the closing paragraph or sentence. Instead, make sure that the final paragraph or sentence clearly signals the end to what you have written.

Summarizing

When you write an ending that summarizes, you can end with a statement that restates the main idea. A nonfiction article about Native American achievements in astronomy ends simply with one statement that reminds the reader of the article's general purpose.

Take a Look

Today we are coming to recognize Native Americans' achievements in astronomical knowledge—and to appreciate the ways in which they used that knowledge.

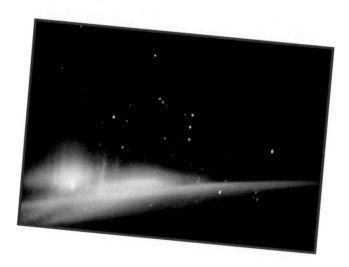

Ending with a Reflective Paragraph

Another way to end is by concluding with a paragraph in which you reflect on or think about what you have written. A final reflection might encourage readers to think about how the information influences the world or them personally.

Take a Look

Once a rain forest is gone, it is gone forever. Plants that live there disappear, and the animals that live there lose their homes and food. For people, that means fewer of the scents, flavors, and valuable medicines we get from the rain forest. Vanishing rain forests affect the world's atmosphere as well. We should take it seriously when we hear of another rain forest being destroyed. When a rain forest disappears, so does a vital part of our planet.

Do you see how the paragraph begins with the plants and animals inside the rain forest and moves outward toward readers and the rest of the world?

Ending for Stories

When writing an ending for your stories, try to increase the tension in the story by using action, dialogue, and details to make the character's struggle more exciting for the reader. Once you have done that, remember to show the reader how the character solves the problem in the story. Be certain to "tie up the loose ends" by making sure the reader gets all their questions about the story answered. Let the reader know what happens to the main characters so they are not left wondering.

Fun Fact

The Amazon Rain Forest produces over one-fifth of the world's oxygen.

Variety in Writing

Variety in writing refers to using sentences and words so they are interesting and not repetitious for readers. You can add variety by using synonyms and appositives. You can also include sentences of different lengths and build sentences in different ways. Readers enjoy reading writing that's varied in the way it is put together.

Use Synonyms

Synonyms are words that mean the same or almost the same as another word. They can help you avoid using the same words over and over. The first example below uses the word *saw* repeatedly. Notice how the second example uses synonyms to improve the revised paragraph.

Take a Look

Example 1
We saw the parade go down Main Street. We **saw** the mayor in a convertible followed by an old-fashioned car carrying the school board president. Next we **saw** a lot more old-fashioned cars. In one of the cars I **saw** a chimpanzee sitting next to the driver. When the chimp **saw** people throwing peanuts, he excitedly pounded his hands on the dashboard.

Example 2
We **watched** the parade go down Main Street. We **saw** the mayor in a convertible followed by an old-fashioned car carrying the school board president. Then a lot more lot more old-fashioned cars **appeared.** In one of the cars I **spied** a chimpanzee sitting next to the driver. When he **spotted** people throwing peanuts, he excitedly pounded his hands on the dashboard.

Change the Length of Sentences

Using sentences of different lengths will improve the rhythm and flow of your writing. Paragraphs with lots of short, same-length sentences can be stiff and boring. Read both paragraphs below. Notice the varied sentence length in the second paragraph.

Example 1
Native Americans of the plains used all buffalo parts. Buffalo horns were used as cooking tools. They were also used to carry hot coals to campgrounds. Hooves made glue. Buffalo fat supplied soap. Bones were made into tools. Backbones with ribs became toboggans.

Example 2
Native Americans of the plains used every part of the buffalo. Buffalo horns were used as cooking tools and to carry hot coals from one campground to the next. Buffalo hooves could be made into glue, while buffalo fat became soap. On the northern plains, backbones with ribs became toboggans for children.

Vary Sentence Beginnings

Another way to create variety in your writing is to vary the beginnings of sentences. When you don't, your writing may sound dull like the paragraph below that uses *we* to begin every sentence. Read both examples below. The second example uses a dependent clause to begin the first sentence and a different subject for the last.

Example 1
We ran out of things to do in our car. **We** forgot to take the things that would entertain us. **We** left books, travel checkers, and electronic games at home.

Example 2
As we traveled in our car, we ran out of things to do. **We** had forgotten to take enough things to entertain us. **Books, travel checkers, and electronic games** had all been left behind at home.

Combining Sentences

Sometimes several sentences share information. For example, they have the same subject or verb. By combining these sentences, you can avoid repeating words. These ideas from shorter sentences can be combined into one sentence by using a series of words.

> In the tidal pool we saw starfish. We also saw sea horses. We also saw sea urchins.
>
> **Better:** In the tidal pool, we saw starfish, sea horses, and sea urchins.

In the first set of sentences, several words are repeated. Each sentence has the same subject and verb. In the improved sentence, the repeated words are left out. A series of words is used to combine the three sentences into one. The meaning is the same, and sentence fluency is improved.

> We swam. We snorkeled. We explored the beach.
>
> **Better:** We swam, snorkeled, and explored the beach.

In the first series of sentences, each one has the same subject. In the improved sentence, the repeated words are left out. A series of words is used to combine the three sentences into one.

> The water sparkled in every direction. The water was clear and calm.
>
> **Better:** The clear, calm water sparkled in every direction.

In the first series of sentences, each one has the same subject. The sentences are combined by adding the adjectives *clear* and *calm* to the first sentence.

Sentence Expansion

Another good way to vary sentences is to expand them. Short sentences can be converted into phrases or clauses and combined with other sentences. The goal is to vary sentence length to add smoothness and to avoid having too many short sentences.

Expanding with Phrases

Participial and prepositional phrases may be combined to vary sentence length. Participial phrases are phrases that begin with a participle and act as adjectives modifying nouns. **Prepositional phrases** are phrases that begin with a preposition and end with a noun or pronoun. They modify nouns, adjectives, adverbs, or verbs. Change short sentences into phrases and attach them to nearby related sentences to improve the flow of your writing.

Notice how the first three of these short sentences convert to **participial phrases** and attach to the last sentence that becomes the main clause.

Dolphins leap high above waves. They spin in the air. They somersault tail over head. Dolphins do a range of spectacular jumps in the wild.

Better: **Leaping high above waves, spinning in the air, and somersaulting tail over head,** dolphins do a range of spectacular jumps in the wild.

Prepositional phrases can also be combined. The information in the second and third sentences of the next example become prepositional phrases attached to the first sentence, which becomes the main clause in the improved sentences.

The gulls searched for food. They were at the beach. It was a hot summer day.

Better: **On a hot summer day,** the gulls searched for food **at the beach.**

Expanding with Clauses

Sometimes two sentences share information. When this happens, one of the sentences can often be made into a dependent clause.

Ted and Jeremy made a large sandcastle.
Ted and Jeremy **are identical twins.**

Better: Ted and Jeremy, **who are identical twins,** made a large sandcastle.

In the example sentences above, the information in the second sentence becomes a dependent clause in the new sentence. The dependent clause modifies *Ted and Jeremy*. When a dependent clause that modifies a noun or pronoun provides information that is not essential to the meaning of the sentence, it is set off by commas. When the dependent clause provides essential information, it is not set off by commas.

More About Expanding with Clauses

Sometimes one sentence explains the action that is going on in another sentence. A sentence that tells how, when, where, or why an action in another sentence is happening can become a dependent clause.

Tony paddled out to the waves breaking on the second sandbar. **Tony wanted to get away from all the other swimmers.**

Better: Tony paddled out to the waves breaking on the second sandbar **because he wanted to get away from all the other swimmers.**

In the example sentences above, the second sentence explains why Tony paddled out to the waves breaking on the second sandbar. The dependent clause modifies the verb *paddled*.

Expanding with Appositives

An **appositive** is a noun placed next to another noun to identify or provide more information about it. An **appositive phrase** is a group of words that includes an appositive and other words that modify it. Use appositives and appositive phrases in your writing to cut down on the need for short explanatory sentences. They give you yet another way to produce writing that is varied and smooth.

Take a Look

Before using an appositive:

> My oldest sister is a marine biologist. Her name is Francesca León.

After using an appositive:

> My oldest sister, **Francesca León,** is a marine biologist.

Before using an appositive phrase:

> The spinner dolphin is a type of dolphin that rotates in the air. Spinner dolphins jump high out of the water and spin up to 14 times before landing.

After using an appositive phrase:

> The spinner dolphin, **a type of dolphin that rotates in the air,** jumps high out of the water and spins up to 14 times before landing.

Do you see how the appositives smoothly provide the information? Appositives are especially helpful when you are trying to produce varied, interesting sentences in small amounts of space.

Reading Your Writing

There are many ways to add variety and smoothness to writing. Without these techniques, you will still be able to write sentences that are grammatically correct. However, these methods will help you produce writing that's more enjoyable to read.

Figurative Language

Figurative language refers to words or groups of words that stand for more than their literal meaning. Writers use figurative language, sometimes called **figures of speech,** to create vivid pictures in readers' minds. Figures of speech frequently make comparisons that rely on the experience of the audience.

Simile

A **simile** is a figure of speech that compares two things that are not alike by using the word *like* or *as*.

> The rug was as soft as a bed of moss.
> The motorcycle rumbled like thunder in the distance.

How does the second example work? Readers are familiar with the sound of thunder. By comparing the sound of the motorcycle to rumbling thunder, the simile creates in the reader's mind a connection to a well-known sound.

Now look at the simile below. Does it work?

> Diego's whistle sounded like that of the crested flycatcher.

Most readers are not familiar with the crested flycatcher bird or its whistle, so they would have no idea how Diego's whistle sounded. Similes are great for creating fresh, clear images, but be sure to base them on your audience experience.

Try It
To what could you compare each of these two things in order to create a simile that your friends would understand?
▶ The heat of a summer day
▶ The screeching brakes of a car

Metaphor

A **metaphor** is a figure of speech that compares two unlike things without using the words *like* or *as*. A metaphor sometimes uses context or the surrounding information to make a comparison. Metaphors also rely on the experience of the audience.

> The air-conditioned waiting room was a refrigerator.
> The trip was a nightmare.

The first example assumes that readers will know from experience and context that the waiting room was not an actual refrigerator but that its temperature was like one. The second example assumes that the audience has experienced a bad dream and can then understand that the trip was not a pleasant experience. When you use metaphors, be sure that the context and the experience of your audience support the image.

Personification

Personification is a figure of speech in which an object or idea is given human qualities. As with other types of figurative language, personification involves making a comparison. Personification relies on context and the ability of readers to relate human qualities to the thing described.

> The old house creaked and complained about its worn and aching joints.
>
> The friendly harbor welcomed us with outstretched arms.

The first example gives something that is not human— a house—the qualities of a person complaining about worn and aching joints. The second example compares a harbor to a friendly person. The comparison works if readers imagine a U-shaped harbor with arms of land, like the hugging arms of a person.

Exaggeration

Exaggeration in writing means stretching the truth to make a strong statement or to add humor. Use exaggeration to add interest to your writing with the understanding that readers are not to take your descriptions literally.

Exaggeration is a great way to capture and hold your reader's attention. Through overstatement, exaggeration can add emphasis to your descriptions and ideas. Readers should understand from their own experience and through context that the description isn't meant to be taken word-for-word. Think of using exaggeration to make readers smile.

> I was so tired I collapsed on the bottom bunk.
>
> My feet were killing me.
>
> The morning sunlight blinded me as it came through the window.

Hyperbole

Hyperbole is a type of extreme exaggeration often used for humorous effect. It is sometimes used in writing to describe the quality of one thing by comparing it to a more extreme quality in another.

> He was so hungry that he ate everything but the table.
>
> My backpack felt as if it had ten bowling balls inside it.

The first example uses hyperbole by making a simple, yet extreme, statement. The second example uses hyperbole by comparing the first item, the weight of a backpack, to that of something far heavier—ten bowling balls. The comparison is so exaggerated that it becomes humorous.

Use exaggeration and hyperbole only at key moments in your writing. If you use it too often, readers may tire of the technique and it will lose its impact.

Idiom

An **idiom** is a word or group of words that cannot be understood by knowing only the literal meaning. People learn idioms or expressions as they learn their language. Idioms can add personality and a natural feel to your writing, although they are not normally used for formal writing. Sometimes idioms say exactly what you want to communicate—just be sure your audience knows what they mean from context and experience.

Read each of the sentences below. The idiom is in bold type. It's meaning is in parentheses.

Our teacher **went out on a limb** for us when she asked the principal if we could have class outside today. (to take a risk)

Nadine had **cold feet** at her piano recital. (to be very nervous)

It never **dawned** on me to try the red button. (to understand)

Could you show Terry **the ropes?** He's never worked at the refreshment stand. (to explain how something is done)

> **Fun Fact**
>
> To know the ropes, meaning to know how something is done, was originally an old sea expression that meant to know how to work the ropes controlling a ship's sails.

Do you see how idioms make writing sound natural, almost like the way people talk?

As you get older, you will understand the meanings of more and more idioms. Younger people and people who have recently learned English have some trouble understanding them. When you use idioms in your writing, use them correctly and in a context that helps make their meaning clear.

Reading Your Writing

Figurative language makes your writing interesting. Simile, metaphor, and personification bring fresh images to the reader's mind. Exaggeration can capture and hold your reader's interest, while using idiom helps make your writing sound natural. When using any of these, be aware of how they match with the experience of your audience and place them in a context that will make their meanings clear.

The Sound of Language

Writers, especially when they're writing poetry, choose words not just for what they mean but also for how they sound. To tune your ear to the sound of language, pay attention to how the words that you read and write create sounds and effects. This lesson includes some special writing devices you can use.

Alliteration

Alliteration is the repetition of the consonant sounds at the beginning words. You may have seen alliteration used in advertising or for movie and book titles such as *Charlie and the Chocolate Factory.*

Alliteration is most often used in poetry, but it can also be used in fiction. Use alliteration when your goal is to have readers be entertained by what you have written.

Take a Look

Below are some more examples of alliteration.

> The **s**nake **s**lithered **s**ideways across the **s**idewalk.
> When my brother **cr**unches **cr**ackers, I go **cr**azy.
> **J**ordan dreamed of a **j**iggling **j**ellyfish.

Try It

What is the beginning sound in your first name? Think of three other words that start with that sound.

Assonance

When you use **assonance** in your writing, you repeat the sounds of vowels. Assonance can add a pleasing sound to your writing and may be used in poetry, and in stories, when you want readers to enjoy the sound of what you've written.

Take a Look

> As the wind continued to b**low**, water r**ose** and fl**ow**ed over the dike.
> D**a**n fl**a**shed a set of br**a**ss keys.
> The br**ee**ze fluttered the palm l**ea**ves.
> They made fine shadows on the b**ea**ch.

Do you see how the first example repeats the long o sound, the second example repeats the short a sound, and the third example repeats the long e sound? The third and fourth sentences show that the repeated vowel sounds of assonance do not have to be contained within one sentence. You may be able to create assonance from nearby words in different sentences. Words should be located close together so readers can hear the repetition of the vowel sounds.

Onomatopoeia

When you use onomatopoeia, you use a word that imitates the sound made by or connected with the thing to which you refer. As with other methods that highlight sound, you will want to use onomatopoeic words most often in writing that entertains. Use onomatopoeia to make sounds come alive for your readers.

Take a Look

> We heard the **pitter-patter** of rain on the tin roof.
> Have you ever heard a bird **jabber** as much as that parrot?
> Alyssa **zoomed** by on her scooter.

A rhyme occurs when words end with the same sound, such as *star* and *guitar*. End rhyme refers to rhyming words that are at the ends of two or more lines of poetry.

Use end rhyme when you want to write rhyming poetry. End rhyme in poetry can be clever and entertaining. At other times, it may sound old-fashioned. Use end rhyme only when you think it will complement what you wish to communicate.

Take a Look

This short poem by Richard Armour shows how end rhyme can add to a poem's cleverness. Notice that the first and third lines and the second and fourth lines rhyme.

> **Good Sportsmanship**
>
> Good sportsmanship we hail, we sing,
> It's always pleasant when you spot it.
> There's only one unhappy thing:
> You have to lose to prove you've got it.

Internal Rhyme

When you use internal rhyme, you rhyme words in the middle of lines. Use internal rhyme in poetry. Like alliteration and assonance, internal rhyme can add to reading enjoyment.

Take a Look

> I'm not a **fool** and I know the **rule**—no trading cards allowed at **school**.
> **Please,** can you **squeeze** me in before I **freeze?**
> We saw a **pale** face peeking from behind the **veil.**

Notice how the last example is not funny like the first two. Rhyme doesn't have to be humorous; sometimes it just adds a pleasant sound to writing.

Repetition of Words and Phrases

When you use repetition in your writing, you repeat words or phrases to add emphasis or rhythm.

Take a Look

> ### The Whole World Is Coming
> a Sioux Indian poem
>
> The whole world is coming
> A nation is coming, a nation is coming,
> the eagle has brought the message to the tribe.
> Over the whole earth they are coming:
> the buffalo are coming, the buffalo are coming,
> the crow has brought the message to the tribe.

Fun Fact

The word *rhythm* comes from the Greek word *rythmos,* which means "measured motion, time, or proportion."

Rhythm

Rhythm is the regular repetition of sounds, accents, or beats. Most writing has a rhythm that imitates natural speech. Poetry is often written with a rhythm that follows a pattern.

Take a Look

Read the lines below. Give stress to the words and syllables in bold type.

> By **caves** where **never sun** has **shone,**
> By **streams** that **never find** the **sea.**

This example from J.R.R. Tolkien's poem "Roads Go Ever Ever On" shows a classic poetry rhythm pattern. The stronger accents create a rhythm by falling on every second syllable.

Reading Your Writing

Writing is more than just words and ideas. Crafting the sound of the language you use results in writing that has a musical, rhythmic flow.

Ways to Develop Expository Text

Expository text is nonfiction writing that informs readers about a topic. You can find expository text in schoolbooks, encyclopedias, newspapers, and magazines and on Web sites that explain or tell "how to." Expository writing sometimes uses diagrams, charts, and maps to help readers understand information. Expository writing may tell about real people and events, provide steps on how to do something, or supply readers with facts and reasons.

Organizing Expository Writing

How you choose to organize your expository writing will be determined by your purpose. Why are you writing? Do you want to compare and contrast two things? Do you want to describe the causes and effects of an event? Do you want to ask a question and present information that helps answer it? Do you want to inform readers about a problem and its possible solutions, or do you want to explain a process? You may be able to think of other ways to organize your writing, but whichever one you choose, keep in mind that your purpose is to give readers information. Knowing what you want to achieve will guide you as you organize the information in a way that is easy for readers to understand.

Try It

For which of these would you use expository writing?

▶ You want to tell a funny story about the time you tried to fry ice cream.

▶ You want to explain how chocolate is made from cocoa beans.

▶ You want to tell how skateboard and in-line skate tricks are alike and different.

Expository text that compares and contrasts describes the similarities and differences between things. When you compare two things, you tell how they are alike. When you contrast, you explain how they are different. If you write an essay or report that includes a section that compares and contrasts, you will want to explain to readers at the beginning *what* you are doing so they know the purpose of the text. Knowing your own purpose will also help you organize your ideas as you write.

Before You Write Brainstorm the important information about your subjects and create separate lists for each.

Sort it Out Look over the details you've listed and sort them by similarities and differences.

Organize and Write When you describe the similarities and differences of a subject, you can do it in one of two ways. 1) Describe your first subject and then discuss the similarities and differences of the second subject. 2) List the similarities and differences of subjects feature by feature as in the following example.

Take a Look

This is how my cat Felicity acts. She likes to lie around during the day, but at night she prowls around the yard. Whenever Felicity is awake, whether it is day or evening, she can be found purring. Although she acts differently during the day than she does at night, she seems happy both times.

Felicity's eyes are very different from day to evening. During the day when she is in bright sunlight, her eyes become thin slits to keep out light. At night when she is outdoors, the pupils of her eyes open wide to let in light. My vet told me cats see almost as well at night as they do during daytime.

When expository text is organized by cause and effect, it describes a **cause**—a condition or event—and also the **effect**—what happens as a direct result of the condition or event. When you write about cause and effect, you explain why one or more things happen.

Organizing Your Writing You may choose to describe the causes first or the effects first. With either approach, make sure the cause-and-effect relationship is clear. Use transition words such as *because, if, then, since, so, therefore,* and *as a result* to guide readers and emphasize the relationships between causes and effects.

Take a Look

This paragraph from a report on tornadoes discusses the causes first and then the effect.

> The air before a violent thunderstorm is unstable. That means it changes direction and moves up and down, mixing with the air above and below it. It moves around **because** two different types of air come into contact with each other. When warm, moist air bumps up against cold, dry air, it rises. As it rises, it cools, sinks, warms up, and rises again. All this moving around of air **results** in strong, vertical wind currents. **If** the currents are big and powerful enough, and **if** the air begins to turn, the **result** is the formation of a violent tornado.

Do you see how the paragraph first describes what causes tornadoes? The cause is unstable, moving air which in turn has its own cause—the collision of warm and cold air. One cause leads to another. Do you see how the transition words emphasize the connections between causes and effects?

Another way to approach a subject for expository writing involves asking a question and attempting to answer it. The attempt to answer some questions may involve stating theories. You could also do research and answer other questions by presenting facts and reasons. Your subject and the type of questions you ask will determine your approach.

Take the Reader with You For example, you could write a piece that begins by asking why people mow their lawns. After capturing your reader's attention with a question, you could come up with your own reasons for why people mow lawns. Walk the reader through your thought process as you give the reasons why you believe people mow lawns. To organize your reasons, use transition words that show order of importance such as *first, second, third, finally,* and *most important.*

Take a Look

Why do people mow their lawns? **First** most people think short, mowed grass looks better. They like how it makes their yard appear neat and under control. **Second** a mowed lawn is a better surface for playing outdoor games like touch football. It's harder to run in long grass. **Third** and **most important,** people mow their lawns because their neighbors do. It's what people expect of them. They don't want to be the ones who stand out with a messy lawn.

Do you see how the example gives reasons in order of importance and uses transition words to signal readers when reasons are presented? Although the example asks just one question and gives three reasons, you may wish to ask more than one question and give any number of reasons when you use the questions/answers approach. Just be sure your writing is organized and clear.

Another way to approach expository writing is to point out a problem and offer one or more solutions. This approach takes a problem and carefully describes it so readers understand why it is a problem. Then it explains how one or more solutions can solve the problem.

Before You Write Begin by asking yourself about the size of the problem. Is it a far-reaching problem or a smaller one? Ask what causes the problem and how many people it affects. Plan to write about things that are as important to your readers.

Gather Your Information and Write Will you need facts and reasons to explain the causes and solutions? Do research in the library or online. Does the topic require observation? Take time to observe, interview others, and take notes. As you write, describe solutions in detail and tell how each will work. If your solutions don't completely solve the problem, let readers know.

The example below relies on personal observation to explain the problem and the solution. It tells about just one solution in detail, but longer expository pieces normally describe more than one solution.

Take a Look

There is a lot of litter at Chadick Park, and the problem seems to be getting worse. Everywhere you look, there is trash. The picnic area is littered with cans and paper. The playing fields don't look much better. Even the walking trails have trash on them. The trash cans that are available are always overflowing.

One way to solve the problem would be to put more trash and recycling bins at the park. I have seen only one recycling bin, and it is off in one corner of the park. Most people won't take the time to go all the way over there to throw away their cans and bottles. Adding more trash bins and placing them conveniently will encourage people to dispose of their trash properly.

Expository text that tells readers how something happens or how to do something step-by-step explains a process. To describe the process, be clear about your purpose and use words that your readers will understand.

To organize, use transition words that show time order such as *first, second, third, then, after, next,* and *last* to list the steps of the process. Clearly defining the steps and listing them in the order they occur will help readers understand and remember what you are trying to explain.

Take a Look

My mom makes great pizza. This is how she does it. First she makes the dough for the crust, which is very hard to do. Second she puts the dough in the oven to bake it a little before she puts the other ingredients on it. Next she spreads really good pizza sauce on the crust. Then she adds shredded mozzarella cheese. Sometimes she tops the pizza with mushrooms and ground beef. Last she bakes the pizza until the cheese is gooey.

Do you see how the example uses transition words to order each step of the process? In expository writing, steps should be listed in the order they should be done and events should be listed in the order they occur.

Reading Your Writing

Expository text tells about real people and events, provides factual information about a topic, or describes a process. Depending on your purpose, you can organize your expository writing in many different ways. The important thing is to organize the information in a straightforward way so readers can understand it.

Ways to Develop Persuasive Writing

Persuasive writing is written for the purpose of influencing its readers to take action. It sometimes has the added purpose of changing the way readers think or feel about a topic. It often does both.

You can use one of two techniques to get readers to think and/or act differently: 1) State an opinion and support that opinion with facts, examples, and reasons. 2) State an opinion and appeal to the audience's interests and emotions.

Take a Look

This paragraph shows persuasive writing that uses facts and reasons.

> The fifth graders at Stetson Elementary School should have a longer lunch break. We are supposed to get twenty-five minutes to eat our lunches. However, since we are the last group to go to the cafeteria, we get less time. The other groups run late and take up extra time. By the time the younger grades finally clear out, and by the time we file in, stand in the food line, and actually sit down, we have only fifteen minutes left to eat. We don't have enough time to finish our food. Just a few more minutes would make a big difference. It might also improve how we do in our afternoon classes.

When you write persuasively, you may need to research your facts by visiting the library, searching online, or by interviewing others. You can also use examples from personal experience or expert opinions such as can be obtained through interviews and research. Use the facts, examples, and expert opinions that will have the most weight with your audience.

Use the second technique when you think your audience will be most influenced by an appeal to their interests or emotions. The example on the next page shows how to support a similar viewpoint by appealing to emotion.

> The fifth graders at Stetson Elementary School should have an earlier and longer lunch break. Have you ever felt so weak from hunger that you couldn't concentrate? What if you then had to wolf down your food in a short amount of time? This is what the fifth graders have to do. We have to wait until all the other groups have eaten their lunches to go to the cafeteria. Then we have to eat in a hurry before the next bell rings. We feel rushed and less important than the other grades. Please, would those who plan the schedule figure out a way to give the fifth graders an earlier or longer lunch break?

Do you see how this example appeals to the emotions. Instead of listing facts, like *fifteen minutes* or the reasons why lunch is too short, it tells how the fifth graders feel and encourages the reader to identify with them. The last line shows how some persuasive writing asks for action on an issue.

Audience and Purpose

Knowing who your audience is and what their interests are will also help you shape your persuasive writing. For example, if your topic is one to which you know your audience feels connected emotionally, you could appeal to their emotions. Knowing how the interests of your audience relate to the topic will also help. For example, if you are writing to persuade the parents of the Home and School Association to donate new gymnastic mats, you could emphasize safety. When writing to persuade, use the approach and language that will influence your audience.

You should also think about the purpose, or reason, you are writing. Do you want to influence the thinking of your audience on a topic? Do you want to get people to act on something? Do you want to point out a problem? Knowing your purpose will guide you and help you organize as you select facts, reasons, or emotional descriptions to influence your readers.

Organizing Your Persuasive Writing: Ask and Answer Questions

One useful way to organize your persuasive writing is to ask and answer a question. When you ask a question, you involve readers and get them immediately thinking about your topic in an active way. The answer or answers you give can be the facts and reasons you use to get your readers to see your point of view and accept it as reasonable. The example shown below tries to persuade the audience to believe that the writer will be old enough to baby-sit in sixth grade.

Take a Look

How old does someone need to be in order to baby-sit? It depends on how mature and well-trained the person is. I think I will be mature enough and have the training to baby-sit when I start sixth grade next year. These are my reasons. First, people tell me that I'm mature for my age. Second, this summer I will be taking the baby-sitting course offered at the YMCA. I'll learn what baby-sitters should and shouldn't do as well as what to do in case of an emergency. Third, I have lots of experience taking care of my younger cousins when my aunt comes over to visit. If a person has both maturity and training and is in at least sixth grade (as I will be next year), she should be allowed to baby-sit.

Do you see the question in the opening sentence? When it asks how old a person should be in order to baby-sit, it states the topic of the persuasive paragraph. The reader expects the information that follows to answer the question. The writer answers the question in the third sentence, mentioning maturity, skills, and being in sixth grade as traits that are generally required. The three reasons that follow answer with specific examples showing why the writer has the maturity and training required. The concluding sentence summarizes the answers/reasons and uses the persuasive word *should* to recommend that he or she should be allowed to baby-sit, restating the paragraph's purpose.

Organizing Your Persuasive Writing: Order Your Reasons

Another way to organize your persuasive writing is to first state your opinion or goal and follow it with the supporting reasons in order of importance. List your reasons—which may be facts or examples—in order of importance from least to most important.

Take a Look

Buckwalter Farm should not be turned into a golf course. It should remain public open space for the following reasons. First another golf course isn't needed. According to the tourist bureau, we have 175 golf courses in the tri-county area. Second most golf courses are not environmentally friendly. They use large amounts of water and chemicals to keep their greens in shape. Their artificial landscape is far more harmful to native plants and animals than that of Buckwalter Farm where chemicals are no longer used. Third people have been going to Buckwalter Farms for years, to fish in the pond, to pick apples in the orchard, and to explore nature by the stream. The farm means a lot to people of all ages in the community—far more than any golf course ever would. Sign the petition to keep Buckwalter Farm from being turned into a golf course.

Reading Your Writing

Use persuasive writing to influence readers to think and act differently by either giving them facts and reasons or by appealing to their interests and emotions. Write with a specific purpose and with your audience in mind. Two ways to organize persuasive writing are asking and answering a question and discussing reasons in order of importance.

Ingredients for Writing a Story

Stories have four major ingredients: **character, plot, setting,** and **point of view.** Carefully develop these components in your fiction writing to create interesting stories that seem real even if they could not possibly happen.

Character

Characters are the people in a story. Create characters with personality who seem as if they could be real. Show, don't tell, readers about the different aspects of a character's personality. Use these five techniques to create lifelike characters.

▶ Show what a character says, and how she or he says it.

"The pitcher's throwing really well, and I'm up next." he said excitedly to his teammate.

▶ Show the way the character acts.

Tom sat alertly in the dugout watching the pitcher.

▶ Show what a character is thinking.

It was the ninth inning and the score was tied. Tom realized that if he could get a base hit, his team could score a run.

▶ Show how a character feels.

Tom was feeling nervous but hopeful. He had already hit two pitches thrown by this pitcher.

▶ Show how other characters respond to or think about the character.

"I'm glad you're up next, Tom," said the coach. "I know you can get a base hit."

Keep this in mind: The goal in creating characters is to make them seem real. Real characters are **well-developed** characters. Characters such as those in *James and the Giant Peach* are not even human, but they seem real because they have interesting personalities that remind us of humans we know.

Plot

The **plot** is what happens in a story. It is the chain of events in which there is both a **problem** and a **solution.** The problem and its solution may involve conflict or struggle that characters must go through before the conclusion. Follow these steps:

Introduce a problem at the beginning. ▶

In **James and the Giant Peach** by Roald Dahl, James, the main character, is sad and lonely. He wants to meet and play with other kids. His aunts mistreat him and don't allow him to leave the garden. James wishes he could go out and explore the world.

In the middle of the story, show how characters go through conflicts as they act or have things happen to them that bring them closer to a solution. ▶

James gets part of his wish, to explore the world, when he goes on a perilous journey on a giant peach. When the peach floats in the ocean, James must figure out how to protect it from attacking sharks. As it floats in the air, he struggles to protect himself and his fellow travelers from angry Cloud-Men. When they finally approach New York, James must figure out how to land.

Most stories have a climax or highest point of interest that takes place near the end of the story, just before the problem is solved. ▶

When an airplane suddenly cuts the strings that carry the peach, James and his friends believe they are finished as they fall to Earth. In a final surprise they are saved when the peach is spiked on the pinnacle of the Empire State Building.

The conclusion happens after the climax, when readers find out how the problem is solved. ▶

James becomes a hero in New York. The peach stone becomes his new home. He is no longer lonely because both his insect friends and hundreds of kids come to visit and play with him.

Setting

The setting is the **time and place** in which story events take place. If your story has more than one setting, you will need to include descriptions for each one. When you write about a setting, use interesting sensory details to make the scene come alive for readers. Include how the setting looks, smells, sounds, and feels.

Time *When* your story takes place is part of setting. Stories may be set in the past, present, or future. For example, a story occurring in a major city in 1900 might tell about horses and buggies in the streets. A story set 300 years into the future might describe transportation that is entirely different. A setting's time can either be general, such as the recent past when most of *James and the Giant Peach* happens or more specific, such as the day the giant peach grows—*a blazing hot day in the middle of summer.*

Place *Where* your story takes place is the other half of setting. It can be general such as "the south of England" where the book begins or specific such as James's peach stone house in Central Park, New York City. Roald Dahl's more detailed descriptions show how setting may relate to the plot. He describes the garden of James's aunts' house as "large and desolate." It covers the whole top of the hill and has only one tree. The setting shows why James is lonely.

> There was no swing, no seesaw, no sand pit, and no other children were ever invited to come up the hill and play with poor James.

Describe each setting in your story with vivid detail to make it real and interesting for readers. Use descriptions that appeal to sight, smell, touch, and sound to give readers the feeling that they are there. Focus on the features of your setting that relate to the plot and, as the action moves, describe each new setting.

Point of View

Point of view is the position from which a story is told. It is *where* the storyteller or narrator is in relation to the story. When you write a story, be consistent with the point of view you choose.

First Person Point of View

The narrator is one of the characters, often the main character, in the story. The narrator, or main speaker, uses the first person pronouns *I, me, my, we, us,* and *our* to describe what he or she says, does, and thinks. Although the actions and words of other characters are described, only the thoughts of the narrator may be. Use the first person "I" in your writing when you want your readers to feel close to and identify with the narrating character.

Second Person Point of View

Stories written in the second person use the pronoun *you* but are awkward to write and very rare. Stories told verbally sometimes use the second person.

Third Person Point of View

The story is told from a point of view outside the action of the story. The narrator is not a character in the story but is instead an outside observer.

Third-person pronouns *he, she, they, him, her,* and *them* describe what characters say, do, and sometimes think. When you write a story in the third person, you may tell the thoughts and emotions of one character, many characters, or none.

Reading Your Writing

In your writing, take the time to develop your characters, plot, and setting, as well as a single, consistent point of view so readers feel like they've entered a world that's complete.

Using Dialogue

Dialogue is the written conversation between characters in stories. Showing characters talking is great way to make them and the events in your stories come to life.

Take a Look

Here's what dialogue can do for your writing.

▶ Dialogue makes the characters seem real by showing what they think and feel.

"That show about eagles last night was great," said Jake.

▶ Dialogue makes stories seem realistic.

"I'd like to have a job working with birds someday," Angie replied.

▶ Dialogue helps keep readers interested.

"That guy in the show will be speaking here next week," announced Jake.

▶ Dialogue moves the action of the story along.

Angie exclaimed, "Oh, good, let's go hear him!"

Punctuating Dialogue

▶ Dialogue should be enclosed in quotation marks.

"He's the best," said Jamie. "He's the best there is."

▶ Commas and periods always go inside the quotation marks.

"Just a minute," said Mr. Sanchez quickly.

▶ Question marks and exclamation points go inside the quotation marks when the dialogue is itself a question or exclamation.

"Are there any other nominations?" he asked.

▶ Use speaker tags, phrases such as *said Mr. Sanchez, he asked,* and *said Jamie* to let your readers know who is speaking.

Placing Dialogue in Your Story

To make clear who says what, be sure to begin a new paragraph every time the speaker changes. Also, speaker tags are sometimes omitted when one or just a few words at a time are spoken.

Take a Look

Notice the use of speaker tags and paragraphs in dialogue from a story.

> "Susie, thanks for coming over," said Jess.
>
> "Hey," Susie said cheerfully, "what are friends for?"
>
> They stared at the book lying on the table.
>
> "Who would have thought this thing could cause so much trouble?" she sighed.
>
> "What are you going to do?" asked Susie.
> "Try to find out who it really belongs to, I guess," Jess replied.
>
> "Good luck on that."
>
> "I know," said Jess. "But I have a few ideas. Let's get started."

Do you see how the dialogue involves the reader and moves the action of the story along? Does it tell you anything about the characters? Does the writing sound natural, like the way people talk?

Reading Your Writing

Use dialogue to keep readers interested, to provide information about characters' moods and personalities, and also to move the action of your story. Write dialogue so that it sounds natural, and be sure to use punctuation, speaker tags, and paragraphing so your readers are clear on who says what.

Vocabulary

If you made a list of every word you know and use, that would be your vocabulary. As a writer, you need to keep adding to that list, no matter how long it is. The more words you know, the better chance you have of communicating exactly what you want to say to your readers.

▶ Compound Words **312**

▶ Antonyms **313**

▶ Synonyms **314**

▶ Analogies **315**

▶ Connotation **316**

▶ Homophones **318**

▶ Homographs **320**

▶ Words with More Than
One Meaning **322**

▶ Greek and Latin Roots **324**

▶ Prefixes **326**

▶ Suffixes **328**

▶ Context Clues **330**

▶ Across-the-Curriculum Words **332**

▶ Adjectives and Adverbs **334**

▶ Precise Verbs **336**

Compound Words

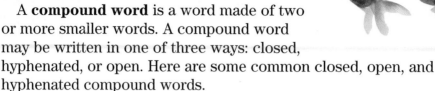

A **compound word** is a word made of two or more smaller words. A compound word may be written in one of three ways: closed, hyphenated, or open. Here are some common closed, open, and hyphenated compound words.

Closed	Open	Hyphenated
barefoot	rain forest	warm-blooded
goldfish	hearing aid	off-season
football	ice storm	play-off

How do you know when a compound should be closed, open, or hyphenated? There are no clear rules, so if you aren't sure, look up the word in the dictionary.

Often, you can tell the meaning of a compound word by studying its smaller words.

At the end of the stream was a **waterfall.** *water* + *fall* = place where *water* is *fall*ing over rocks

You can't always figure out a compound word's meaning based on the words that make it up. For example, *headquarters* doesn't mean "the *heads* of *quarters*"; it means "the main center of command or operations."

Try It

Snowdrift is a common compound word. Based on its two smaller words, what is the definition of *snowdrift*?

Writing Connection

Compound words can help make your writing more specific. For example, its much clearer and easier to write "I put some twigs and leaves in the fireplace" rather than "I put some twigs and leaves in the place inside where we make fires."

Antonyms

Antonyms are words with opposite, or nearly opposite, meanings. The following are pairs of antonyms.

near, far	fast, slow	odd, even	happy, sad

Some words have more than one meaning, and therefore they have more than one antonym.

start, stop	fair, cloudy
start, end	fair, unjust

Antonyms are useful for contrasting things or ideas. Notice how antonyms are used in the paragraph below to contrast two dogs.

The two dogs were different in many ways. Ranger was tall and husky, whereas Muffy was short and dainty. Ranger had short, black fur, whereas Muffy's fur was long and white.

Some words have many synonyms, or words with the same or similar meanings. These words often have many antonyms, too.

brave, courageous, daring	timid, fearful, cowardly

When you choose an antonym in your writing, make sure that it means exactly what you want to express. Often, only one antonym is the best choice for the exact meaning you want to express.

Try It

Replace the underlined words with antonyms to express the opposite meaning.

▶ The <u>old</u> house was <u>small</u> and <u>shabby</u>.

Synonyms

Synonyms are words that have the same, or nearly the same, meanings. For example, *work*, *labor*, and *toil* are synonyms. Here are more groups of synonyms.

> huge, enormous, gigantic   old, aged, ancient

Even though words are synonyms, they are not always interchangeable. You must decide which words express your thoughts most exactly. For example, some words whose meanings are similar to *unhappy* include *gloomy*, *sullen*, and *dismal*. However, because these words all have slightly different meanings from *unhappy*, they can't be substituted for one another.

Read the paragraphs below. Notice how the first is different from the second, even though the ideas are basically the same.

> It was a hot day, and the waves were rolling up on the beach. We ran into the ocean and dunked our heads under the cold water. The cold waves felt soothing against our sunburned skin.

> It was a sweltering day, and the waves were crashing onto the beach. We dashed into the ocean and dunked our heads under the cold water. The cold waves felt refreshing against our hot skin.

Writing Connection

When you use synonyms, rather than using the same words over and over, your writing is much more interesting.

Analogies

An **analogy** is a comparison of two words based on how the two words are related. Here are some examples of how words can be related.

Synonyms

The relationship between the words in the pairs below is that they are synonyms, or mean the same thing.

> *neat* is to *tidy* as *tiny* is to *small*

Antonyms

The relationship between the words in the pairs below is that they are antonyms, or opposites.

> *kind* is to *cruel* as *noise* is to *quiet*

Part to Whole

The relationship between the words in the pairs below is that the first word names something that is a part of the whole thing named by the second word.

> *sleeve* is to *coat* as *arm* is to *body*

Object to Group

The relationship between the words in the pairs below is that the first word is an object that is part of the larger group named by the second word.

> *cat* is to *animal* as *banana* is to *fruit*

Try It

What word best completes the following analogy?

▶ *Hammer* is to *tool* as *sweater* is to _____.

Connotation

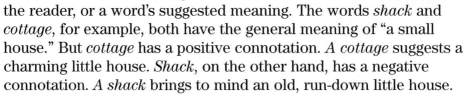

Would you rather be called called "clever" or "cunning"? You likely would rather be called "clever" because of its connotation. **Connotation** is the feeling a word creates in the reader, or a word's suggested meaning. The words *shack* and *cottage*, for example, both have the general meaning of "a small house." But *cottage* has a positive connotation. *A cottage* suggests a charming little house. *Shack*, on the other hand, has a negative connotation. *A shack* brings to mind an old, run-down little house.

Here are some more words with similar meanings but different connotations.

Positive	Negative
slender	skinny
fragile	weak
confident	conceited
thrifty	stingy
determined	stubborn
brave	reckless

When you write, you often choose a word from among a group of synonyms because of its connotation. For example, the words *small* and *puny* have similar meanings, but you would use the word *puny* only if you wanted to express a negative image.

In the sentence below, depending upon what you mean to say, one word fits better than the other because of the words' connotations.

My friends were (**chatting/gossiping**) about me when I joined them.

Although both *chatting* and *gossiping* have the basic meaning of "talk," *chatting* suggests a light-hearted, friendly conversation. *Gossiping* suggests an unkind and even harmful conversation. You would choose the word that most exactly communicates what you want to say.

Using Connotation in Your Writing

Writers use the connotations of words to produce positive or negative images in readers' minds. For example, if a writer wants readers to like a certain character in a story, the writer will use words with positive connotations to describe that character. If you read that a character is cheerful, kind, and helpful, you probably will like that character.

Here are two paragraphs that present the same basic information. Because some of the words have different connotations, the tone and meaning of each paragraph is different. Which paragraph produces a negative image in your mind? Why?

As I approached the house of the people who live next door, their hound began to growl. It glared fiercely and aggressively at me. Just as the beast lunged at me, the woman shrieked at it to stop.

As I approached my neighbors' house, their dog began to bark. It gazed steadily and confidently at me. Just as the dog approached me, my neighbor commanded it to stay.

Try It

Read the sentences below. How do the underlined words affect the meaning of the sentences?

▶ The boy gobbled his sandwich and then slurped his milkshake.

▶ The boy ate his sandwich and then drank his milkshake.

Writing Connection

Knowing the connotations of words helps you choose words that express your ideas exactly. It also helps you create positive or negative images in your readers' minds.

Homophones

What's wrong with the sentence below? If you say it out loud, it seems to be fine. In written form, it doesn't make sense.

Theirs two** much **reign too** play **bawl.

The italicized words are homophones. Homophones are two or more words that sound the same but that have different meanings and spellings. Because homophones sound the same, it is easy to write one word when you mean another.

Some Common Homophones

to	I took my little brother <u>to</u> the baseball game.
too	I had <u>two</u> tickets.
two	My sister wanted to come <u>too</u>.
by	I walked <u>by</u> the bakery after school.
buy	I wanted to <u>buy</u> some bagels.
hole	The bagel has a <u>hole</u> in the middle.
whole	I didn't eat the <u>whole</u> bagel.
their	Did the girls forget <u>their</u> books?
they're	<u>They're</u> going to the library.
there	They go <u>there</u> every Thursday.
your	Where is <u>your</u> coat?
you're	<u>You're</u> going to need it today.
its	The dog wagged <u>its</u> tail.
it's	<u>It's</u> time to feed the dog.
hear	Did you <u>hear</u> that noise?
here	I think it came from over <u>here</u>.

More Homophones

Even when you know the different meanings of homophones, they can still cause spelling problems because they sound the same. When you proofread your writing, be alert for homophones. More common homophones are listed below. These are a little trickier than the homophones on the previous page because they aren't used as often.

pair	I have a new pair of shoes.
pear	This pear is ripe and juicy.
pare	I will pare the potatoes before I boil them.
rain	The gentle rain fell softly on the grass.
reign	The reign of Queen Victoria lasted for more than fifty years.
rein	The rider tightened the left rein to turn the horse to the left.
whether	Do you know whether rain is expected today?
weather	The weather has been sunny all week.
knight	A knight wore armor for protection.
night	Owls usually hunt at night.

Try It

Which homophones correctly complete the sentence?
Do you know (weather/whether) you can (buy/by) a new bike?

Writing Connection

Because homophones sound the same, it's easy to make a mistake by writing one homophone when you really mean another. When you proofread your writing, you can make sure that you've used the correct spelling of a word that has homophones.

Homographs

Some words are spelled exactly the same way but have different meanings and origins. These words are called **homographs.** For example, the word *arms* has two meanings: "human upper limbs" and "weapons."

Many homographs also are pronounced the same way. Some of these are shown below.

The <u>duck</u> waddled back to the pond. (large, wild bird) He had to <u>duck</u> his head when he entered the house. (lower suddenly)
What is the <u>date</u> of your birthday? (time at which an event occurs) A <u>date</u> is similar to a raisin, only larger. (sweet, dark fruit)
The ice is <u>firm</u> enough for us to go ice-skating. (solid; hard) My mother works for a law <u>firm</u> downtown. (company)
The gardener will <u>prune</u> the rose bushes. (trim) I had a sandwich, a salad, and a <u>prune</u> for lunch. (a dried plum)
The water in the <u>pool</u> is refreshingly cool. (tank filled with water) My dad taught me to play <u>pool</u>. (game played with balls on a table)
My mother likes to <u>rest</u> after dinner. (relax) I will eat the <u>rest</u> of my sandwich later. (remainder)
I like raspberry <u>jam</u> on my toast. (fruit preserve) Mother tells me not to <u>jam</u> all my clothes together in the closet. (squeeze)
I will <u>clip</u> my younger sister's hair. (cut; trim) I need to <u>clip</u> these papers together. (attach)
I <u>felt</u> the icy wind stinging my cheeks. (did feel) A pool table is usually covered with <u>felt</u>. (soft cloth)
I <u>left</u> early for the party. (did leave) I turned <u>left</u> at the intersection. (direction)
Complete solar eclipses are <u>rare</u>. (uncommon) Do you like your steak cooked <u>rare</u>? (not cooked much)
I can hardly hear you above that <u>racket</u> coming from the stadium. (noise) I brought my <u>racket</u> and balls so we can play tennis. (paddle used in tennis)

More Homographs

Some homographs are pronounced differently.

A single <u>tear</u> slid down the baby's cheek. (drop of moisture from the eye) Did you <u>tear</u> your new coat? (rip)
The girls <u>wound</u> ribbons in their hair. (wrapped) Did you <u>wound</u> your knee when you fell? (hurt)
Pencils used to be made of <u>lead</u>. (metallic element) Will you <u>lead</u> the hikers along the trail? (show the way)
The <u>dove</u> flew away to its nest. (bird) We <u>dove</u> into the cool water. (did dive)
Will you please <u>close</u> the door? (shut) Make sure no one is standing <u>close</u> to it. (near)

Some homographs that have more than one syllable are pronounced differently because the accent shifts.

I will <u>record</u> the results of my science experiment. (write down) I played an old <u>record</u> that my dad used to listen to. (music disk)
Our test will cover the <u>content</u> of this science chapter. (all things inside) I will be <u>content</u> to sit here and enjoy the sunshine. (satisfied)
The Sahara is the world's largest <u>desert</u>. (hot, dry area) Please don't <u>desert</u> me now! (leave)

Try It

How is the word *wound* pronounced in each use below?
▶ The nurse wound a bandage around the wound on my arm.

Writing Connection

You don't have to worry about spelling mistakes when you use homographs in your writing. You only need to know the different meanings.

Words with More Than One Meaning

Some words are spelled the same way and have the same origins but different meanings. For example, the word *engage* has two meanings: "to bind oneself to do something," as in engage oneself to be married, and "to arrange for the use or services of," as to engage a gardener to take care of a garden.

Most words that have more than one meaning and the same origin are also are pronounced the same way. Some of these are shown below.

The band's music was very <u>loud</u>. (noisy) The singer wore a <u>loud</u> checkered shirt. (unpleasantly bold or bright in color)
My friends and I are going shopping at the <u>mall</u>. (a group of stores) The cherry trees were in full bloom all along the <u>mall</u>. (a grassy strip between two roadways)
My brother is big and <u>strong</u>. (having great physical power) A <u>strong</u> wind shook the leaves from the tree. (moving with great speed or force) By the time we finished our game, I had built my army to 500 soldiers <u>strong</u>. (having a specified number)
I finally figured out the <u>solution</u> to the math problem. (answer) I washed the car with a strong cleaning <u>solution</u>. (a liquid in which something has been dissolved)
We viewed the ruins of an ancient <u>pueblo</u> in Arizona. (a village of Native Americans) The <u>Pueblo</u> make beautiful silver and turquoise jewelry. (Native American people of Arizona and New Mexico)

More Multiple-Meaning Words

Many words that have more than one meaning are related to science. These words often have a second meaning that describes a specific scientific concept. Some of these are shown below.

I cannot <u>force</u> my brother to help me. (to make someone do something) The <u>force</u> of the moon's gravity acts on Earth's oceans. (an influence that produces a change in speed or direction of motion on an object)
My grandmother appreciates the <u>frequency</u> of my visits. (the condition of happening often) Radio waves have low <u>frequency</u>. (the number of waves that pass a fixed point each second)
The constant barking of our neighbors' dog has caused <u>friction</u> between them and my parents. (disagreement) The <u>friction</u> of the book against the floor caused the book to stop sliding. (the force that resists motion between two bodies in contact)
The pilot had to <u>circle</u> the plane over the airport. (move around) We must measure the diameter of the <u>circle</u>. (a closed curve, every point of which is equidistant from the center)

Try It

What are two related but different meanings of the word *lid?*

Writing Connection

Many related words with more than one meaning have very specific definitions for one of their meanings. Learning these meaning will help you express specific concepts in your writing.

Greek and Latin Roots

Many English words have Greek and Latin roots. When you know the meanings of a word's root or roots, you can sometimes figure out the word's general meaning.

Greek Roots

Study the Greek roots and their meanings given below.

Root	Meaning	Sample Words and Definitions
bio	life	*biology:* the study of life *biologist:* a scientist who specializes in biology
geo	earth	*geology:* the study of the history of the earth *geothermal:* heated by Earth
graph	write	*autograph:* a person's signature *telegraph:* a written message sent a long distance
mech	machine	*mechanic:* a person who works on machines *mechanism:* a tool or device
meter	measure	*diameter:* the width of a circle *barometer:* an instrument that measures the pressure of the atmosphere
phon	sound	*phonics:* the study of sound *telephone:* an instrument used for speaking over long distances

In your reading, look for words that have the roots described in this lesson. Try to figure out the meanings of the words based on their roots.

Latin Roots

Study the Latin roots and their meanings given below.

Root	Meaning	Sample Words and Definitions
aqua	water	*aquarium:* tank in which animals that live in water are kept *aquatic:* growing or living in water
aud	hear	*audiocassette:* a cassette that is listened to *inaudible:* not able to be heard
dic	speak	*dictate:* to say something aloud to be recorded *diction:* the way in which words are pronounced
form	shape	*transform:* to change the shape or appearance of *reform:* to change one's habits for the better
ject	throw	*eject:* to throw out; cause to leave *reject:* to throw out or discard
ped	foot	*pedal:* a lever worked by the foot *pedestrian:* a person walking
struct	build	*structure:* anything that is built *construct:* build

Fun Fact

More than 60 percent of English words are based on Latin words, and many others are based on Greek roots.

Try It
Based on its roots, what is the definition of the word biography?

Writing Connection
When you know the meanings of Latin and Greek roots, you can figure out the meanings of many unfamiliar words that have these roots. As you learn new words, you will expand the vocabulary that you use in writing.

Prefixes

A **prefix** is one or more letters added to the beginning of a root or base word that changes the word's meaning. For example, when the prefix *re-* is added to the word view, the meaning becomes "view again." When the prefix *pre-* is added to *view*, the meaning becomes "view before."

Some prefixes have the same or similar meanings. Knowing the meanings of prefixes will help you figure out the meanings of unfamiliar words. Look at the list of prefixes below. Notice how each prefix changes the meaning of the base word.

Prefix	Meaning(s)	Sample Words
anti-	against	antibacterial, antifreeze
bi-	two	bicycle, bipartisan
dis-	not; opposite	disagree, disapprove
im-	not	impractical, impossible
in-	not	inactive, inexact
inter-	among; between	interweave, interstate
mis-	not; wrong	miscalculate, misbehave
non-	not	nonpoisonous, nonstop
over-	too much	overdo, overworked
pre-	before	preheat, predate
re-	again	redo, repaint
semi-	half	semicircle, semimonthly
tri-	three	triplet, tricycle
un-	not; the opposite of	unwise, unhappy

Prefixes Change the Meaning of Words

Below are some words with prefixes used in sentences. Notice how each prefix changes the meaning of the word.

> The coach <u>approved</u> of his players' behavior.
> The coach <u>disapproved</u> of his players' behavior.

> The child was <u>impatient</u> and <u>unhappy</u>.
> The child was <u>patient</u> and <u>happy</u>.

Keep in mind that you can't add all prefixes to all words. For example, although you might want to combine the prefix *un-* with the word *appear*, *unappear* is not a word. The word that correctly expresses this meaning is *disappear*. If you are unsure about adding a prefix to a word, check the dictionary.

Even when you know the meaning of a prefix, you might not be able to figure out a word's meaning. This sometimes happens because the base word also has an ending. Other times, you may not know the meaning of the base word. You must then look up the meaning of the base word with its prefix in the dictionary.

Look at the words below. Which meanings could you figure out if you separated the base word from its ending?

Word	Meaning	Prefix	Base Word
illegible	not readable	*il-*	legible
overprotected	too much protected	*over-*	protected

Writing Connection

By learning the meanings of prefixes, you will understand how they change the meanings of words, which will increase your vocabulary.

Suffixes

A **suffix** is one or more letters added to the end of a root or base word that changes the word's meaning. A suffix can also change the part of speech of a word. For example, adding *-ful* to the noun *hope* makes the word *hopeful*, an adjective.

Knowing the meanings of suffixes will help you figure out the meanings of unfamiliar words. Look at the chart below and notice how each suffix changes the meaning of the base word.

Suffix	Meaning	Sample Words
-able/-ible	is, able to	workable, sensible
-er/-or	one who	singer, actor
-ful	full of	careful, graceful
-ish	relating to	selfish, childish
-ist	one who performs or practices	guitarist, geologist
-less	without	helpless, tireless
-ly	like; resembling	motherly, slowly
-ment	state or condition of	enjoyment, contentment
-ness	state; condition; quality of	goodness, fairness
-ure	action; process	enclosure, procedure
-y	being or having	sticky, funny

Try It

How does the suffix change the meaning of the word?

▶ I spent a <u>restful</u> night at the inn.

I spent a <u>restless</u> night at the inn.

Rules for Adding Suffixes

When you add suffixes to base words, follow the rules below.

If a suffix begins with a vowel and the base word ends with a silent *e,* drop the *e* before adding the suffix:
    desire + able = desirable
    blue + ish = bluish
    expose + ure = exposure

If a base word ends with a *y,* change the *y* to *i* before adding the suffix—unless the suffix begins with an *i:*
    beauty + ful = beautiful
    rely + able = reliable
    geology + ist = geologist
    fury + ious + furious

Keep in mind that you can't add all suffixes to all words. For example, although you might want to add the suffix *-ful* to the base word *friend, friendful* is not a word. If you are unsure about adding a suffix to a word, look it up in the dictionary.

Even if you know the meaning of a word's suffix, you might not be able to figure out the word's meaning because you don't know the meaning of the base word. For example, you may come across the word *perishable.* Even though you know that the suffix *-able* means "is" or "able to," if you don't know that *perish* means "spoil" or "die," you won't be able to define the word. In this case, you must look up the meaning of the base word or the word with its suffix in the dictionary.

Writing Connection

By learning the meanings of suffixes, you will understand how they change the meanings of words. As you learn these new meanings, you will increase your vocabulary. The more words you know, the better you will be able to express yourself in writing.

Context Clues

What do you do when you come across an unfamiliar word in your reading? Before you reach for a dictionary, you probably try to figure out the meaning of the word by looking at the context. The **context** is the words and sentences that surround the unfamiliar word. The context usually gives you clues about the meaning of the unfamiliar word.

There are different kinds of context clues. In this lesson, you will learn some tips for finding and using context clues to figure out the meanings of unfamiliar words.

Tips for Using Context Clues

Some writers use a *definition*. They give the meaning of the word within the sentence or surrounding sentences. Look for clue words such as *or*, *that is*, and *in other words*. These all point to a definition.

> Frogs are *amphibians*, or animals that live both on land and in the water.

Some writers *compare* or *contrast* the unfamiliar word with another word. Look for comparison and contrast words, such as *also*, *like*, *too*, *but*, *unlike*, and *on the other hand*.

> Unlike many other *predatory* birds, owls hunt at night.

Cause-and-effect relationships may also be used to explain an unfamiliar word. Look for words such as *because*, *as a result*, and *therefore*.

> Because owls are *nocturnal*, their eyes are well adapted to darkness.

More Tips for Using Context Clues

Often an unfamiliar word appears in a *series*. Sometimes you can figure out the meaning of the word based on the other words in the series.

> The crown was made of diamonds, rubies, emeralds, and *amethysts*.

Sometimes you have to use the general context to figure out the meaning of a word because there are no specific clues available.

> Our cancelled flight put us in a difficult *predicament*.

Another example is the word *pound*. It has several different meanings, including "a unit of weight," "to hit again and again," "to drive into," as to *pound* a stake into the ground, and "pen or fenced area." How can you tell which meaning fits this sentence?

> We chose our pet from among the dogs at the pound.

First you can tell that *pound* is used as noun. From this context clue, you know that *pound* in this sentence does not mean "to hit again and again" or "to drive into." By further studying the word's context, you can tell that the meaning "a unit of measure" doesn't make sense. Thus, you can determine that the meaning of *pound* in the sentence above is "a pen or fenced area."

Try It

Use the context clues in the sentence below to figure out the meaning of *legumes* in the sentence below.

▶ I like peas, beans, and other *legumes*.

Across-the-Curriculum Words

In school you use vocabulary words that are specific to each subject that you study. In this lesson you will learn some words commonly used in math, science, social studies, and health.

Math

combine: add together

denominator: the part of a fraction written below the line

division: the mathematical operation of finding out how many times one number is contained in another number

equivalent: equal

minimum: the least amount

maximum: the greatest amount

numerator: the part of a fraction written above the line

percent: one part of 100

sequence: an ordered set of numbers

Science

carnivore: an animal that eats other animals

constellation: a group of stars

habitat: a place where an animal or plant naturally lives

herbivore: an animal that eats only plants

iceberg: a large floating mass of ice detached from a glacier

mammal: a warm-blooded animal that nurses its young

omnivore: an animal that eats both plants and other animals

parasite: an organism that lives off another organism

reptile: a cold-blooded animal

Social Studies

candidate: a person running for office

civil rights: the individual rights of citizens guaranteed by the U.S. Constitution

Congress: the chief law-making body of the United States made of the Senate and House of Representatives

currency: money

export: to sell or carry goods to other countries

import: to buy or bring goods into a country

frontier: the imaginary line that marks division between settled and unexplored territory

government: the laws and customs of a political unit and the people who enforce them

urban: relating to a city

veto: to refuse to approve a bill

Health

bacteria: tiny organisms that can cause disease

cardiovascular: related to the heart and blood vessels

contagious: easily spread from one person to another

carcinogen: something that causes cancer

diagnosis: the act of identifying a disease based on symptoms

digestion: the process of converting food into simpler forms

epidermis: the outer layer of skin

molar: large tooth located in the rear of mouth

symptom: a change in normal body functions that indicates disease

Fun Fact

A majority of science, math, health, and social studies words have Greek or Latin origins.

Try It

Choose a word from each of the lists in this lesson. Define the words using your own words.

Adjectives and Adverbs

Adjectives and adverbs describe, or modify, other words. Adjectives modify nouns. Adverbs modify verbs, adjectives, and other adverbs. When adjectives and adverbs appeal to the senses, writing is more specific, vivid, and interesting.

Adjectives and adverbs limit the meanings of the words they describe. In other words, they make the meanings of the words they describe more specific. Read these sentences.

> The rain fell onto the soil.
> The light rain fell silently onto the parched soil.

In the first sentence, the noun *rain* could mean any kind of rain—heavy rain, steady rain, light rain, damaging rain, and so on. Also, the verb *fell* could mean fell in any way—continuously, loudly, and so on. The same is true of the general word *soil*. Because *rain*, *fell*, and *soil* are so general, the reader comes away with a fuzzy picture after reading this sentence.

In the second sentence, the meaning of the general noun *rain* is now limited to mean only rain that is light and gentle. The general verb *fell* is now limited by the adverb *silently. Also*, the general noun *soil* is now limited to soil that is parched. These modifiers appeal to the senses. They give the reader a much clearer and more vivid image of the scene.

Choose adjectives and adverbs in your writing that will give specific information to your readers. What exactly do you want your readers to visualize?

The noun and verb in the group of sentences below are the same, but the adjectives and adverbs are different. Notice how the different adjectives and adverbs communicate different ideas.

> The rider stopped his bike.
> The *nervous* rider stopped his bike *shakily* and *suddenly*.
> The experienced rider stopped his bike *smoothly* and *easily*.

Words to Avoid

Try not to use adjectives and adverbs that are overused, especially those that don't appeal to the senses. Adjectives such as *nice*, *good*, *pretty*, and *bad* are used so much that they don't have much meaning. They aren't specific, so they don't give the reader a clear image. The same is true of overused adverbs such as *very*, *really*, and *quite*.

Connotation

Sometimes you choose between two modifiers that are similar in meaning based on what *feeling* is connected with each. This feeling is called the word's **connotation**. (See pages 316–317 for more on connotation.) By choosing words that express certain feelings, you relay these feelings to your reader. For example, although *stingy* and *thrifty* both have the general meaning of "frugal," *stingy* has a negative connotation, while *thrifty* has a positive connotation. You would choose one word over the other based on whether you wanted to express a positive image or a negative image.

Try It

What adjectives and adverbs could you add to the sentence below to express a positive image?

▶ The girl sang a song.

Writing Connection

When you use precise adjectives and adverbs in your writing, you give your readers clear images. You can convey positive or negative images of things or actions simply by choosing accurate words to describe them. Vivid, specific adjectives and adverbs also make your writing more enjoyable for your readers.

Precise Verbs

Most verbs express action. They tell what is going on. The verb is therefore the word in the sentence that usually communicates the most meaning. This is why you should be especially careful in choosing verbs.

When you choose a verb, think about exactly what kind of information you want to give your readers. What exactly do you want your readers to visualize?

Study the verbs below. Notice how each group of verbs has a slightly different meaning. Visualize each action as you read.

As a writer, you know exactly what you want to communicate. Choosing precise verbs gives you the ability to connect with your readers in the most effective way.

look	gaze	glare	stare
take	grab	seize	retrieve
like	enjoy	adore	cherish
shine	glisten	glow	radiate
eat	nibble	gobble	munch
run	race	sprint	jog
hold	cradle	grasp	clutch
throw	heave	toss	hurl
cut	hack	split	trim
make	create	construct	build
come	arrive	appear	approach
say	state	remark	speak

Let's Get Specific

Read each of the following descriptions. Notice how the choice of verbs affects your idea of what's happening.

The puppy *approached* the boy. It *hesitated* before getting onto his lap.

The puppy *ran* to the boy and *scrambled* onto his lap.

Often, the most precise verb is the verb that is most specific.   In the examples above, the words *approached* and *hesitated* communicate a very different image than *ran* and *scrambled*.

Verbs and Connotations

Sometimes you choose between two verbs that are similar in meaning based on the connotation that is connected with each.

What connotation is associated with the verb in each sentence?

The girl *tattled* about what happened.
The girl *told* what happened.

The word *tattled* has a negative connotation. The reader gets the feeling that the girl told what happened to get other people in trouble. However, the word *told* is general. It doesn't express much information.

Try It

Replace the verbs to create a more positive image.
▶ The boy glared at his friend as he grabbed his coat.

Rules for Writing:
Grammar, Usage, and Mechanics

You know about rules. When you know and follow the rules of a game, you're better at the game. It's the same with writing. Knowing the rules and following them will make you a better writer.

▶Grammar **340**

▶Usage **364**

▶Mechanics **378**

Grammar

Grammar is about how language is organized. Parts of speech, such as nouns and verbs, are grammar. The names for different parts of a sentence, such as subject and predicate, are grammar. The names for different types of sentences, such as simple, compound, and complex, are grammar. Knowing about grammar helps you understand how to build sentences that make sense to your readers.

▶ Nouns **342**

▶ Pronouns **344**

▶ Verbs **346**

▶ Adjectives and Adverbs **348**

▶ Prepositions **350**

▶ Conjunctions and Interjections . . . **351**

▶ Subjects and Predicates **352**

▶ Direct Objects
and Indirect Objects **354**

▶ Modifiers—Words and Phrases . . . **355**

▶ Clauses **356**

▶ Sentences: Simple,
Compound, and Complex **358**

▶ Problems with Sentence
Structure **360**

▶ Kinds of Sentences **363**

Nouns

Nouns name everything. For example, nouns name persons, places, things, and ideas.

Person	niece, Gabriella, dentist, soccer coach
Place	San Diego, camp, race track, beach
Thing	skateboard, jewelry, sand, picture
Idea	freedom, stubbornness, decade

A **common noun** names *any* person, place, thing, or idea. It is *general*.

A **proper noun** names a *particular* person, place, or thing. It is *specific*. Notice the two words in the above chart that are capitalized. They are the only proper nouns. Proper nouns are always capitalized. All the rest are common nouns. A common noun isn't capitalized unless it's the first word in a sentence.

	Common noun	Proper noun
(person)	principal	Ms. Garcia
(place)	school	Barkley Elementary
(thing)	tour	Statue of Liberty Tour
(idea)	war	Civil War

Remember, common nouns begin with lowercase letters, unless they begin a sentence. Proper nouns are always capitalized.

Common nouns can be concrete or abstract. **Concrete nouns** name the things you can see, touch, hear, smell, or taste. **Abstract nouns** name ideas, qualities, and feelings. You cannot normally perceive them with your senses.

Try It

Which nouns are concrete and which are abstract?
water, confidence, smoke, beauty, whisper, wood

Singular and Plural Nouns

If a noun names one person, place, thing, or idea, it is a **singular noun.** If it names more than one, it is a **plural noun.**

▶ Most of the time, a singular noun can be made plural by adding *s*.

Examples: horse → horses   orange → oranges

▶ Some nouns add *es* to form the plural.

Examples: glass → glasses   tax → taxes   ditch → ditches tomato → tomatoes

▶ Other nouns change the end of the word before adding *s* or *es*.

Examples: calf → calves   country → countries

▶ Some nouns do not add *s* or *es* to form the plural.

Examples: child → children   man → men   goose → geese foot → feet

▶ Some nouns do not change at all. The singular and plural forms are the same.

Examples: moose, deer, salmon

▶ Compound nouns that are hyphenated or written as more than one word become plural by adding *s* to the main noun.

Examples: sister-in-law → sisters-in-law   vice president → vice presidents

Possessive Nouns

A noun that shows ownership or possession of things or qualities is a **possessive noun.** Possessive nouns can be singular or plural. Singular possessive nouns are formed by adding *'s*.

Kyle wanted to go to **Cameron's** house.

Plural possessive nouns are formed by adding *'s* to plural nouns not ending in *s*. Plural nouns already ending in *s* simply add an apostrophe to the end.

The geese's eggs were outside my cousins' tent.

Writing Connection

Do not write *it's* when you mean *its*. *It's* is a contraction and *its* is a possessive pronoun.

Pronouns

A **pronoun** is a word used in place of one or more nouns.

Cody ate a large slice of blueberry pie. **He** even asked for seconds.

He is the pronoun that replaces **Cody,** the antecedent.
An **antecedent** is the word referred to or replaced by a pronoun.

Personal Pronouns

Pronouns that refer to people or things are called **personal pronouns.** The three types of personal pronouns—subject pronouns, object pronouns, and possessive pronouns—perform different functions in sentences.

Use a **subject pronoun** as the subject of a sentence and also as the predicate noun. **I** would love to go to the laser show. (subject)

It is **I.** (predicate noun)

Use an **object pronoun** as a **direct object** or as an **indirect object.**

We remember **him.** (direct object)

The neighbors gave **us** tickets. (indirect object)

I hiked to the cliff, and the view gave **me** goose bumps.

Notice how *I* and *me* are used in this compound sentence. *I* and *me* mean the same thing, but *I* functions as the subject of one clause, and *me* functions as the indirect object of the other clause.

Type	Pronouns	Function
Subject Pronouns	I, you, she, it, we, they	subject or predicate noun
Object Pronouns	me, you, her, him, it, us, you, them	direct object, indirect object, object of preposition

Possessive Pronouns

A **possessive pronoun** shows ownership. It can be used alone or before a noun.

> She gave me **his** beach towel. Where is **mine?**

These possessive pronouns go before nouns: *my, your, her, his, our, your,* and *their.*

Use these alone: *mine, yours, hers, his, its, ours, yours,* and *theirs.*

More Types of Pronouns

Reflexive and Intensive Pronouns A reflexive pronoun ends with -self or -selves and refers back to the subject.

> Example: Gabe and Ian made **themselves** co-captains of the soccer team.

An **intensive pronoun** ends with *-self* or *-selves* and emphasizes a noun or pronoun.

> Example: Gabe and Ian **themselves** cleaned the field.

Interrogative Pronouns An interrogative pronoun asks a question.

> Example: ***Whose*** shin guards are these?

Relative Pronouns A relative pronoun introduces a word group called a relative clause.

> The captains organized the team members, **who** were eager to play.

Demonstrative Pronouns A demonstrative pronoun points out a specific person, place, thing, or idea.

> **That** was an extraordinary shot.

Indefinite Pronouns An indefinite pronoun doesn't refer to a specific person, place, thing, or idea.

> **Everybody** on the team wants to go to the soccer clinic.

Soccer is the number-one sport in the world. It is called *football* or *futbol* in many countries.

Writing Connection
Pronouns provide variety and prevent the repetition of nouns.

Verbs

A **verb** is a word that shows action or expresses a state of being.

Action Verbs

Action verbs add energy and precision to sentences. The action of the verbs can be seen or unseen. *I* **understand** *the problem.* **Understand** is a verb in which the action is unseen. *The bottle* **fell** *from the rack.* **Fell** is a verb in which the action is seen.

State-of-Being Verbs

State-of-being verbs do not show action. They express a condition of existence.

> Olivia **was** on a vacation.

Forms of *be* are the most commonly used state-of-being verbs. The forms of *be* are *is, am, are, was, were, be, being,* and *been*. *Seem* and *become* are also state-of-being verbs.

Some verbs can function either as an action verb or a state-of being-verb.

remain appear look turn stay taste smell feel sound grow

> The dog **smells** the skunk. (action verb)
>
> It **smells** like a skunk. (state-of-being verb)

Linking Verbs

A **linking verb** is a state-of-being verb that connects the subject to a noun, pronoun, or adjective in the predicate.

> Janice **is** an artist.

Auxiliary Verbs

An **auxiliary,** or helping, **verb** helps the main verb show action or express a state of being.

> Jane and Emilio **are** painting a mural.

> **Common Auxiliary Verbs**
> do, did, does, am, is, are, was, were, be, being, been, have, has, had, may, might, must, can, could, will, would, shall, should

Helping verbs can help show **when** something happens.

> Jane and Emilio **were** painting a mural. (action continuing in the past)
>
> Jane and Emilio **are** painting a mural. (action continuing in the present)
>
> Jane and Emilio **will** paint a mural. (action to happen in the future)

Verb Phrases

One or more auxiliary verbs combined with the main verb make a verb phrase. We **have been watching** their progress.

Notice that the verb phrase, *have been watching*, has two helping verbs.

Active and Passive Voice

The **active voice** of a verb is used when the subject performs the verb's action.

> Emilio **brushed** the dog.

Emilio is the subject performing the verb's action: *brushed*.

The **passive voice** of a verb is used when the subject receives the verb's action.

> The dog **was brushed** by Emilio.

Dog is the subject receiving the action of the verb *was brushed*.

Writing Connection

To keep readers involved, use the active voice in your writing as often as possible.

Adjectives and Adverbs

An **adjective** is a word that describes or modifies a noun or pronoun. Adjectives modify in three ways. They show **what kind, how many,** and **which one.**

> Hurricanes create **rough** seas. **(what kind)**
>
> Last year the flooding destroyed **fifteen** houses. **(how many)**
>
> **That** hurricane hit harder than most. **(which one)**

Adjectives usually, but not always, come before the nouns they modify. Notice how these adjectives follow the verb but modify the noun.

> The waves are **strong.** (modifies waves)
>
> The mayor looks **tired.** (modifies mayor)

Articles

The, *a*, and *an* belong to a special group of adjectives called **articles.**

A and *an* are called indefinite articles. They refer to one of a group of people, places, things, or ideas. Use *a* before nouns beginning with a consonant sound. Use *an* before nouns beginning with a vowel sound. Examples: **a** hurricane, **an** overcoat

The is the definite article because it identifies specific people, places, things, or ideas. Examples: **the** storm, **the** houses

Adjectives

Adjectives such as *this, these, that,* and *those* point out particular nouns.

> **These** moccasins are mine. **That** horse is his.

This, these, that, and *those* are demonstrative pronouns when they take the place of a noun in a sentence.

> **These** are my moccasins. **That** is his horse.

Proper Adjectives

Proper adjectives are adjectives formed from proper nouns. They are almost always capitalized.

> Examples: *Chinese lantern, Japanese beetle, English muffin*

Hyphenated Adjectives

Adjectives can be created by combining words with hyphens. **Fresh-picked** zucchini, **gale-force** winds, **less-than-friendly** lion.

Adverbs

An **adverb** is a word that modifies a verb, an adjective, or another adverb. Adverbs often tell *how, when, where,* or *to what extent* an action is performed.

The Girl Scouts **carefully** cleaned up the city park. (modifies verb *cleaned*)

They picked up trash stuck in the **extremely** muddy ground. (modifies adjective *muddy*)

The troop leader **very** proudly awarded them badges. (modifies adverb *proudly*)

The girls **happily** accepted their awards. (tells how)

As a result of the troop's hard work, the park cleanup ended **early.** (tells when)

The scouts decided to stay **there** for the afternoon. (tells where)

Adverbs often have *-ly* endings: *frequently, calmly, wisely, shyly.* Watch for the few *-ly* words that are adjectives: *lonely, friendly, lively, kindly,* and *lovely.* You can tell they are adjectives because they describe nouns and pronouns.

Try It

Identify the adjectives and adverbs in these sentences.

▶ The friendly troop leader carefully explained that cleaning the park was the girls' idea.

▶ The proud parents listened happily as the troop leader spoke kindly about their children.

Writing Connection

Adjectives and adverbs make your writing more powerful. They help the reader to understand your meaning more clearly.

Prepositions

A **preposition** relates a noun or pronoun to the rest of a sentence. The noun or pronoun that follows the preposition is called the **object of the preposition.**

The actors waited **behind** the curtain. The preposition is **behind.** It connects the noun *curtain* to the rest of the sentence. *Curtain* is the object of the preposition.

Common Prepositions

aboard	around	by	inside	through
about	at	down	into	to
above	before	during	like	unto
across	behind	except	of	under
after	below	for	off	up
against	beneath	from	on top of	upon
along	beside	in	over	with
among	between	in front of	since	within

Prepositional Phrases

A **prepositional phrase** is a group of words that begins with a preposition and ends with the object of the preposition.

Akiko climbed **over the boulders.**

Writing Connection

Prepositions help the reader organize characters and events in your writing. They provide order for and show the position of the things you write about.

Conjunctions and Interjections

A **conjunction** is a word used to connect words or groups of words.

Coordinating Conjunctions A **coordinating conjunction** connects independent parts, or clauses, that have equal importance in a sentence. *And, but,* and *or* are coordinating conjunctions.

> Would you like a scavenger hunt **or** a long hike?
>
> The scavenger hunt sounds like fun, **but** I would like to hike.
>
> To begin the hunt, walk to the bridge **and** look for a message.

Correlative Conjunctions **Correlative conjunctions** work in pairs to join words and groups of words. *Either-or* and *neither-nor* are correlative conjunctions.

> **Neither** Abby **nor** Lena looked under the log.
>
> **Either** hunt for small sticks **or** begin digging the fire pit.

Subordinating Conjunctions A **subordinating conjunction** joins two clauses, or groups of words, in a way that makes one dependent on the other. The clause that a subordinating conjunction introduces is said to be "subordinate," or dependent, because it cannot stand by itself as a complete sentence. The words *after, although, as, because, before, since, so, until, when,* and *whenever* are subordinating conjunctions.

> The counselors led activities **until** it was time for lunch.
>
> **After** we set up our tents, the campfire meeting will start.

Interjections An **interjection** is a word or group of words that expresses strong emotion.

Separated from the rest of the sentence, an interjection is punctuated by a comma or exclamation point.

> **Oops,** I dropped it. **Ha!** I tricked you.

Subjects and Predicates

A sentence expresses a complete thought. A sentence has a subject and a predicate.

Subjects

The **subject** tells whom or what the sentence is about. The **simple subject** is the key noun or pronoun that does something or is described.

> A skinny **dog** limped up the driveway.

Some simple subjects are made of more than one word.

> **Mrs. Rodrigo** said she saw a strange dog on her porch.

Some sentences look as if they don't have a subject. That's because the subject is understood.

> Set the cooler under the trees.

Here, the subject *you* is understood.

The **complete subject** is the simple subject plus all of its modifiers.

> **The hot, muggy evening** brought everyone to the pool.

> **The sign near the entrance** was brightly lit.

A **compound subject** is made of two or more simple subjects. The subjects are linked by a conjunction and share the same verb.

> **Masks** and **snorkels** are not allowed at the pool.

Try It

Locate the compound subject in this sentence. Do you see the two simple subjects? Do you see the complete subject with all of its modifiers?

▶ The YMCA staff and the new lifeguards worked on an activities calendar.

Predicates

The **predicate** is the part of the sentence that describes or tells what the subject does. The **simple predicate** is the verb or verb phrase that expresses an action or a state of being about the subject.

> Dylan **raked** leaves all afternoon.

> He **will rake** leaves tomorrow, too.

The **complete predicate** is the simple predicate plus all the words that modify it or add to its meaning.

> The leaf piles **grew higher than the trampoline.**

> Leaf burning **releases too much pollution into the air.**

A **compound predicate** is made of two or more simple predicates that are joined by a conjunction and have the same subject.

> We **jumped** into the leaf piles and **scattered** the leaves.

> He **raked** the leaves, **piled** them into rows, and **made** a maze.

Fun Fact

Leaves and other yard waste represent 20% of the waste sent to U.S. landfills.

Try It

Locate the compound subject and compound predicate.

▶ The leaves and tree limbs were gathered and taken away after the storm.

Inverted Order of Subject and Predicate

The predicate often, but not always, comes after the subject in a sentence. Sometimes the order of the subject and predicate is inverted, or reversed. Questions often begin with part of a verb phrase. Example: Will you find another rake? The subject, *you*, stands in the middle of the verb phrase, *will find*.

A sentence may also be written in inverted order to add emphasis to the subject. Example: Across the yard **ran** a squirrel.

The simple predicate *ran* comes before the subject, *squirrel*.

Writing Connection

Understanding subjects and predicates helps us build strong sentences. Strong sentences are the backbone of good writing.

Direct Objects and Indirect Objects

Direct Objects

A **direct object** is a noun or pronoun that receives the action of a verb. It answers the question what? or whom? and always comes after an action verb.

We bought **tickets.**
The Insectarium opened its **doors.**
The staff welcomed **us.**

A sentence may have more than one direct object.

We watched the **bees** and **beetles.**

Indirect Objects

An **indirect object** is a noun or pronoun for or to whom something is done. It answers the question to whom? for whom? to what? or for what?

The bees gave the **people** quite a show.
Siri saved **Lena** a place in line.
The teachers gave the **exhibit** a thumbs-up.

Indirect objects occur only in sentences with direct objects, and they appear *between* an action verb and the direct object.

Try It

Locate the indirect and direct object in this sentence.

▶ The museum staff gave the students a tour.

Writing Connection

A direct object and an indirect object show the reader how the action of a verb affects the rest of the words in a sentence.

Modifiers— Words and Phrases

A **phrase** is a group of words. Some phrases are modifiers. A **modifier** describes another word in a sentence.

Prepositional Phrases

A **prepositional phrase** is a group of words that begins with a preposition and ends with a noun or pronoun. Prepositional phrases function as adverbs or adjectives.

The trail leads **down the mountain.**

(adverb phrase modifying *leads*)

A peregrine falcon **with a broken claw** flew overhead.

(adjective phrase modifying *falcon*)

Participial Phrases

A **participial phrase** includes a participle and other words that complete its meaning. It always functions as an adjective.

We heard something **shrieking in the woods.**

The trail leader, **concerned about safety,** went to investigate.

The noise was made by hungry baby hawks, **waiting in their nest for food.**

Appositives

An **appositive** is a noun that follows another noun to modify or rename it. An **appositive phrase** includes an appositive and the words that modify it.

The trail leader, **Ben,** told us he likes birds. (appositive)

The bird book, **a wonderful resource,** is available at most libraries. (appositive phrase)

Writing Connection

Modifiers provide important details for the reader. They make your writing much more interesting.

Clauses

A **clause** is a group of words that has a subject and a verb. The two types include independent clauses and subordinate, or dependent, clauses.

Independent Clause

An **independent clause** has a subject and a verb and can stand alone as a sentence.

> Juan Delgado arrived from Puerto Rico.

More than one independent clause may appear in a sentence. Independent clauses are usually connected by a comma and a conjunction. Sometimes they are connected by a semicolon.

> His mother met him at the door, and the rest of his family greeted him warmly.

The two independent clauses can stand as independent thoughts. They are connected by a comma and the conjunction and.

> We were happy to see Juan; he had been away for a long time.

The two independent clauses are connected by a **semicolon.**

Dependent Clauses

A **dependent clause** is a group of words that has a subject and a verb but cannot stand alone as a sentence. A dependent clause always connects to a word or words in the independent clause in a sentence.

> Juan, **who went to Puerto Rico,** returned home in July.

The dependent clause, in bold, cannot stand alone as a sentence. It is dependent on the independent clause and describes the noun *Juan*.

Adjective Clauses

An **adjective clause** is a dependent clause used as an adjective. It modifies a noun or pronoun.

The meal **that Mrs. Delgado cooked** made everyone smile.

The adjective clause, *that Mrs. Delgado cooked*, tells more about the noun, *meal*, in the main clause. The word that introduces the adjective clause in the example above, *that*, is called a **relative pronoun.** The relative pronouns are ***that, which, who, whom, where,*** and ***whose.***

Adverb Clauses

An **adverb clause** is a dependent clause that is used as an adverb. It modifies the verb.

Juan helped with the chores **as if he had never been away.**

The adverb clause modifies the verb *helped* in the main clause. It tells *how* he helped with the chores. The words *as if*, which introduce the adverb clause in the example above, act as a **subordinating conjunction.** Subordinating conjunctions introduce adverb clauses. Below are some examples of subordinating conjunctions.

after	as though	since	unless	where
although	because	than	until	whereas
as	before	though	when	wherever
as if	if	till	whenever	while

Writing Connection

Independent clauses provide the basic information in a sentence. Relating dependent clauses to independent clauses adds information to single sentences and helps you avoid short, choppy sentences in your writing.

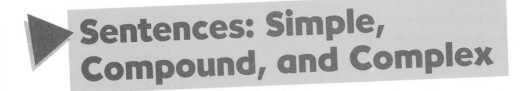

Sentences: Simple, Compound, and Complex

Simple Sentences

A **simple sentence** contains only one independent, or main, clause. It contains one subject and one predicate. The single subject may be compound. The single predicate may also be compound.

The breeze blew steadily.

This simple sentence has just one subject (*breeze*) and one predicate (*blew*).

Maya and Alicia walked to the park and flew their kites.

This simple sentence has a compound subject (*Maya, Alicia*) and a compound predicate (*walked, flew*).

One kite dipped and drifted downward.

This simple sentence has a single subject (*kite*) and a compound predicate (*dipped, drifted*).

Compound Sentences

A **compound sentence** consists of two or more simple sentences (also called independent clauses). The sentences are connected by a comma and a conjunction or by a semicolon.

The kite was caught in a current of air, **and** we watched it soar upward.

The conjunction **and** connects the two simple sentences.

Maya changed her kite design; she added two tails.

This compound sentence combines its clauses with a semicolon. Semicolons connect two closely related sentences.

Complex Sentences

A **complex sentence** consists of one simple sentence (independent clause) and one or more dependent clauses. Remember, a dependent clause is a group of words that cannot stand alone as a sentence. The complex sentence below has one dependent clause with the independent clause.

Although the breeze was steady, both kites continued to dive.

Compound-Complex Sentences

A **compound-complex sentence** has two or more independent clauses and at least one dependent clause.

As the storm approached, the wind blew with great force, and Alicia pulled her kite in to safety.

Try It

Rewrite these sentences so they don't sound choppy. Add, delete, or change words and punctuation to create new sentences out of both the dependent clauses and the independent clauses.

▶ We arrived at the kite festival. We parked our car. We saw the most amazing kite. It was a Chinese dragon kite. It poked out its tongue. It rolled its eyes. It flew in the air the whole time.

Writing Connection

Compound, complex, and compound-complex sentences help avoid repetition and provide a way to smoothly and accurately connect ideas.

Problems with Sentence Structure

Fragments

A **fragment** does not express a complete thought and should not be written as a sentence.

▶ The canoe leaning against the shed.

The sentence fragment lacks a predicate. To form a complete sentence, add a verb.

The canoe leaning against the shed **leaks.**

▶ Wanted to take out a kayak.

This fragment is missing a subject. Adding a subject forms a complete sentence.

Sean and Kate wanted to take out a kayak.

▶ When they paddled through the marsh.

This fragment is a dependent clause; it cannot stand alone as a sentence. To form a complete sentence, add an independent clause.

They took care not to disturb wildlife when they paddled through the marsh.

Run-On Sentences

A **run-on sentence** is two or more sentences written as though they are one.

▶ Sean saw a giant nest it belonged to a mute swan.
This run-on sentence is really two sentences. Here are the ways to correct it.

Sean saw a giant nest. It belonged to a mute swan.

Sean saw a giant nest; it belonged to a mute swan.

The following run-on sentence can also be corrected.

▶ The swan grew agitated it couldn't make a sound.

Insert a period and create two sentences *or* fix it by adding a comma and a conjunction.

The swan grew agitated, **but** it couldn't make a sound.

Rambling Sentences

A **rambling sentence** goes on and on. It connects too many thoughts with the words *and, but,* or *or.*

> We came to a patch of mud and had to drag our kayak and our arms hurt and we became tangled in weeds and it took a while to get to deeper water but we made it. (incorrect)

> We came to a patch of mud and had to drag our kayaks. Our arms hurt and we became tangled in weeds. It took a while to get to deeper water, but we made it. (correct)

Awkward Sentences

An **awkward sentence** is one that is unclear because of its construction. An awkward sentence makes the reader stumble and stop to think about its meaning. The use of *only* in the following sentence can be very confusing to readers.

> I only have one kayak.

Does the sentence mean that the only thing the writer owns in the world is one kayak? Does it mean that the writer has lots of boats but just one kayak? Small changes can help make the meaning more clear.

> The only thing I have is one kayak. (only thing the speaker owns)

> I have only one kayak. (lots of boats but just one kayak)

This example below is another awkward sentence with a corrected version:

> Incorrect: The kayaks belong to the state park, and they close at 8 P.M.

> Correct: The kayaks belong to the state park, which closes at 8 P.M.

Double Subjects

Be careful not to use a pronoun right after the subject of a sentence.

> Incorrect: Sean he wants to race kayaks someday.

> Correct: Sean wants to race kayaks someday.

Using <u>Of</u> When You Mean <u>Have</u>

Incorrect: We could **of** taken the longer kayak trail.

Correct: We could **have** taken the longer kayak trail.

Unnecessary Words and Phrases

It is tempting to throw in extra words when we want to emphasize something. Avoid using words and phrases that repeat what has already been written.

Incorrect: It was the most ultimate rescue ever made.

Correct: It was the ultimate rescue.

Incorrect: The state park advertised itself as providing a lot of activities and the state park did provide more activities than any state park we had visited.

Correct: The state park advertised its range of activities, and it did offer more to do than any park we had visited.

Try It

Reword these sentences so that they are correct.

▶ The park it didn't have a campground but it had a lodge though which is like a hotel so that's where we stayed. Stayed for two nights. We would of liked to of camped.

Writing Connection

Writing that is redundant or has rambling and awkward sentences is hard to read and understand. Clear, readable writing effectively avoids these traps.

Kinds of Sentences

There are four kinds of sentences: declarative, interrogative, imperative, and exclamatory.

Declarative Sentences

A **declarative sentence** makes a statement. It always ends with a period.

> Meindert DeJong wrote <u>The Wheel on the School</u>.

Interrogative Sentences

An **interrogative sentence** asks a question. It ends with a question mark.

> Did you enjoy reading the book?

Imperative Sentences

An **imperative sentence** gives a command or makes a request. Imperative sentences usually end with a period, but sometimes imperative sentences end with an exclamation point. The subject *you* is usually understood.

> Please read the first four chapters by tomorrow. Begin now!

Exclamatory Sentences

An **exclamatory sentence** expresses a strong feeling. It ends with an exclamation point.

> I couldn't believe the teacher let his students put a wagon wheel on the school roof!

Fun Fact

Meindert DeJong, the author of *The Wheel on the School,* supported himself after graduating from college by tinning, grave digging, and farming.

Try It

What kind of sentence is this?

▶ Sit down with me and tell me all about it.

Think of examples for the other three kinds of sentences.

Writing Connection

Use different kinds of sentences to add variety and interest to your writing.

Usage

Usage is about how we use language when we speak and write. For example, the rules of usage tell you when to use *was* and when to use *were*. They tell you when to use *broke* and when to use *broken*. They tell you when to use *smaller* and when to use *smallest*. Learning and using the rules of usage will make it easier for people to understand what you say and what you write.

▶ Verb Tenses **366**

▶ Subject-Verb Agreement **368**

▶ Using Pronouns **370**

▶ Comparative and
Superlative Adjectives **372**

▶ Comparative and
Superlative Adverbs **373**

▶ Contractions **374**

▶ Double Negatives **375**

▶ Misused Words **376**

Verb Tenses

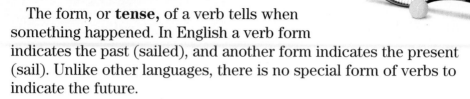

The form, or **tense,** of a verb tells when something happened. In English a verb form indicates the past (sailed), and another form indicates the present (sail). Unlike other languages, there is no special form of verbs to indicate the future.

Present Tense

A **present-tense verb** shows action that is happening now or on a regular basis.

> Jade **runs** to the net for the winning shot.
> (what is happening now)

> Selena often **runs** to the net.
> (a regular action)

Past Tense

A **past-tense verb** shows action that has already happened.

> Jade **won** the first three games.
>
> (what already happened)

Future Tense

A **future-tense verb** shows action that will happen. Use the auxiliary verb *shall* or *will* with the main verb to show what will happen in the future.

> I **will attend** the tennis tournament.
>
> (what will happen)

Perfect Tense

▶ The **present-perfect tense** shows an action completed in the present or one that began in the past and is continuing in the present. Use the auxiliary verb has or have before the main verb to form the present perfect tense.

> Jade **has studied** for the test.
> (a completed action)

> Selena **has played** tennis for four years.
> (a continuing action)

▶ The **past-perfect tense** shows an action that began and ended in the past. Use the auxiliary verb *had* with the main verb for the past-perfect tense.

We **had cleared** the puddles off the court.

▶ The **future-perfect tense** shows an action that will begin and end in the future, usually before another future event begins. Use the auxiliary verbs *will have* or *shall have* before the main verb.

By the end of the day, they **will have practiced** for five hours.

Forming Tenses of Regular and Irregular Verbs

Regular verbs add *-ed* to the present-tense verb to form the past tense or (with an auxiliary verb) one of the perfect tenses.

The forms of some common irregular verbs are listed below. There are many others.

Present Tense	Past Tense	Past-Perfect Tense
*I **watch** tennis.*	*I **watched** tennis.*	*I **have watched** tennis.*

Irregular verbs do not add *-ed.* Instead, they change their form.

Present Tense *I **take** lessons.*	Past Tense *I **took** lessons.*	Past-Perfect Tense *I **have taken** lessons.*
begin	began	begun
drink	drank	drunk
ring	rang	rung
sing	sang	sung
sink	sank	sunk
swim	swam	swum

Try It

What verb tenses will make these sentences correct?

▶ We practiced with our tennis coach tomorrow.

▶ She joins us for an hour yesterday.

Writing Connection

Keep the verb tenses consistent in your writing so your readers are sure about when events happened.

Subject-Verb Agreement

A subject and a verb must agree in number. The present-tense verb form used is determined by whether the subject of a sentence is singular or plural. The verb form for regular **present-tense verbs** usually ends in *s* or *es*.

Singular Subject and Verb	Plural Subject and Verb
A **pioneer searches** for a new way of life.	**Pioneers search** for a new way of life.
He **swings** a rope.	**They swing** ropes.

▶ **Irregular verbs,** such as *be, have,* and *do,* take different forms in order to agree with the subject.

I **am** a cowboy. He **is** a cowboy. They **are** cowboys.

She **has** many books. We **have** many books.

It **does** sound interesting. They **do** listen.

Agreement with Compound Subjects

A **compound subject** is made of two or more simple subjects that use the same verb. Two or more subjects connected by *and* use the form of the verb that agrees with a plural subject.

Songs **and** stories **spark** Bill's imagination.

Both Bill Pickett **and** his show horse, Spradley, **are** a hit.

▶ Compound subjects joined by *or* or by *nor* use the verb form that agrees with the subject closest to the verb.

Sometimes, the bull rider or a rodeo **clown gets** caught by the angry animal.

A coyote or **wolves creep** into the hen houses.

Agreement with Indefinite Pronouns

When an **indefinite pronoun** is the subject of a sentence, the verb must agree with the indefinite pronoun in number. Below is a chart showing singular and plural indefinite pronouns.

Singular		Plural
another	much	both
anyone	neither	few
anything	no one	many
each	nothing	others
either	one	several
everybody	somebody	
everything	something	

Everybody leaves the stadium at the end.

Everybody is a singular indefinite pronoun. The verb must agree with a singular subject.

A **few leave** early.

Few is a plural indefinite pronoun. The verb must agree with a plural subject.

Try It

Choose the correct verb in the sentence below.

▶ Everybody (is,are) seeking autographs.

Writing Connection

Taking the time to find and use the correct verb form, even with tricky indefinite pronouns, results in good, consistent writing.

Using Pronouns

Pronoun/Antecedent Agreement

The words or word referred to by a pronoun is called the **antecedent.** *Antecedent* means "going before."

Dad and Liana went to the mall. ***They*** love to shop.

Dad and Liana are the antecedent of *They.*

▶ A pronoun must agree with its antecedent in **person** and **number.**

Dad likes to shop more than anyone in **his** family.

The pronoun *his* and its antecedent *Dad* are both singular.

Liana spends **her** entire allowance every week.

The pronoun *her* and its antecedent *Liana* are both singular.

The **Changs** do most of **their** shopping in department stores.

The pronoun *their* and its antecedent *Changs* are both plural.

If there is a new **gadget** out, **it** will surely tempt them.

The pronoun *it* and its antecedent *gadget* are both singular.

Agreement with Indefinite Pronouns

▶ Pronouns such as *another, anybody, each, either, everyone, one, someone, something, much, no one,* and *nothing,* which do not refer to a particular person, place, or thing, are singular indefinite pronouns.

When the antecedent is a singular indefinite pronoun, use a singular personal pronoun.

One of the girls lost **her** money.

The pronoun *her* and its antecedent *One* are both singular.

Each of the stores had a sale sign in **its** window.

The pronoun *its* and its antecedent *Each* are both singular.

▶ When the antecedent is a plural indefinite pronoun, use a plural personal pronoun. Plural indefinite pronouns include *both, few, many, others,* and *several.*

> **Several** of the students spent **their** money on trading cards.

> The pronoun *their* and its antecedent *Several* are both plural.

The indefinite pronouns *all, any, enough, most, none,* and *some* can be singular or plural.

> Will **any** of the boys eat **his** lunch in the food court?

> The pronoun *his* and its antecedent *any* are both singular.

> **Some** of the boys ate **their** lunch in the food court.

> The pronoun *their* and its antecedent *Some* are both plural.

Agreement with Demonstrative Pronouns

The demonstrative pronouns *this, that, these,* and *those* point out something. They must agree with their antecedent. *This* and *that* are singular. *These* and *those* are plural.

> **These** are the **books** I need.

> The demonstrative pronoun *these* agrees with the plural noun *books.*

> **That** is my favorite **book.**

> The demonstrative pronoun *that* agrees with the singular noun *book.*

Try It
Complete the following sentence using the correct pronoun.
▶ Many of the girls brought _____ CDs to the party.

Writing Connection
Pronouns save time and space. They improve the flow of writing by helping you avoid repeating words.

Comparative and Superlative Adjectives

The **comparative** form of an adjective compares one person or thing with another. The **superlative** form of an adjective compares one person or thing with several others.

For most adjectives with one syllable and some with two syllables, add *-er* to form the comparative and *-est* to form the superlative.

The sun is high**er** than it was an hour ago.

Today is the hott**est** day of the week.

Adjectives with two or more syllables form the comparative by using *more* before the adjective. Form the superlative by using *most* before the adjective.

Today's climb was **more** difficult than yesterday's climb.

Tomorrow's climb will be the **most** difficult of all.

Fun Fact

The adjective *good* has twenty-four different meanings.

Irregular Comparative and Superlative Adjectives

Some adjectives do not follow a specific pattern. It helps to remember their forms.

That was a **bad** mistake. His mistake was worse. Mine was the **worst** of all.

Base Form	Comparative	Superlative
good	better	best
bad	worse	worst
many	more	most
little	less	least

Try It

Complete the sentence below using the superlative form of an adjective.

He ran the _____ of all the athletes.

Comparative and Superlative Adverbs

The **comparative** form of an adverb compares one action with another. The **superlative** form of an adverb compares one action with several others.

For most adverbs with one syllable and some with two syllables, add -er to form the comparative and -est to form the superlative. Use an adverb to modify a verb, an adjective, or another adverb.

> I arrived earli**er** for practice than most of the players.

> Kyle was the earli**est** player to arrive at the field.

Adjectives with two or more syllables form the comparative by using *more* before the adverb. Form the superlative by using *most* before the adverb.

> Kyle runs the bases **more quickly** than I do.

> Nate runs the bases **most quickly.**

Irregular Comparative and Superlative Adverbs

Some adverbs do not follow a specific pattern. It helps to remember their forms.

> Kyle usually plays **better** than everyone else.

> Jose played **best** in the last game.

Take care not to use the adjectives *good* and *bad* as adverbs. Use the words *well* and *badly* as adverbs and *good* and *bad* only as adjectives.

> Our team played **well.** (adverb)

> It was a **good** game. (adjective)

> The other team did not play **badly.** (adverb)

> They made a **bad** play at the end. (adjective)

Base Form	Comparative	Superlative
well	better	best
badly	worse	worst
little	less	least

Contractions

A **contraction** is a word that is usually formed by combining two words and replacing one or more letters with an apostrophe. Some contractions use the word *is*.

> **Sam is** going to the competition. —► Sam's going to the competition.

Many common contractions are formed with the word *not*.

> I **do not** want to go. —► I **don't** want to go.

Contractions help writing and speaking sound natural and less choppy.

Common Contractions	
are not ➤ aren't	have not ➤ haven't
did not ➤ didn't	was not ➤ wasn't
has not ➤ hasn't	would not ➤ wouldn't
should not ➤ shouldn't	could not ➤ couldn't
will not ➤ won't	does not ➤ doesn't
cannot ➤ can't	is not ➤ isn't
do not ➤ don't	were not ➤ weren't

Try It

Write this sentence with contractions.

▶ I could not go to the competition with Sam because I was not allowed.

Common Contractions	
I am ➤ I'm	they are ➤ they're
I have ➤ I've	you are ➤ you're
I will ➤ I'll	you would ➤ you'd
he is ➤ he's	we will ➤ we'll
she is ➤ she's	we have ➤ we've
they will ➤ they'll	it is; it has ➤ it's

Double Negatives

Use a **negative word** to express the idea of *no* or *not*.

That team **never** wins any games.

Nobody attends their competitions.

Negative Words
no never nobody none no one nothing nowhere hardly

A **double negative** occurs when *two* negative words are used to express a single idea when *one* negative word should do the job. Many contractions use the negative word *not*. As a result, double negatives sometimes find their way into our speech and writing. Watch for the contraction trap, however, to avoid double negatives.

Incorrect: Sam did**n't** do **nothing** wrong while winning his match.

Correct: Sam did**n't** do anything wrong while winning his match.

Correct: Sam did **nothing** wrong while winning his match.

Incorrect: He does**n't** know **nothing** about karate.

Correct: He doesn't know anything about karate.

Correct: He knows nothing about karate.

Incorrect: We do**n't** have **no** lesson today.

Correct: We don't have a lesson today.

Correct: We have no lesson today.

Try It

Fix these sentences.

▶ We don't have no place for our lesson.

Our instructor doesn't see nothing wrong with practicing tomorrow.

Misused Words

This lesson will help you choose between words that are often misused.

To, Too, Two

To suggests direction.
Go **to** the kitchen.

Too shows degree or means "also."
Make sure the gravy isn't **too** thin.
Check the roast, **too.**

Two is the number before *three*.
Add **two** tablespoons of flour to the gravy.

Sit and Set

Sit is what you do when you place yourself on a chair. Sit does not take a direct object. These are the verb forms of *sit*: **sit, sitting, sat.**

Will you please sit here? No! I've been sitting all day.

Set involves putting something somewhere. Set usually has a direct object. These are the verb forms of *set*: **set, setting.**

I set my helmet on the counter. He was setting up the goal.

Rise and Raise

Rise means "to move upward." It does not take a direct object. These are the verb forms of *rise*: **rise, rose, rising, risen.**

Blue smoke will rise from the fire. The bread dough is rising.

Raise means "to cause something to move upward or to grow." *Raise* normally has a direct object. These are the verb forms of *raise*: **raise, raising, raised.**

Jeb will raise corn this year. The runner raised the torch.

More Misused and Confusing Words

▶ **can, may** If you have the ability, you *can*. If you have permission, you *may*. I **can** leave the building whenever I'm ready. You **may** join me if you like.

▶ **its, it's** To make *it* possessive, use *its*. To form the contraction of *it is* or *it has*, use it's with an apostrophe. Our dog has **its** fur shaved in the summer. **It's** funny when you see her for the first time.

▶ **many, much** Use *many* for things that can be counted. Use *much* for things that cannot be counted. I have too **many** apples for one pie. The apples I have won't make **much** applesauce.

▶ **which, who** *Which* refers only to things. *Who* refers only to people. Use the small bottle, **which** is almost empty. After you wash the dishes, hand them to Carmen, **who** will dry them.

▶ **then, than** Use *then* as an adverb to suggest another time. Use *than* as a conjunction to make a comparison. The chili was spicy enough **then.** This chili is spicier **than** last week's.

▶ **lay, lie** Use *lay* when you mean "to put or place." Just **lay** the books on the table. Use lie when you mean "to rest or recline." I think I will **lie** down.

Try It

Review the commonly misused words that were covered in this lesson. Choose the words that cause you the most problems, then use them correctly in sentences.

Writing Connection

To prevent misunderstanding, take the time to spell the word you mean. Look it up, if you must.

Mechanics

The rules of mechanics are very important in writing. Imagine a paragraph with no capital letters at the beginnings of sentences and no punctuation at the ends of sentences. How confusing would that be? Of course, there is a lot more to mechanics than capitalizing the first word of a sentence and using end marks. The following lessons will give you what you need to know to understand and use the rules of mechanics to improve your writing.

▶ End Marks **380**

▶ Abbreviations **382**

▶ Commas **384**

▶ Colons and Semicolons **388**

▶ Quotation Marks, Underlining,
and Apostrophes **389**

▶ Parentheses, Hyphens, Dashes,
and Ellipses **390**

▶ Capitalization **391**

End Marks

The Period (.)

The **period** is the most frequently used end punctuation mark. Use a period to end a sentence that makes a statement (declarative) or one that makes a command or polite request (imperative).

Anjuli invented a new way to tie-dye T-shirts. (statement)

Please buy five yellow T-shirts. (request)

Put the new T-shirts on that shelf. (command)

Periods in Outlines

Use a period after every Roman numeral that labels a main topic and after every letter or Arabic numeral that labels a subtopic or subdivision.

I. Main topic
      A. Subtopic
           1. Subtopic division
               a. Subdivision of a subtopic
               b. Subdivision of a subtopic

Periods as Decimal Points

Use a period as a decimal point, between the whole number and fractional figure.

8.5 kilometers   75.5 percent $5.50

The Question Mark (?)

A **question mark** ends a sentence that asks a question (interrogative). Use a question mark only at the end of a sentence that asks a direct question.

When will we ever tie-dye our T-shirts?

May I sit next to Kailey?

Do not use a question mark after an indirect question. Indirect questions are usually reworded statements (declarative sentences) or commands (imperative statements).

She asked to borrow some rubber bands.

The Exclamation Mark (!)

Use an **exclamation point** after a word, short phrase, or sentence to show strong feeling. The word or short phrase that an exclamation point follows may be an interjection, expressing strong emotion.

Good Grief! Wow! Ouch!

Used with a sentence, an exclamation point may express strong feeling or make a command.

Get down from there right now!

Try It

Add the correct end punctuation to each of these sentences.

▶ We sold our tie-dyed T-shirts at the fundraiser

▶ Did you hear what happened

▶ Wow

▶ We sold them all in 15 minutes

Writing Connection

Knowing when *not* to use punctuation is just as important as knowing when to use it. That may make all the difference between strong, clear writing and writing that exhausts its readers. For instance, overused exclamation points leave readers gasping for breath. For greater impact, use them only when they are absolutely needed.

Abbreviations

An **abbreviation** is a shortened form of a word. Most abbreviations use periods.

If an abbreviation occurs at the end of a sentence, use only one period.

Ms. Kurz asked us to meet at 5 **A.M.**

▶ Use periods for titles used before a person's name.

Dr. Strauss   **Mrs.** Jagdish   **Mr.** Foreman

▶ Use periods for abbreviations that follow a person's name.

Martin Luther King, **Jr.**   Jill Theophano, **M.D.**

▶ Use periods when using initials for a person's first and/or middle name.

Ursula **K.** LeGuin   **H.G.** Wells

▶ Use periods for these time and date abbreviations.

12:15 **A.M.**   7:34 **P.M.**   1100 **B.C.**   **A.D.** 1066

Abbreviations for Specific Uses

The following abbreviated words may be used for charts, envelopes, maps, and scientific writing. Most other times, these words should be spelled out.

Days and Months

Thurs., Fri., Sat., Sept., Oct., Nov.
Use the longer form in your writing. Example: **Mon.** ➔ **Monday**

Streets and Roads

(printed on maps): St., Ave., Blvd., Rd., Ct., Ln.
Spell these out in your writing.
Example: Mulberry **St.** ➔ Mulberry **Street**

U.S. Units of Measure

Notice that an abbreviation may be different from the actual word.
oz. (ounce), *lb.* (pound), *in.* (inch), *ft.* (foot), *yd.* (yard)

teaspoon ➔ *tsp.*   tablespoon ➔ *tbsp.*
pint ➔ *pt.*   quart ➔ *qt.*   gallon ➔ *gal.*

Abbreviations That Do Not Use Periods

Acronyms

An **acronym** is a word created from the first letters or syllables of other words. Acronyms are abbreviations, but they do not require periods.

scuba (self-contained underwater breathing apparatus)
NASA (National Aeronautics and Space Administration)
AWOL (absent without leave)

Initialisms

An **initialism** is formed from the first letters of the words it represents. Pronounce each letter of an initialism when speaking; when writing, do not use periods.

ATM (automatic teller machine)
UFO (unidentified flying object)
SUV (sport utility vehicle)

Postal Abbreviations

These two-letter state abbreviations used by the U.S. Postal Service save space on envelopes. Avoid them elsewhere in writing.

CA (California)   DE (Delaware)
ID (Idaho)   SC (South Carolina)

Metric Units of Measure

Metric system abbreviations do not use periods.

cm (centimeter)   **L** (liter)   **m** (meter)

Other Units of Measure

C (Celsius)   **F** (Fahrenheit)   **mph** (miles per hour)

Writing Connection

Abbreviations can help us write things such as telephone messages more quickly. Use abbreviations only if readers will easily understand the abbreviation.

Commas

Commas are punctuation marks that help organize thoughts and items. They show the reader where to pause and what thoughts go together.

Commas in a Series

Use a comma to separate three or more items in a series. A series of three or more groups of words also uses a comma after each group.

> Please grab the leash, collar, and treats. (series of words)

> Was it a toy poodle, miniature poodle, or standard poodle? (series of phrases)

Commas also separate the items in a series of three or more predicates.

> The dogs stepped out of their crates, sniffed the ground, and began to play.

Commas After Introductory Phrases or Clauses

Use a comma after a long introductory phrase or clause. A short introductory phrase or clause does not need a comma.

> **When you become really good at handling dogs,** I will let you show them. (long introductory clause)
> **Until we arrived at the dog show,** we had no idea what the schedule was. (long introductory phrase)

> **At 12:00** the show began. (short introductory phrase)
> **When it started** we had a schedule. (short introductory clause)

Commas in Compound Sentences

Compound sentences contain two or more independent clauses. Use a comma and a connecting word, such as *and, but,* or *or,* to join the independent clauses.

> The Irish terrier wanted to play catch, **and** the beagle wanted to chase him.

> I would really like to see the Weimaraners, **but** the Saint Bernards are showing next.

Do **not** use commas to separate the compound subjects or compound predicates of simple sentences.

Jed **brushed his dog from head to tail** and **walked it outside near the barn.** (compound predicate)

Commas and Interjections

Use a comma to set off an interjection not followed by an exclamation point.

Oh, well, I came to the dog show mostly for fun.

Commas with Appositives

Use two commas to set off an appositive, a word or phrase placed next to a noun to provide extra information.

Roger's dog, **a German Shepard,** is my favorite.

Commas with Direct Address

Direct address is a name or phrase used in speaking directly to a person. Use one or two commas to set off a noun of direct address (the person being spoken to) from the rest of the sentence.

Kara, which is your favorite breed?

Actually, **Mariah,** I really like mixed breeds.

Commas Used to Separate Adjectives

Use commas to separate two or more adjectives that have equal importance in modifying the same noun.

The **sleek, fast** greyhound easily outran the basset hound.

Do not use a comma between adjectives when the adjective closer to the noun functions as a part of it.

She is an experienced dog trainer.

Commas with Interrupters

Use commas to set off interrupters, words or phrases that interrupt the central idea of a sentence.

English Setters, **on the other hand,** require lots of exercise.

They will be quite happy, **however,** in a large yard.

Commas with Introductory Words

Use a comma to set off the introductory words *yes*, *no*, and *well*.

No, I have never seen that type of dog.

Well, would you like to see it?

Yes, I would.

Commas in Dialogue

Use one comma to set off a direct quotation when the speaker is named at the beginning or end of a quotation. Use two commas, one on either side of the speaker tag, in the middle of a quotation.

Jasmine asked, "When will we get to see the greyhounds?"

"They will be in the show area," he answered, "when the whippets are finished."

"That will be about thirty minutes from now," he added.

Commas with Parts of a Letter

Use a comma after a friendly letter's greeting and after the closing of all letters.

Dear Mrs. Woodhouse,
Dear Ted,
Sincerely,
Yours truly,

Commas with Dates

Use a comma between the day and year of a complete date. Do not use a comma when you write only the month and year.

Champion Master Briar was born April 12, 1996.

In August 1999 he won the best-of-breed award.

Commas in Large Numbers

Use commas in numbers with four digits or more, except for years.

Barbara Woodhouse trained more than 17,000 dogs and their owners.

In 2000 Mr. Singer left an inheritance of $50,000 to his dog.

Commas in Addresses

Use a comma after a street address when it is followed by the name of a city. Use a comma to set off the name of a state or country when it follows the name of a city. Do not use a comma between a state and a ZIP code.

Regal Rustin prefers to live in Tiverton, England, with his owners.

Write to Ruff and Ready at 236 Lonesome Highway, Cut Bank, MT 59736

Try It

Add commas to these sentences.

▶ The teacher Mrs. Liu handed me my certificate.

▶ Madonna my best friend said "Good job Violet."

▶ Well I think I saw Jesse yesterday.

▶ I'll bring cheese fruit and salad for the picnic.

▶ After we count all the votes Ms. Ryan will announce the winner.

Writing Connection

Commas help organize writing into ideas so readers know when to separate thoughts or items and when to pause.

Colons and Semicolons

Introduce a List with a Colon

To introduce a list with a colon, use the words *the following* or *as follows* at some point in the sentence before the colon and list.

> The things you will need for the sleepover are **as follows:** a toothbrush, pajamas, a sleeping bag, and a change of clothes.

Colons After Salutations

Use a colon after a business letter salutation.
Dear Ms. Pulaski:

Colons Between Hours and Minutes

Use a colon to separate the hour and the minutes of a precise time.

> Drop your daughter off at 6:15 P.M. and pick her up at 9:30 A.M. tomorrow.

Semicolons (;)

A **semicolon** is a punctuation mark used to join the independent, or main, clauses in a sentence and to help separate clauses joined by some adverbs.

> Connect independent clauses not joined by *and, but, or,* or *nor.*
> Everyone finally fell asleep; some of the girls snored.

Try It

Add a colon and a semicolon to these clauses.

▶ The alarm clock went off at 8 15 I realized I had missed the play.

Writing Connection

Colons and semicolons save space and help organize writing. They are not used often.

Quotation Marks, Underlining, and Apostrophes

Quotation Marks

Use **quotation marks** to enclose the exact words of a speaker. Periods and commas should be inside closing quotation marks. Question marks and exclamation points should be inside the quotation marks if they are part of the quotation.

Dana said, "Let me show you my telescope."

"May I look through it?" asked Tiana.

"Look at the moon!" she said excitedly.

Quotation Marks for Titles

Use quotation marks for the titles of poems, songs, and short stories.

"Wander-Thirst" (poem) "Vergil, the Dog" (short story)

"Yankee Doodle" (song)

Underlining Italics

Use underlining or italics for book titles.

<u>Julie of the Wolves</u>   *Mrs. Frisby and the Rats of NIMH*

The Apostrophe

To show **possession,** add an apostrophe and **s** to the end of singular indefinite pronouns and most singular nouns.

Someone**'s** constellation chart

Joshua**'s** glasses

Saturn**'s** rings

Possessive pronouns do not have apostrophes.

its size   **whose** notebook   The telescope is **hers.**

In **contractions,** apostrophes take the place of missing letters.

It's is formed from *it is* or *it has*. *I'm* is formed from *I am*.

Parentheses, Hyphens, Dashes, and Ellipses

Parentheses

Parentheses are punctuation marks used to enclose information that either adds to or helps explain other words in a sentence.

> The introduction (p. 6) tells where some lynx live (North America).

Hyphens

Use a **hyphen** to divide a word between syllables when you run out of space on a line.

> Tigers once roamed across almost all of Asia, from Si-beria in the north to Indonesia in the south.

▶Use a hyphen for some compound nouns.

> good-bye   teeter-totter   sister-in-law

▶Use a hyphen when creating a compound modifier, usually an adjective formed from two words written in front of a noun.

> second-place finish   orange-red sun   New York-style pizza

▶Use hyphens for numbers and fractions that are written out.

> ninety-nine pins   forty-six eggs   one-fourth

Dashes

Use a **dash** to show an interruption in speech or a sudden change of thought.

> Pumas—people rarely see them—live in these mountains.

Ellipses

Ellipses consist of what look like three periods, each one with a space before and after it. Use ellipses to show a pause in speech.

> It's interesting . . . Does it climb trees?

Capitalization

When you **capitalize,** you make the first letter of a word a capital letter. Letters that are not capitalized are called lowercase.

Capitalize the first word of every sentence.

The bicycle race takes place tomorrow.

Capitalize the first word in a direct quotation.

Mom shouted, "Don't forget your water bottle and your helmet!"

Capitalize proper nouns and proper adjectives.

> **Proper Nouns:** Brazil, Texas, Yankee Stadium
>
> **Proper Adjectives:** Brazil nuts, Texas resident, Yankee fan

Capitalize the pronoun *I.*

Once **I** start one of her books, **I** can't put it down.

Capitalize initials that stand for part of a person's name.

J.R.R. Tolkien   L. Frank Baum

Titles

Capitalize people's titles.

Houston Baker, **Jr.**   Wendy Falb, **Ph. D.**
Dr. Alexis Mazza
Councilwoman Hannah Fernandez

Do not capitalize titles used as common nouns or those following names.

Joan Cohen, a **d**octor of pediatrics, is running for **c**ouncilwoman.

Capitalize titles used in place of names.

Will you change your vote, **S**enator?

Capitalize words used in place of names.

Will **G**randpa ask Sergi's grandmother to go?

Notice that *grandpa* used as a name is capitalized. *Sergi's grandmother* describes a person; it is not capitalized.

Geographical and Historical Terms

Capitalize the names of historic periods.

Stone Age
Great Depression
Harlem Renaissance
Victorian period

Capitalize the names of historic events.

Holocaust
Pearl Harbor Day
American Revolution
Battle of Bunker Hill

Capitalize geographic place names.

These include bodies of water, mountains, and other features that have been named.

Great Salt Lake	Everglades
Snake River	Chesapeake Bay
Atlantic Ocean	Mt. Hood
Blue Ridge Mountains	Death Valley

Capitalize the regions of a country.

Snow Belt   New England   Pacific Northwest   Mid-Atlantic

Capitalize direction words used for a specific place.

the South of France
the North Pole
the East
the West

Use lowercase for general direction words.

eastern shore

northwest current

south side of the mountain

Capitalize the names of holidays and special events.

Labor Day   Fourth of July
Olympics   World Series

Capitalize the names of months and days.

May   September
Tuesday   Saturday

Capitalize the names of countries, cities, states, and counties.

Portugal   Seattle
Kentucky   Orange County

Capitalize titles of businesses, institutions, and organizations.

Salvation Army
Cook County Hospital
Westminster College

Capitalize brand names.

Crazy Crunch cereal
Super Spin yo-yos
Speedy sneakers

Capitalize the titles of books, movies, magazines, and newspapers.

Harriet the Spy (book)
Spider Magazine (magazine)
Chicago Tribune (newspaper)

Capitalize the titles of musical compositions and works of art.

The Magic Flute (opera)
Starry Night (painting)
The Thinker (statue)

Capitalize the names of important documents and awards.

Magna Carta
Nobel Peace Prize
Declaration of Independence
Bill of Rights

Capitalize the names of important structures.

Vietnam Memorial
the Pentagon
Golden Gate Bridge
Lincoln Tunnel
St. Louis Arch

Capitalize Religions, Nationalities, and Languages

Religions	Nationalities	Languages
Judaism	Polish	Mandarin
Islam	Colombian	English
Hinduism	Senegalese	Russian
Christianity	Norwegian	Spanish
Buddhism	Malaysian	Japanese

Capitalize only those school subjects that refer to a language.

English   Spanish
German   French

Use lowercase letters for most school subjects.

math   science
social studies   reading

Capitalize greetings and closings in letters.

Use a capital letter to begin the greeting or salutation and also the first and last name of the person to whom you are writing. The first letter of every word in the salutation of a business letter should be capitalized.

Dear Ms. Valente,   To Whom It May Concern:

Dear Sir: Dear John,

Capitalize the parts of a topic outline.

Use capital Roman numerals and capital letters to label main topics and subtopics. Use lowercase letters for the subdivisions of the subtopics. The first word of each heading, subheading, and subdivision should also be capitalized.

- I. Swimming for fun
  - A. Provides exercise
    1. Effects on whole body
       a. Low impact on joints and muscles
       b. Works wide range of muscles
    2. Heart benefits
       a. Strengthens the heart
       b. Increases red-blood cell production
  - B. Provides relaxation
    1. Soothing effects of water
    2. Stress-relieving effects of the exercise
- II. Swimming for competition

Note: Only the subdivision labels (a., b.) are lowercase.

Try It

Add the correct capitalization to this sentence.

▶ we were driving over the golden gate bridge when i realized that i had left my math book, spanish homework, and ranger magazine at uncle charlie's house.

Writing Connection

When you capitalize correctly in your writing, you alert your readers when sentences begin and when you are being specific.

Glossary

A

abbreviation   the shortening of a word, such as St. for Street. Most abbreviations are followed by a period.

abstract nouns   words that name ideas, qualities, and feelings

acronym   the short form of several words, usually as in the name of an organization, such as NASA for National Aeronautics and Space Administration

active voice   when the subject performs the verb's action

adjective clause   a dependent clause that modifies a noun or pronoun in the main clause of a sentence

adverb clause   a dependent clause that modifies the verb in the main clause of a sentence

alliteration   the repetition of the consonant sounds at the beginning of words

analogy   a comparison of two words based on how the two words are related

antecedent   a word referred to or replaced by a pronoun

appositive   a noun that follows another noun to modify or rename it

appositive phrase   includes an appositive and the words that modify it

assonance   the repetition of the sounds of vowels in words

auxiliary verb   a helping verb that helps the main verb show action or express a state of being

B

bibliography   a list of research materials used and referred to in the preparation of an article or report

byline   the place where a reporter writes his/her name in a news story

C

callout   in a news story, a quotation or interesting portion of a sentence printed in large, bold type in the middle of a column

caption   a sentence or phrase written under a picture or illustration that tells more about the picture

cause-and-effect chart   a type of graphic organizer that shows the cause and possible effect or effects of that event

character analysis   looking closely at a character in a piece of writing to learn as much as you can about that character

chronological order　an organizational pattern that tracks events in time order

cinquain　a poem that has five lines and follows a special pattern

clause　a group of words that has a subject and a verb

closed compound word　a compound word that has no space between the words, such as *popcorn*

collecting grid　a type of graphic organizer used to record information gathered from many different sources

comparative form　the form of an adjective or adverb that compares two of something

complex sentence　a type of sentence that is made of an independent clause and one or more dependent clauses

compound predicate　two or more simple predicates joined by a conjunction that share the same subject

compound sentence　two or more simple sentences joined by a conjunction

compound subject　two or more simple subjects connected by a conjunction that share the same verb

compound-complex sentence　a sentence that has two or more independent clauses and at least one dependent clause

concrete nouns　words that name things you can see, touch, hear, smell, or taste

connotation　the feeling a word creates in the reader, or a word's suggested meaning

context clue　words or sentences that surround an unknown word that give the reader clues about the meaning of the unknown word

conventions　the mechanics of writing that include spelling, punctuation, grammar, capitalization, and usage

coordinating conjunction　a word used to connect compound parts of a sentence, such as *and, but,* and *or*

correlative conjunction　words that work in pairs to join words and groups of words, such as *either . . . or* and *neither . . . nor*

couplet　a type of poetry that has two lines that rhyme

D

declarative sentence　a sentence that makes a statement and ends with a period

definite article　the article *the* that identifies specific people, places, things, or ideas

demonstrative pronoun   points out something. *This, that, these,* and *those* are demonstrative pronouns when they take the place of a noun.

dependent clause   part of a sentence containing a subject and a verb that cannot stand alone as a sentence

dialogue journal   a type of journal in which two people write back and forth about a subject as if they were having a conversation

diamante   a diamond-shaped, seven-line poem that has specific information in each line and an exact number of words

direct object   a noun or pronoun that receives the action of the verb

drafting   the second stage, or phase, in the writing process, in which the writer starts writing

E

editing/proofreading   the fourth stage, or phase, in the writing process, in which the writer makes corrections in spelling, grammar, usage, capitalization, and punctuation

end rhyme   rhyming word at the end of two or more lines of poetry

expository writing   a form of writing used for giving information or explaining something, such as newspaper and magazine articles, textbooks, and biographies

F

fantasy   a story that has characters, places, or events that could not exist in the real world

figurative language   words or groups of words that stand for more than their literal meaning, such as similes, metaphors, and personification

fragment   a group of words that does not express a complete thought and is missing a subject, a predicate, or both

free verse   a type of poetry that doesn't follow any specific form and usually does not rhyme

H

haiku   a three-line poem about nature that has a specific number of syllables for each line

heading   the part of a letter that includes the address of the writer and the date the letter was written

helping verb   a verb that helps the main verb

historical fiction   a story that takes place in an actual time and place in the past. The story gives lots of accurate details about the period in which the events take place.

homographs   words that are spelled the same but have different meanings and origins

homophones   two or more words that sound the same but have different meanings and spellings

hyperbole   an extreme exaggeration often used for humorous effect

I

idiom   a word or group of words that cannot be understood by knowing only the literal meaning, such as *being in the dog house*

imperative sentence   a sentence that gives a command or makes a request and ends with a period or exclamation point

indefinite article   the articles *a* and *an* that refer to a general group of people, places, things, or ideas

indefinite pronoun   a pronoun that does not refer to a specific person, place, thing, or idea, such as *everyone* or *something*

independent clause   a group of words that has a subject and a predicate and can stand alone as a sentence

indirect object   a noun or pronoun for whom or to whom something is done

initialism   formed from the first letters of the words it represents, such as *ATM* (Automatic Teller Machine)

intensive pronoun   a pronoun that ends with *-self* or *-selves* and is used to draw special attention to a noun or pronoun already mentioned

interjection   a word or group of words that shows strong feeling

internal rhyme   words that rhyme in the middle of lines of poetry

interrogative pronoun   a pronoun that asks a question, such as *whose*

interrogative sentence   a type of sentence that asks a question and ends with a question mark

interrupter   a word or phrase that interrupts the central idea of a sentence

irregular plural nouns   nouns that do not follow the rule for most plural nouns, such as *child* and *children*

irregular verb   a verb that does not follow the rule for adding *-ed* to form the past tense

L

lead   the first paragraph of a news story that answers the "five Ws": *who, what, when, where, why*

learning log   where you write about something you are studying, such as a science experiment.

linking verb   a state-of-being verb that links the subject of the sentence with a word in the predicate

lyric   a type of poem that expresses strong personal emotions, often using details of the five senses

M

memo (memorandum)   a short message that communicates something to a person or group of people with whom you are working

metaphor   a figure of speech that compares two unlike things without using the words *like* or *as*

N

narrative writing   a form of writing that tells a story or gives an account of an event

nonrhyming poetry   poetry in which the words at the ends of the lines do not rhyme

O

object of the preposition   the noun or pronoun that follows the preposition in a prepositional phrase

object pronoun   a pronoun used as a direct object, object of the preposition, or indirect object, such as *him* or *us*

onomatopoeia   a word that imitates the sound made by or connected with the thing to which you refer, such as the *pitter-patter* of rain

open compound word   a compound word that has a space between the two smaller words, such as *rain forest*

order of importance   a way of organizing information by putting ideas from least important to most important

outline   a type of graphic organizer used to show main topics and subtopics. An outline uses Roman numerals, capital letters, Arabic numerals, and lowercase letters to label these ideas.

P

participial phrase   includes a participle and other words that complete its meaning and always functions as an adjective

passive voice   when the subject receives the verb's action

pattern poetry   poetry in which the lines use the pattern or format of another poem or song to create a new poem

personal narrative a piece of writing that is a story about something that happened in the writer's life

personification a figure of speech in which an object or idea is given human qualities

persuasive report a report that is written to change the thinking, feelings, or actions of the readers about a specific issue or to get the reader to recognize the writer's point of view

persuasive writing a type of writing in which the writer tries to change the way the readers think or feel about a topic, inspire action, or get the reader to recognize the writer's point of view

phrase a group of words that does not have a subject and predicate

plot analysis the process of identifying the problem, conflict, climax, and conclusion of the plot

point of view the viewpoint from which a story is written, either as the first person telling the story as it happens to them or third person as an observer of the story

portfolio a type of folder or notebook in which a writer keeps his/her pieces of writing

possessive nouns shows who owns something

possessive pronoun a pronoun that shows who owns something

predicate the part of a sentence that tells what the subject is or does

predicate noun a noun in the predicate that tells about the subject. It is linked to the subject by a linking verb.

prefix one or more letters added to the beginning of a root or base word that changes the word's meaning

preposition a word that shows position or direction

prepositional phrase a phrase that begins with a preposition and ends with a noun or pronoun

presentation how your writing looks in its final form

prewriting the first stage, or phase, of the writing process, in which the writer thinks, brainstorms, and makes a list or web to write down thoughts he/she wants to include in the piece of writing

proofreading marks a set of commonly agreed upon marks that are used to show where corrections are needed in a piece of writing

proper adjective an adjective made from a proper noun that always starts with a capital letter

proper noun a noun that names a specific person, place, thing, or idea and always start with a capital letter

prose all types of writing that are not considered poetry

publishing   the final stage, or phase, of the writing process, in which the writer makes a final and correct copy of the piece of writing and then shares it with the selected audience

purpose   the reason for writing something, usually to inform, to explain, to entertain, or to persuade

Q

quatrain   a four-line poem or a stanza of a longer poem that expresses one thought and has a variety of rhyming patterns

quotation   the exact words a person speaks

R

reflective paragraph   a paragraph that ends a piece of writing and causes the reader to reflect on or think about what has been written

reflexive pronoun   a pronoun that ends with *-self* or *-selves* and refers to the subject of the sentence

relative pronoun   a pronoun that introduces a word group called a dependent clause that modifies a noun or pronoun used in the main part of the sentence

research report   a report that gives information about real facts, ideas, or events

revising   the third stage, or phase, of the writing process in which the writer improves the writing by adding, deleting, consolidating, rearranging, and/or clarifying material

rhythm   the beat or pattern in a song or poem

run-on sentence   two or more sentences incorrectly written as one sentence

S

salutation   the greeting of a letter

sentence fluency   a quality of writing in which the sentences flow smoothly

signal words   words that tell the order in which things happen in a process, such as *first, next,* and *last,* also called transition words

signature   the part of a letter in which the writer signs his/her name

simile   a figure of speech that compares two or more things that are not alike by using the word *like* or *as*

simple sentence   has one subject and one predicate

singular noun   a word that names one person, place, thing, or idea

source a place where one seeks information when doing research, such as encyclopedias, dictionaries, books, almanacs, atlases, videos, magazines, newspapers, personal interviews, and the Internet

state-of-being verb a verb that does not show action but shows a condition or state of being

story map a type of graphic organizer that is used to outline the events of a story

subject the part of a sentence that tells who or what the sentence is about

subject-verb agreement when the verb agrees with the subject of the sentence. They both must be singular or plural.

subordinate clause another name for dependent clauses that are introduced by a subordinating conjunction

subordinating conjunction a word that introduces an adverb clause

subtopic a subdivision of the main topic of a piece of writing

suffix one or more letters added to the end of a root or base word that changes the word's meaning

superlative form the form of an adjective or adverb that compares three or more of something

supporting sentences the sentences in a paragraph that tell more about the paragraph's main idea

T

topics-and-subtopics chart a type of graphic organizer that lists topics and subtopics in an outline form

topic sentence states the paragraph's main idea. Topic sentences are often used in expository and persuasive writing.

triplet a type of poetry that has three lines of rhyming words

V

Venn diagram a type of graphic organizer used to compare and contrast two items

verb phrase a main verb plus one or more helping verbs

verb tense the time of the verb, such as present, past, and future

voice the trait that makes a piece of writing your very own

W

word choice the words a writer uses to have the maximum effect on the reader

writing process a process used to develop writing. The stages, or phases, of the writing process are prewriting, drafting, revising, editing/proofreading, and publishing.

Index

The index is a list of words and page numbers. It lists the different things that are in the Handbook. The words are in alphabetical order. You look in the list for the word you want to find. Then you look at the page number of the Handbook where it can be found. The index is a good tool. Learn to use it. It can save you a lot of time.

A

abbreviations, 382–383
abstract nouns, 342
acronyms, 383
across-the-curriculum words, 332–333
action verb, 346
active voice, 347
ad copy, 214
adding, 38–39
addresses, 387
addressing an envelope, 90
adjective clause, 284, 356–357
adjectives, 201, 242, 334–335, 348, 372, 385
adventure story, 170–175
adverb clause, 284, 357
adverbs, 242, 334–335, 349, 373
advertisement, 214–215
alliteration, 290
analogies, 315
analyzing fiction, 100–105
antecedent, 344, 370
antonym, 313, 315
apostrophe, 343, 374, 389
appositive, 280, 285, 355, 385
appositive phrase, 285, 355
articles, 348
assonance, 291
audience, 19–20, 31, 44, 50, 51, 114–116, 118, 120–121, 127, 133, 143, 188, 213, 215, 219, 221, 225, 264–267, 300–301
autobiography, 152–157

auxiliary verb, 347
awkward sentences, 360–361

B

bibliography, 141–143
biography, 106, 158–163
birthday cards, 79
body (letter), 82–83, 85, 86, 88–89, 91–92, 216
body (news story), 124
book reviews, 110–115
brainstorm, 18
business letter, 58–65, 86–91. See also,
    letter of complaint, 58–59, 87–89
    letter of concern, 87, 89
    letter of request, 87, 89
    letter to the editor, 87, 216–219
    memo, 92–93
byline, 124

C

callout, 124
capitalization, 391–395
captions, 54
cards, 76–81
cast of characters, 189
cause and effect, 36–37, 260, 296, 330
cause-and-effect chart, 260
chain-of-events organizer, 153, 157
character, 27, 75, 164, 166, 168–169, 171, 174–177, 180–183, 186–189, 195, 197, 279, 304

character analysis, 100–105
character web, 100–101
chart, 26, 260–261
chronological order, 132–133, 156–158, 162–163
cinquain, 233
clarifying, 10, 38, 42
clarity, 10
clauses, 356–357, 384
climax, 102–103, 105, 305
closed compound word, 312
closing (letter), 82–83, 85–86, 88, 91, 216, 219, 386, 395
closing (news story), 124
closing paragraph, 222
closing sentence, 248, 251
clues, 165–169
collecting grid, 261
collecting information, 25
colon, 91, 388
combining sentences, 242, 245, 282
comma, 85, 242, 244, 247, 308, 351, 356, 358, 384–387
common nouns, 342
comparative form, 372–373
compare, 272, 275, 286–287, 294–295, 372–373
compare/contrast, 258, 330
complete predicate, 353
complete subject, 352
complex sentence, 244, 359
compound predicate, 353, 358
compound sentence, 244, 358, 384
compound subject, 242, 352, 358, 368
compound words, 312, 390
compound-complex sentence, 359
computer, 49, 53–54, 70, 84
conclusion, 102–103, 105, 156, 207–209, 222, 278
concrete nouns, 342
conferencing, 45
conflict, 27, 102–103, 105, 182, 187–188

conjunctions, 242, 244, 247, 351, 356, 358, 360
connotation, 316–317, 335, 337
consolidating, 38, 41
context clues, 330–331
contractions, 374–375, 389
contrast, 272, 274, 294–295
conventions, 14, 85, 91, 93, 99, 105, 109, 114–115, 120–121, 127, 133, 143, 151, 157, 163, 169, 175, 181, 187, 197, 205, 209, 219, 225
coordinating conjunctions, 351
correlative conjunctions, 351
couplet, 229

D

dash, 390
dates, 386
deadline, 21
decimal points, 380
declarative sentence, 240, 363, 380
definite article, 348
definition, 330
deleting, 38, 40
demonstrative adjective, 348
demonstrative pronoun, 345
dependent clause, 244, 356
descriptions, 200–205, 271
descriptive paragraphs, 200, 253
descriptive writing, 150, 198–209, 252–253. See also,
　　　descriptions, 200–205, 271
　　　observation report, 206–209
details, 10, 39, 127
diagram, 74
dialogue, 188–189, 195, 197, 279, 308–309, 386
dialogue journal, 72
diamante, 232
direct address, 385

direct object, 344, 354
direct quotes, 391
directions, 116, 118–119
double negative, 375
double subjects, 361
draft, 19, 32–33
drafting, 19, 32–37, 60–61, 85, 91, 93, 99,
    105, 109, 114–115, 120–121, 127, 133,
    143, 151, 157, 163, 169, 175, 181, 187,
    197, 205, 209, 219, 225

E

editing, 19, 46–49, 63, 85, 91, 93, 99, 105,
    109, 114–115, 120–121, 127, 133, 143,
    151, 157, 163, 169, 175, 181, 187, 197,
    205, 209, 219, 225
editing checklist, 48
effective beginnings, 276–277
effective endings, 276–279
ellipsis, 390
E-mail, 84
end marks, 380
end rhyme, 292
entertain, 9, 264–265
evidence, 250–251
exaggeration, 288–289
examples, 214, 250–251, 300
exclamation point, 241, 308, 351, 363,
    380–381
exclamatory sentence, 241, 363
expert opinion, 212, 214, 221
explain, 9, 254, 264–265, 271, 294
explaining a process, 116–117, 120
expository essay, 128–133
expository paragraph, 254
expository writing, 94–143, 212, 254,
    294–299. See also,
        book reviews, 110–115
        directions, 118–119, 121
        expository essay, 128–133
        news story, 122–127
        process, 116–117, 120

research report, 134–143
responding to nonfiction,
    106–109
summary, 96–99

F

facts, 214, 216, 250–251, 265, 277, 300
fantasy, 182–187
fiction, 100–105, 110–111, 115, 164, 168,
    170–171, 176, 182–183
figurative language, 286–289. See also,
    exaggeration, 288–289
    hyperbole, 288
    idiom, 289
    metaphor, 201, 287, 289
    personification, 287, 289
    simile, 201, 286, 289
figures of speech, 286–289
first-person point of view, 307
focus, 10, 23
forms of writing, see
    descriptive writing, 150, 198–209,
        252–253
    expository writing, 94–143, 212,
        254, 294–299
    narrative writing, 144–197, 252,
        265
    personal writing, 68–93
    persuasive writing, 210–225, 255,
        300–303
    poetry, 226–237, 291–293
fragment, 246, 360
free verse, 234
friendly letter, 82–85
future perfect tense, 366
future tense, 366

G

get-well cards, 78
giving directions, 116, 118–119

grammar, 340–363. See also,
    adjectives, 201, 242, 334–335, 348, 372, 385
    adverbs, 242, 334–335, 349, 373
    clauses, 356–357, 384
    conjunctions, 242, 244, 247, 351, 356, 358, 360
    direct object, 344, 354
    indirect object, 344, 354
    interjections, 351, 381, 385
    kinds of sentences, 240–241, 363
    nouns, 284, 342–343
    phrases, 243, 283, 355, 384
    predicate, 240, 245–246, 352–353
    prepositions, 350
    pronouns, 284, 344–345
    sentence problems, 360–362
    subject, 240, 246, 352
    types of sentences, 358–359
    verbs, 284, 336–337, 346–347
graphic organizer, see
    cause-and-effect chart, 260
    chain-of-events organizer, 153, 157
    character web, 100–101
    collecting grid, 261
    story map, 27–28, 147, 151, 169, 175, 181, 187, 257
    time line, 159, 162–163, 258
    topics-and-subtopics chart, 259
    topic webs, 22, 56
    Venn diagram, 258
    web, 18, 22, 56, 256
Greek roots, 324–325
greeting, 386, 395

H

haiku, 233
heading, 58, 82–83, 85–86, 88, 91–92, 216, 219
headline, 124–125
helping verb, 346–347
historical fiction, 176–181

homograph, 320–321
homophone, 318–319
hyperbole, 288
hyphen, 312, 349, 390
hyphenated adjectives, 349
hyphenated compound word, 312

I

I, 391
ideas, 10, 44, 132–133, 151, 157, 163, 169, 175, 181, 187, 197
idiom, 289
imperative sentence, 241, 363, 380
indefinite articles, 348
indefinite pronoun, 345, 369–370
indent, 34
independent clause, 244, 356, 388
indirect object, 344, 354
inform, 264–265, 294
informational writing, 29
initialism, 383
inside address, 58, 86, 88, 91, 216, 219
intensive pronoun, 345
interjections, 351, 381, 385
internal rhyme, 292
interpreting data, 207, 209
interrogative pronoun, 345
interrogative sentence, 241, 363, 380
interrupters, 385
interview, 128, 158, 221
introductory words, 386
inverted order, 353
invitations, 81
irregular plural nouns, 343
irregular verbs, 368

J

journal entry, 70–71, 146
journals, 70–75

K

key words, 136
kinds of sentences,
  240–241, 363

L

Latin roots, 324–325
lead, 11, 124–127
learning log, 73–74
letter of complaint, 58–59, 87–89
letter of concern, 87, 89
letter of request, 87, 89
letters, see
    business letters, 58–65,
      86–91
    friendly letters, 82–85
letter to the editor, 87, 216–219
linking verb, 346
list, 18, 388
literature response journal, 75
location words, 36–37, 116, 204–205,
  271–274
lyric, 231

M

main idea, 99, 109, 248, 250–251
mechanics, 378–395. See also,
    capitalization, 391–395
    punctuation marks, 19, 240–241,
      380–390
memo, 92–93
metaphor, 201, 287, 289
misused words, 376–377
modifier, 242, 355
mood, 164, 168–169
multiple-meaning words,
  322–323
mystery, 164–169

N

narrative paragraph, 252
narrative writing, 144–197, 252, 265.
  See also,
    adventure story, 170–175
    autobiography, 152–157
    biography, 158–163
    fantasy, 182–187
    historical fiction, 176–181
    mystery, 164–169
    personal narrative, 146–151
    play, 188–197
narrator, 190, 195–196, 307
negative word, 375
news story, 122–127
nonfiction, 106–109, 112–114, 122
nonrhyming poetry, 232–235
note cards, 137
note taking, 122
notes, 34, 127, 133, 143, 209
nouns, 284, 342–343
numbers, 387, 390

O

object of the preposition, 350, 355
object pronouns, 344–345
observation, 206–209
observation report, 206–209
onomatopoeia, 291
open compound word, 312
opening paragraph, 222
opinion, 110, 113–115, 126, 212, 214, 219,
  265, 300
order of importance, 270, 297, 303
order words, 36–37, 116, 269, 272
ordering information, 268–271.
  See also,
    compare, 272, 275, 286–287,
      294–295, 372–373
    contrast, 272, 274, 294–295

location words, 36–37, 116, 204–205, 271–274

order of importance, 270, 297, 303

order words, 36–37, 116, 269, 272

time words, 36–37, 268, 272–273, 299

transition words, 14, 35–37, 116, 118, 121, 150, 156–157, 162–163, 268–275, 297, 299

organization, 11, 27, 44, 85, 91, 93, 99, 105, 109, 114–115, 120–121, 127, 133, 143, 157, 163, 169, 174–175, 187, 197, 205, 209, 219, 225

organization of details, 201–205

origins of words, 324–325

outline, 380, 395

P

page design, 52, 54

paragraphs, 34–35, 37, 248–255

paragraphs, types of, 252–255

parentheses, 390

participial phrase, 283, 355

passive voice, 347

past perfect tense, 366

past tense, 366

paste-up, 53

pattern poetry, 236–237

peer conferencing, 45

perfect tense, 366

period, 240–241, 363, 380, 382–383

personal narrative, 146–151

personal note, 76–81

personal pronouns, 344

personal writing, 68–93. See also,
   birthday cards, 79
   business letter, 59–65, 86–91
   dialogue journal, 72
   E-mail, 84
   friendly letters, 82–85
   get-well cards, 78
   invitations, 81
   journals, 70–75
   learning log, 73–74
   literature response journal, 75
   memo, 92–93
   notes and cards, 76
   telephone messages, 80
   thank-you notes, 77

personification, 287, 289

persuade, 58–61, 113, 219, 255, 264–265

persuasion in advertising, 214

persuasive letter, 58–61

persuasive paragraph, 255

persuasive report, 220–225

persuasive writing, 210–225, 255, 300–303. See also,
   advertisement, 214–215
   letter to the editor, 216–219
   persuasive report, 220–225

photo caption, 124

phrases, 243, 283, 355, 384

play, 188–197

plot, 102–105, 110, 165, 171, 174, 176–177, 180–183, 186–188, 195, 197, 304–305

plot analysis, 105

plural nouns, 343

poetry, 226–237, 291–293. See also,
   nonrhyming poetry, 232–235
   pattern poetry, 236–237
   rhyming poetry, 228–231

point of view, 180, 304, 307

possession, 389

possessive nouns, 343

possessive pronouns, 344–345

postal abbreviations, 383

precise verbs, 336–337

predicate, 240, 245–246, 352–353

predicate pronoun, 344

prefix, 326–327

prepositional phrase, 283, 350, 355

prepositions, 350

present perfect tense, 366

present tense, 366

presentation, 15, 50, 52, 85, 91, 93, 99,
  105, 109, 114–115, 120–121, 127, 133,
  143, 151, 157, 163, 169, 175, 181, 187,
  197, 205, 209, 219, 225
prewriting, 18–31, 56–59, 85, 91, 93, 99,
  105, 109, 114–115, 120–121, 127–128,
  133, 143, 151, 157, 163, 169, 175, 181,
  187, 197, 205, 209, 219, 225
problem, 102–103, 105, 305
problems and solutions, 298
process, 116–117, 120, 299
pronoun/antecedent agreement,
  370
pronouns, 344–345
proofreading, 46–49, 85, 91, 93, 105, 109,
  114–115, 120–121, 127, 133, 143, 151,
  157, 163, 169, 175, 181, 187, 197, 205,
  209, 219, 225
proofreading marks, 47, 62–63
proper adjectives, 348
proper nouns, 342
prose, 228
public service ad, 215
publishing, 19, 50–55, 64–65, 85, 91, 93,
  99, 105, 109, 114–115, 120–121, 127,
  133, 143, 151, 157, 163, 169, 175, 181,
  187, 197, 205, 209, 219, 225
punctuation marks, 19, 240–241,
  380–390. See also,
    apostrophe, 343, 374, 389
    colon, 91, 388
    comma, 85, 242, 244, 247, 308, 351,
      356, 358, 384–387
    dash, 390
    ellipsis, 390
    exclamation point, 241, 308, 351,
      363, 380–381
    hyphen, 312, 349, 390
    parentheses, 390
    period, 240–241, 363, 380, 382–383
    question mark, 241, 308, 363, 380
    quotation marks, 308, 389
    semicolon, 356, 358, 388
    underlining, 389

purpose, 20–21, 24, 44, 112, 114, 116, 127,
  133, 143, 264, 267, 301. See also,
    entertain, 9, 264–265
    explain, 9, 254, 264–265, 271, 294
    inform, 9, 264–265, 294
    persuade, 9, 58–61, 113, 219, 255,
      264–265

Q
quatrain, 230
question mark, 241, 308, 363, 380
questions and answers, 297, 302
quotation, 123, 389
quotation marks, 308, 389

R
rambling sentence, 247, 361
rearranging, 38, 43
reasons, 216, 300, 303
reflection, 150, 278–279
reflexive pronouns, 345
relative pronoun, 244, 345, 357
repetition, 290, 293
research, 122, 220, 261
research report, 134–143
resolution, 27, 102, 180, 188, 195
responding to nonfiction, 106–109
revising, 19, 38–45, 62, 85, 91, 93, 99, 105,
  109, 114–115, 120–121, 127, 133, 143,
  151, 157, 163, 169, 175, 181, 187, 197,
  205, 209, 219, 225
revising checklist, 44
rhyme, 228–237, 292
rhyming poetry, 228–231
rhythm, 14, 228, 293
RSVP, 81
run-on sentence, 246–247, 360

S
salutation, 58, 82–83, 85–86, 88, 91, 216,
  219, 388
scene (in plays), 188, 197
second-person point of view, 307

semicolon, 356, 358, 388
sentence expansion, 283–285
sentence fluency, 14, 44, 85, 99, 109, 115, 127, 133, 175, 282
sentence length, 281
sentences, 240–247, 281–285, 358, 363
setting, 27, 164, 166, 168–169, 171, 174–176, 180, 182–183, 186, 188, 195, 197, 304, 306
signal words, 14, 36–37, 118, 120.
    See also,
        transition words, 14, 35–37, 116, 118, 121, 150, 156–157, 162–163, 268–275, 297, 299
signature, 82–83, 85, 88, 91, 216, 219
simile, 201, 286, 289
simple predicate, 353
simple sentence, 358
singular noun, 343
skimming tips, 136
solution, 168, 216, 218, 305
sound of language, 290–293. See also,
        alliteration, 290
        assonance, 291
        end rhyme, 292
        internal rhyme, 292
        onomatopoeia, 291
        repetition, 290, 293
        rhythm, 14, 228, 293
sources, 135, 141–142, 158, 220
speaker tags, 308–309
spelling, 19, 46
stage directions, 189, 195–197
state-of-being verb, 346
story map, 27–28, 147, 151, 169, 175, 181, 187, 257
story writing, 304–307. See also,
        character, 27, 75, 164, 166, 168–169, 171, 174–177, 180–183, 186–189, 195, 197, 279, 304
        dialogue, 188–189, 195, 197, 279, 308–309, 386
        plot, 102–105, 110, 165, 171, 174, 176–177, 180–183, 186–188, 195, 197, 304–305

point of view, 180, 304, 307
setting, 27, 164, 166, 168–169, 171, 174–176, 180, 182–183, 186, 188, 195, 197, 304, 306
structures of writing, 238–261. See also,
        paragraphs, 34–35, 37, 248–255
        sentences, 240–247, 281–285, 358, 363
subject, 240, 246, 352
subject pronouns, 344–345
subject-verb agreement, 368–369
subordinate clause, 284, 356
subordinating conjunction, 244, 351, 357
subtopic, 29–31, 35, 106, 259
suffix, 328–329
summary, 74, 96–99, 108, 110, 113, 115, 213, 219, 272, 275, 278
superlative form, 372–373
supporting details, 99, 107, 109, 124, 127, 143
supporting sentence, 34–35, 248, 251
surprise, 164, 169
survival story, 170
suspense, 165, 167–169, 174
synonyms, 280, 314–316

T

telephone messages, 80
thank-you notes, 77
third-person point of view, 307
time line, 159, 162–163, 258
time words, 36–37, 268, 272–273, 299
titles, 389, 391
tone, 85, 92
topic, 23–24, 134, 220, 249
topic (choosing) 20, 23, 29–31, 44, 56
topic sentence, 34–35, 105, 107, 127, 136, 143, 248, 251
topic web, 22, 56
topics-and-subtopics chart, 259

traits of good writing, see

    conventions, 14, 85, 91, 93, 99, 105,
        109, 114–115, 120–121, 127, 133,
        143, 151, 157, 163, 169, 175, 181,
        187, 197, 205, 209, 219, 225

    ideas, 10, 44, 132–133, 151, 157, 163,
        169, 175, 181, 187, 197

    organization, 11, 27, 44, 85, 91, 93,
        99, 105, 109, 114–115, 120–121,
        127, 133, 143, 157, 163, 169,
        174–175, 187, 197, 205, 209, 219,
        225

    presentation, 15, 50, 52, 85, 91, 93,
        99, 105, 109, 114–115, 120–121,
        127, 133, 143, 151, 157, 163, 169,
        175, 181, 187, 197, 205, 209, 219,
        225

    sentence fluency, 14, 44, 85, 99,
        109, 115, 127, 133, 175, 282

    voice, 12, 44, 85, 91, 99, 105, 109,
        114–115, 131, 151, 157, 169, 219,
        225

    word choice, 13, 44, 93, 127,
        131–133, 151, 175, 181, 197, 205,
        209

transition words, 14, 35–37, 116, 118,
    121, 150, 156–157, 162–163, 264,
    268–275, 297, 299

triplet, 229

U

underlining, 389

units of measure, 383

usage, 364–377. See also,

    comparative/superlative form,
        372–373

    contractions, 374–375, 389

    misused words, 376–377

    pronoun/antecedent agreement,
        370

    subject-verb agreement, 368–369

    verbs, 284, 336–337, 346–347

V

variety in writing, 14, 44, 280–285

Venn diagram, 258

verb phrases, 347

verb tenses, 366–367

verbs, 284, 336–337, 346–347

vocabulary, 310–337. See also,

    across-the-curriculum words,
        332–333

    analogies, 315

    antonyms, 313, 315

    compound words, 312, 390

    connotation, 316–317, 335, 337

    context clues, 330–331

    Greek and Latin roots,
        324–325

    homographs, 320–321

    homophones, 318–319

    multiple-meaning words,
        322–323

    prefixes, 326–327

    suffixes, 328–329

    synonyms, 280, 314–316

voice, 12, 44, 85, 91, 99, 105, 109,
    114–115, 131, 151, 157, 169, 219,
    225

W

web, 18, 22, 56, 256

word choice, 13, 44, 93, 127, 131–133,
    151, 175, 181, 197, 205, 209

word origins, 324–325

word web, 74

words to avoid, 335

working title, 27

writing process, 16–65

    drafting, 19, 32–37, 60–61, 85, 91,
        93, 99, 105, 109, 114–115, 120–121,
        127, 133, 143, 151, 157, 163, 169,
        175, 181, 187, 197, 205, 209, 219,
        225

editing, 19, 46–49, 63, 85, 91, 93, 99, 105, 109, 114–115, 120–121, 127, 133, 143, 151, 157, 163, 169, 175, 181, 187, 197, 205, 209, 219, 225

prewriting, 18–31, 56–59, 85, 91, 93, 99, 105, 109, 114–115, 120–121, 127–128, 133, 143, 151, 157, 163, 169, 175, 181, 187, 197, 205, 209, 219, 225

publishing, 19, 50–55, 64–65, 85, 91, 93, 99, 105, 109, 114–115, 120–121, 127, 133, 143, 151, 157, 163, 169, 175, 181, 187, 197, 205, 209, 219, 225

revising, 19, 38–45, 62, 85, 91, 93, 99, 105, 109, 114–115, 120–121, 127, 133, 143, 151, 157, 163, 169, 175, 181, 187, 197, 205, 209, 219, 225